First World War
and Army of Occupation
War Diary
France, Belgium and Germany

2 INDIAN CAVALRY DIVISION
Divisional Troops
Headquarters (427 Company A.S.C.),
Divisional Supply Column (71 & 83 Companies A.S.C.)
and 2 Divisional Ammunition Park (72 Company A.S.C.)
19 September 1914 - 31 October 1916

WO95/1184

The Naval & Military Press Ltd
www.nmarchive.com
Published in association with The National Archives

Published by

The Naval & Military Press Ltd

Unit 10 Ridgewood Industrial Park,

Uckfield, East Sussex,

TN22 5QE England

Tel: +44 (0) 1825 749494

www.naval-military-press.com

www.nmarchive.com

This diary has been reprinted in facsimile from the original. Any imperfections are inevitably reproduced and the quality may fall short of modern type and cartographic standards.

Contents

Document type	Place/Title	Date From	Date To
Heading	B.E.F. 2 Ind. Cav. Div. O.C.-A.S.C. To (427 Coy A.S.C) 1914 Dec to 1916 Dec		
Heading	War Diary of A.S.C. 2nd Indian Cavalry Division. From 13th December 1914 To 31st January 1915		
War Diary	Southampton	13/12/1915	13/12/1915
War Diary	Roven	15/12/1915	30/12/1915
War Diary	Rebecques	31/12/1915	31/12/1915
War Diary	Berguette	01/01/1915	02/01/1915
War Diary	Rebecques	03/01/1915	03/01/1915
War Diary	Mametz	04/01/1915	31/01/1915
Heading	War Diary of A.S.C. 2nd Indian Cavalry Division From 1st February 1915 To 28th February 1915		
War Diary	Mametz	01/02/1915	28/02/1915
Heading	War Diary of Supply & Transport 2nd Indian Cavalry Division From 1st March 1915 To 31st March 1915		
War Diary	Mametz	01/03/1915	12/03/1915
War Diary	Lozinghem	12/03/1915	15/03/1915
War Diary	Norrent Fontes	15/03/1915	18/03/1915
War Diary	Roquetoire	19/03/1915	31/03/1915
Heading	War Diary of Army Service Corps 2nd Indian Cavalry Division From 1st April 1915 To 30th April 1915		
War Diary	Rocquetoire	01/04/1915	25/04/1915
War Diary	Wemaers-Cappel	26/04/1915	30/04/1915
War Diary	Houtkerque	30/04/1915	30/04/1915
Heading	War Diary of Army Service Corps 2nd Indian Cavalry Division. From 1st May 1915 To 31st May 1915		
War Diary	Houtkerque	01/05/1915	02/05/1915
War Diary	Waemers-Cappel	03/05/1915	04/05/1915
War Diary	Dennebroecq	05/06/1915	17/06/1915
War Diary	Coyecque	17/05/1915	18/05/1915
War Diary	Bomy	19/05/1915	31/05/1915
Heading	War Diary of A.S.C. 2nd Indian Cavalry Division. From 1st June 1915 To 30th June 1915		
War Diary	Bomy	01/06/1915	30/06/1915
Heading	War Diary of Army Service Corps. 2nd Indian Cavalry Division. From 1st July 1915 To 31st July 1915		
War Diary	Bomy	01/07/1915	31/07/1915
Heading	War Diary of Army Service Corps. 2nd Indian Cavalry Division From 1st August 1915 To 31st August 1915		
War Diary	Bomy	01/08/1915	01/08/1915
War Diary	Royon	02/08/1915	02/08/1915
War Diary	Gorenflos	03/08/1915	03/08/1915
War Diary	Belloy-Sur-Somme	03/08/1915	21/08/1915
War Diary	Belloy	22/08/1915	31/08/1915
Heading	War Diary of A.S.C., 2nd Indian Cavalry Division From 1st September 1915 To 30th September 1915		
War Diary	Belloy-Sur-Somme	01/09/1915	22/09/1915
War Diary	Ribeaucourt	23/09/1915	25/09/1915
War Diary	Auxi Le Chateau-Doullens Road	26/09/1915	27/09/1915
War Diary	Ribeaucourt	28/09/1915	30/09/1915

Heading	War Diary of Army Service Corps 2nd Indian Cavalry Division From 1st October 1915 To 31st October 1915		
War Diary	Ribeaucourt	01/10/1915	13/10/1915
War Diary	Frohen Le Grand	14/10/1915	22/10/1915
War Diary	Oissemont	23/10/1915	31/10/1915
Heading	War Diary of O.C. A.S.C. 2nd Indian Cavalry Division From 1st November 1915 To 30th November 1915		
War Diary	Oisemont	01/11/1915	30/11/1915
Heading	War Diary of O.C. Army Service Corps. 2nd Indian Cavalry Division From 1st December 1915 To 31st December 1915		
War Diary	Oisemont	01/12/1915	31/12/1915
Heading	War Diary of A.S.C. Headquarters 2nd Indian Cavalry Division From 1st January 1916 To 31st January 1916		
War Diary	Oisemont	01/01/1916	31/01/1916
Heading	War Diary of O.C. Army Service Corps. 2nd Indian Cavalry Division From 1st February 1916 To 29th February 1916		
War Diary	Oisemont	01/02/1916	29/02/1916
Heading	War Diary of O.C. A.S. Corps. 2nd Indian Cavalry Division From 1st March 1918 To 31st March 1916		
War Diary	Oisemont	01/03/1916	31/03/1916
Heading	War Diary of O.C. Army Service Corps. 2nd Indian Cavalry Division From 1st April 1916 To 30th April 1916		
War Diary	Oisemont	01/04/1916	30/04/1916
Heading	War Diary of O.C. A.S. Corps. 2nd Indian Cavalry Division From 1st May 1916 To 31st May 1916		
War Diary	Oisemont	01/05/1916	07/05/1916
War Diary	St. Riquier	08/05/1916	13/05/1916
War Diary	Oisemont	14/05/1916	31/05/1916
War Diary	War Diary of O.C. A.S.C, 2nd Indian Cavalry Division From 1st June 1916 To 30th June 1916		
War Diary	Oisemont	01/06/1916	04/06/1916
War Diary	Senarpont	05/06/1916	21/06/1916
War Diary	Pont Remy	22/06/1916	26/06/1916
War Diary	Bussy-Les-Daours	27/06/1916	30/06/1916
Heading	War Diary of O.C. Army Service Corps, 2nd Indian Cavalry Division From 1st July 1916 To 31st July 1916		
War Diary	Bussy-Les-Daours	01/07/1916	18/07/1916
War Diary	Dernancourt	19/07/1916	24/07/1916
War Diary	Bussy-Les-Daours	25/07/1916	31/07/1916
Heading	War Diary of O.C. A.S.C. 2nd Indian Cavalry Division From 1st August 1916 To 31st August 1916		
War Diary	Bussy-Les-Daours	01/08/1916	07/08/1916
War Diary	Longpre	08/08/1916	08/08/1916
War Diary	Rieux	09/08/1916	31/08/1916
Heading	War Diary of Headquarters, A.S.C. 2nd Indian Cavalry Division From 1st September 1916 To 30th September 1916		
War Diary	Rieux	01/09/1916	06/09/1916
War Diary	Bussy	07/09/1916	13/09/1916
War Diary	Fricourt	14/09/1916	16/09/1916
War Diary	Bussy	17/09/1916	25/09/1916
War Diary	Dreuil	26/09/1916	27/09/1916
War Diary	Cavillon	28/09/1916	30/09/1916

Heading	War Diary of A.S.C. Hd. Qrs., 5th Cavalry Division (Late 2nd Ind. Cavy. Divin.) From 1st October 1916 To 30th November 1916.		
War Diary	Cavillon	01/10/1916	31/10/1916
War Diary	Dargnies	01/11/1916	30/11/1916
Heading	War Diary of Headquarters, A.S.C, 5th Cavalry Division From 1st December 1916 To 31st December 1916		
War Diary	Dargnies	01/12/1916	31/12/1916
Heading	B.E.F. 2 Ind. Cav. Div. Troops (71 Coy A.S.C 83 Coy A.S.C.) Section No 2 Div Supply Col 1914 Sept To 1915 Mar & 1916 July to 1916 Oct To 5 Cav Divn 74 Divn Supply Column Box 1163		
Miscellaneous	Div Supply Column War Diary of O.C. 71 M.T. Coy.	04/03/1915	04/03/1915
Heading	War Diary of 2nd Indian Divisional Supply Column From 1st July 1916 To 31st July 1916		
War Diary	Amiens-Bussy Road	28/06/1916	31/07/1916
Heading	War Diary of 2nd Indian Cavalry Division Supply Column From 1st August 1916 To 31st August 1916		
War Diary	Bussy-Allonville Road.	01/08/1916	08/08/1916
War Diary	Watterblery	09/08/1916	09/08/1916
War Diary	Bouillancourt	10/08/1916	31/08/1916
Heading	War Diary of 2nd Indian Cavalry Supply Column From 1st September 1916 To 30th September 1916		
War Diary	Bouillancourt	01/09/1916	06/09/1916
War Diary	Bussy-Allonville Road	07/09/1916	13/09/1916
War Diary	Albert Millencourt Road.	14/09/1916	18/09/1916
War Diary	Bussy-Allonville Road	19/09/1916	25/09/1916
War Diary	Camps En Amienois	26/09/1916	30/09/1916
Heading	War Diary of Supply Column 5th Cavalry Divn (Late 2nd Ind Cavy. Divn) From 1st October 1916 To 30th November 1916		
War Diary	Camp En Amienois	01/10/1916	01/11/1916
Heading	2nd Indian Cav. Ammn Park (72 Coy A.S.C.) 1914 Sep 1916 Oct To 5 Cav Div Box 1163		
Heading	2 Ind Cav Division Ammunition Park 72 Coy A.S.C. 1914 Sept-1916 Oct		
War Diary	Portsmouth	19/09/1914	31/12/1914
Miscellaneous	Appendix "A" to Vol. 1 of War Diary of Secunderabad Cavalry Brigade Amtn. Park.		
Heading	War Diary with Appendix of 2nd Indian Cavalry Ammunition Park From 1st February 1915 To 28th February 1915		
War Diary	Aire	07/02/1915	29/02/1915
Miscellaneous	2nd Indian Cavalry Am Park. Appendix "A"		
Heading	War Diary of 2nd Indian Cavalry Ammunition Park From 1st March 1915 To 31st March 1915		
War Diary	Aire	01/03/1915	14/03/1915
Miscellaneous	2nd Indian Cavalry Amm Park. Appx "A" to Cav. Division Dates 31-3-15		
Heading	War Diary with Appendices of 2nd Indian Cavalry Ammunition Park From 1st April 1915 To 30th April 1915		
War Diary	Aire	00/04/1915	00/04/1915
Miscellaneous	2nd Ind. Cavy. Ammn. Park. Appendix "A" to War Diary For April 1915		

Miscellaneous	C Form (Original). Messages And Signals. Appendix XVIII		
Heading	War Diary with Appendices of Ammunition Park 2nd Indian Cavalry Division From 1st May 1915 To 30th June 1915		
War Diary	Aire	02/05/1915	25/05/1915
Miscellaneous	2nd Indian Cavalry Ammn. Park. Appendix "A" to War Diary For May 1915. Ammunition Issues		
War Diary	Aire	03/06/1915	17/06/1915
Miscellaneous	2nd Indian Cavalry Ammn. Park. Appendix "A" to War Diary For month of June 1915. Ammunition Issues		
Miscellaneous	War Diary with Appendices of 2nd Indian Cavalry Ammunition Park. From 1st July 1915 To 31st July 1915		
War Diary	Aire	01/07/1915	30/07/1915
Miscellaneous	2nd Indian Cavalry Ammn. Park. Appendix "A" to War Diary For month of July 1915. Ammunition Issues		
Heading	War Diary with Appendices of 2nd Indian Cavalry Ammunition Park. From 1st August 1915 To 31st August 1915		
War Diary	Aire	01/08/1915	01/08/1915
War Diary	Humbert	02/08/1915	02/08/1915
War Diary	Domquer	03/08/1915	03/08/1915
War Diary	Longpre	07/08/1915	07/08/1915
War Diary	Fourdrinoy	13/08/1915	15/08/1915
War Diary	Pont Noyelle	15/08/1915	31/08/1915
Miscellaneous	2nd Indian Cavalry Ammn. Park Appendix "A" to War Diary For month of August 1915. Ammunition Issues		
Heading	War Diary of 2nd Ind. Cavalry Divnl. Ammunition Park From 1st September 1915 To 30th September 1915		
War Diary	Pont Noyelle	01/09/1915	13/09/1915
War Diary	Fourdrinoy	15/09/1915	17/09/1915
War Diary	Camps-En-Amienois	17/09/1915	22/09/1915
War Diary	Domart	23/09/1915	30/09/1915
Miscellaneous	2nd Indian Cavalry Ammn. Park Appendix "A" to War Diary For month of September 1915		
Heading	War Diary with Appendices of 2nd Indian Cavalry Ammunition Park From 1st October 1915 To 31st October 1915		
War Diary	Domart	01/10/1915	12/10/1915
War Diary	L'Etoile	13/10/1915	21/10/1915
War Diary	Bienecourt	22/10/1915	31/10/1915
Miscellaneous	2nd Indian Cavalry Ammn. Park Appendix "A" to War Diary For month of October 1915		
Heading	War Diary with Appendices of 2nd Indian Cavalry Ammunition Park From 1st November 1915 To 30th November 1915		
War Diary	Biencourt	01/11/1915	17/11/1915
War Diary	Drueil	19/11/1915	30/11/1915
Miscellaneous	2nd Ind. Cavy. Ammn. Park. Appendix "A" to War Diary For month of November 1915		
Heading	War Diary of Detachment 2nd Cav. Div. Amm. Pk. Attached To 46th Div. Amm. Sub Pk. From 30-11-15 to 31-12-15 Volume I		
War Diary	Avroult (map Hazebrouck 5 A, B 5,8,6,	30/11/1915	30/11/1915
War Diary	St. Venant	01/12/1915	31/12/1915

Heading	War Diary of Detachment 2nd Cav. Div. Ammn. Pk. Attached To 46th Div. A.S.P. From 30-11-15 to 06-01-16		
War Diary	St. Venant	01/01/1916	06/01/1916
Heading	War Diary of 2nd Indian Cavalry Ammunition Park From 1st December 1915 To 31st December 1915		
War Diary	Drueil	01/12/1916	31/12/1916
Miscellaneous	2nd Indian Cavalry Ammn. Park. Appendix "A" to War Diary For month of December 1915.		
Heading	War Diary of 2nd Indian Cavalry Ammunition Park From 1st January 1916 To 31st January 1916		
War Diary	Senarpont	01/01/1916	31/01/1916
Miscellaneous	2nd Indian Cavalry Ammn. Park. Appendix "A" to War Diary For January		
Heading	War Diary of 2nd Indian Cavalry Ammunition Park. From 1st February 1916 To 29th February 1916		
War Diary	Senarpont	01/02/1916	29/02/1916
Miscellaneous	Appendix "A" To War Diary For month of February.		
Heading	War Diary of 2nd Indian Cavalry Ammunition Park (Detached Section) From 18th February 1916 To 29th February 1916		
Heading	War Diary of Detachment 2nd Indian Cavalry Amm. Park Attached To 38th Division Feb 18th To Feb 29th 1916 Volume I		
War Diary		18/02/1916	29/02/1916
Heading	War Diary of 2nd Indian Cavalry Ammunition Park From 1st March 1916 To 31st March 1916		
Heading	War Diary of 2nd Ind. Cav. Div. Amn. Park 1st March to 31st March 1916 Vol XV		
War Diary	Senarpont	01/03/1916	31/03/1916
Miscellaneous	Appendix "A" to "War Diary" For the month of March 1916 for 2nd Indian Cavalry Ammunition Park.		
Heading	War Diary of Detachment 2nd Indian Cavalry Amm Park. March 1916. Volume II.		
War Diary		01/03/1916	31/03/1916
Heading	War Diary of 2nd Indian Cavalry Divisional Ammunition Park From 1st April 1916 To 30th April 1916		
War Diary	Senarpont	01/04/1916	30/04/1916
Miscellaneous	Appendix "A" to War Diary For month of April 1916 2nd Indian Cavalry Ammunition Park.		
Heading	War Diary of 2nd Indian Cavalry Ammunition Park (Detachment) From 1st April 1916 To 3rd April 1916		
War Diary		01/04/1916	03/04/1916
Heading	War Diary of 2nd Indian Cavalry Divisional Ammunition Park From 1st May 1916 To 31st May 1916		
War Diary	Senarpont	01/05/1916	31/05/1916
Miscellaneous	2nd Indian Cavalry Ammunition Park. Appendix "A" to War Diary For month of May. 1916.		
Heading	War Diary of 2nd Indian Cavalry Divisional Ammunition Park From 1st June 1916 to 30th June 1916		
War Diary	Senarpont	01/06/1916	04/06/1916
War Diary	Gamaches	05/06/1916	22/06/1916
War Diary	Oisemont	23/06/1916	27/06/1916

War Diary	Bussy Les Daours	28/06/1916	30/06/1916
Miscellaneous	Appendix "A" to War Diary For the month of June 1916 For 2nd Indian Cavalry Ammn. Park.		
Heading	War Diary of 2nd Indian Cavalry Ammunition Park From 1st July 1916 To 31st July 1916		
War Diary	Bussy Les Daours	01/07/1916	17/07/1916
War Diary	Mericourt	18/07/1916	31/07/1916
Miscellaneous	2nd Indian Cavalry Ammunition Park. Appendix "A" to War Diary July 1916		
Heading	War Diary of 2nd Indian Cavalry Division Ammunition Park From 1st August 1916 To 31st August 1916		
War Diary	Mericourt	01/08/1916	08/08/1916
War Diary	Bouillancourt	09/08/1916	10/08/1916
War Diary	Rambures	11/08/1916	31/08/1916
Miscellaneous	2nd Indian Cavy. Ammn Park Appendix "A" to War Diary For month of August 1916		
Heading	War Diary of 2nd Indian Cavalry Ammunition Park From 1st September 1916 To 30th September 1916		
War Diary	Rambures	01/09/1916	06/09/1916
War Diary	Bussy-Les-Daours	07/09/1916	14/09/1916
War Diary	Albert	14/09/1916	22/09/1916
War Diary	Meaulte	23/09/1916	23/09/1916
War Diary	Bussy-Les-Daours	23/09/1916	30/09/1916
Miscellaneous	2nd Indian Cavalry Ammunition Park Appendix "A" to War Diary For month of September 1916		
Heading	War Diary of 2nd Indian Cavalry Amn. Park October 1st to 31st 1916 Vol XXI		
War Diary	Bussy Les Daours	01/10/1916	06/10/1916
War Diary	Montagne	07/10/1916	31/10/1916
Heading	B.W.F France & Flanders. 2 Ind Cav. Div. Troops. O.C. Army Service Corps. 1914 Dec To 1916 Dec. Divisional Supply Column (71 Coy A S C) 1914 Sept To 1915 Mar. 1916 July To 1916 Sept. 2 Indian Cav. Ammunition Park (72 Coy ASC) 1914 Sept To 1916 Oct.		
Heading	B.W.F. France & Flanders 2 Ind Cav. Div Troops. O.C Army Service Corps 1914 Dec To 1916 Dec. Divisional Supply Col (71 Coy A.S.C.) 1914 Sept To 1915 Mar. 1916 July To 1916 Sept 2 Indian Cav Ammunition Park (72 Coy A.S.C.) 1914 Sept To 1916 Oct.		

B.E.F.

2 IND. CAV. DIV

O.C. – ASC

(427 COY ASC)

~~1915 OCT~~ TO ~~1916 APR~~

1914 DEC TO 1916 DEC

~~NO BOX~~

121/4

123

WAR DIARY

OF

O.C. A. S. C. 2nd Indian Cavalry Division.

From. 13th December 1914 To, 31st January 1915.

Instructions regarding War Diaries and Intelligence Summaries are contained in F. S. Regs., Part II. and the Staff Manual respectively. Title pages will be prepared in manuscript.

WAR DIARY

INTELLIGENCE SUMMARY

(Erase heading not required.)

Army Form C. 2118.

Hour, Date, Place	Summary of Events and Information	Remarks and references to Appendices
13th Dec. Southampton –	Horse Transport ~~for~~ 2nd Indian Cavalry Division left in S. S. Kephern i/c of Lieut Col. C H G Moore D.S.O. S+T Corps. Six horses short of complement 1 sick left at Southampton	
15th Dec. Rouen –	Horse Transport arrived and proceeded to Camp Bruyeres	
16th Dec. Rouen	Captain A.S. Crawford reports his arrival on appointment as Adjutant – Ten horses sick of which one died	
17th Dec "	Thirty seven horses sick Total 37 sick and ten short	Regimental officers arrived to take over their Regimental Transport
18th Dec "	Thirty three horses sick Total 80 sick and 10 short	
19th Dec "	Fifteen horses sick Total 95 sick and 10 short.	
20th Dec "	Thirteen horses sick Total 108 sick + 10 short – S Sergt Addison appointed to Division for Transport Duty –	
21st Dec "	Forty four horses were received from Orleans – A batch of fifty were sent, but six rejected as unsuitable – 198 Horses were present in camp on this date, the balance having been supplied by Remount Depot, Rouen –	
22nd Dec – "	The animals were fitted with harness and exercised in the carts –	
23 / 24 Dec	Several unsuitable animals were returned to ~~Ordnance~~ Remounts and others drawn in exchange – S+T Supply Personnel at Rouen left for Orleans –	

Instructions regarding War Diaries and Intelligence Summaries are contained in F. S. Regs., Part II. and the Staff Manual respectively. Title pages will be prepared in manuscript.

WAR DIARY
or
~~INTELLIGENCE SUMMARY~~
(Erase heading not required.)

Army Form C. 2118.

Hour, Date, Place	Summary of Events and Information	Remarks and references to Appendices
Dec 25th Rouen -	General Holiday observed as far as possible - Princess Marys gifts distributed to all A.S.C. men.	
Dec 26th, 27th, 28th } Rouen -	Horse Transport was placed at Disposal of A D T for local use - and employed mainly in taking Hay to Remount Camp.	
	Charger drawn for Captain Crawford -	
Dec 29th Rouen - 10.30 am	Orders received for entrainment of Horse Transport 2nd Indian Cavalry Division on 30th January in 3 Trains -	
Dec 30th Rouen -	The horse Transport 2nd Indian Cavalry Division entrained & left Rouen as under.	
	No 1 Train Rive Gauche Station Entrainment commenced 8.45 am Train left 12.45 pm	
	4 officers (Lt Col Moore?) 112 ~~Horses~~ men 103 Horses 33 vehicles 1 Motor Car	
	This train contained Divisional Troop Transport - also Batmen & Horses for Divisional H.Q.	
	No 2 Train Martainville (Gare du Nord) Entrainment commenced 10 am Train left 14.25	
	3 officers 43 men 72 Horses 24 Vehicles for Mhow Brigade	
	No 3 Train Rive Gauche Station Entrainment commenced at 13 o'clock Train left 17.05.	
	3 officers 43 men 72 Horses 24 vehicles for Meerut Brigade -	
Dec 31st REBECQUES	No 1 Train arrived at ~~REBECQUES~~ BERGUETTES STATION at 6.30 am - Detrainment commenced at 7 am and the whole Transport was ready to leave at 8.45 am, but owing to no orders having been received no movement was possible -	
	No 3 Train arrived about 8.30 am and was ready to leave station yard by 10.30 am.	
	About 1 pm as no orders had been received arrangements	

Instructions regarding War Diaries and Intelligence Summaries are contained in F. S. Regs., Part II. and the Staff Manual respectively. Title pages will be prepared in manuscript.

WAR DIARY
or
~~INTELLIGENCE SUMMARY~~
(Erase heading not required.)

Army Form C. 2118.

Hour, Date, Place	Summary of Events and Information	Remarks and references to Appendices
1st 31st Dec ~~Rebecques~~	were made for billetting temporarily and parking horses & vehicles. The ~~third~~ second train detrained at Blandecques.	
4 pm	A.Q.M.G. ~~Indian~~ Cavalry Corps arrived and informed A.D.S.&T. that Lt Col E.G. Vaughan had been appointed to 2nd Ind. Cav. Division & Lt Col C.H. Moore to 1st Ind. Cav. Division.	
1st Jan BERGUETTE ~~[illegible]~~	Transport was handed over to units of Meerut Cavalry Bde viz 13th Hussars, 18th Lancers & 3rd Skinners Horse. Capt Henry arrived from Orleans for duty as Brigade Transport Officer Meerut Brigade	
2nd Jan BERGUETTE ~~[illegible]~~	Transport handed over to Divisional Head Quarters, R.A. Head Quarters, Cavalry Field Ambulances 'X' 'V' Battery R.H.A. Transport for one Field Ambulance & 'V' Battery R.H.A. proceeded by road to BLANDECQUES.	
3rd Jan. REBECQUES	Capt Crawford with Divisional A.S.C. Head Quarter Transport proceeded to REBECQUES. Capt Hall Divisional Transport Officer arrived at REBECQUES.	
4th Jan. HAMETZ	7th Grade Clerk Wali Ullah Khan joined Head Quarters Divisional S&T Corps. Lt Col E.G. Vaughan took over complete charge as A.D.S.&T. of 2nd Ind. Cav. Division. Lt Col C.H. Moore took over charge ~~of~~ as A.D.S.&T. 1st Ind. Cav. Division. S. Sergt Addison and Clerk A.C. Ankers(?) transferred to 1st Division.	
5th Jan. HAMETZ	A.D.S.&T.'s office established at HAMETZ. Conductor J.A. Bosworth joined from 1st Indian Cav. Division. 4th Grade Clerk Ambica Charan Ghose joined from 1st I.C. Division. Capt Rendall Supply Officer Divisional Troops	Authority Indian Cavalry ~~Army~~ Corps letter Q V 100 / 4-1-15.
6th Jan "	Information received that Troops of MHOW & MEERUT Brigades would shortly proceed to the Trenches. A.D.S.&T. proceeded to AIRE to arrange for extra rations for these troops. Supply officers Mhow and Meerut Brigades notified(?) H.Q. with reference to same arrangement.	

Instructions regarding War Diaries and Intelligence Summaries are contained in F. S. Regs., Part II. and the Staff Manual respectively. Title pages will be prepared in manuscript.

WAR DIARY
or
INTELLIGENCE SUMMARY
(Erase heading not required.)

Army Form C. 2118.

Hour, Date, Place	Summary of Events and Information	Remarks and references to Appendices
8th January Mametz –	Morning Routine Work – at 3 pm AD S+T attended conference with reference to movement of troops to the trenches and issued instructions to Brigade Supply with regard to necessary Supply details rendered necessary by the move –	
5.30 pm	2 Lieut Pratt reported Division had all received its rations –	a.c.
9th January – MAMETZ	AD S+T proceeded to ST OMER and visited Secunderabad Brigade Supply Officer at MAZINGHEM –	
	OC MT arranged to supply 3 lorries for advanced Party of MHOW Brigade –	
	AD S+T visited Secunderabad Head Quarters –	a.c.
10th January – MAMETZ	Advanced party proceeded to Bethune on motor Lorries –	
	Reports required received from all Brigades except Secunderabad	
2 p.m	Wire received from Corps H.Q. requiring ~~altering~~ details of animals in Ration Return – necessary action by wire – Personal visit to S'bad Brigade for details which could not be supplied	a.c.
11th January – MAMETZ	AD S+T proceeded to BETHUNE to inspect arrangements for Troops proceeding to Trenches – The lorries arrived with Supplies about 12 noon direct from Rail Head under the personal supervision of O.C. M.T. Supply Column – Supplies then loaded on to Regimental Wagons. Supplies arrived before the troops –	a.c.
12th January – MAMETZ	AD S+T proceeded to ~~Mazingh~~ MAZINGHEM with reference to failure of O.C. Supplies SECUNDERABAD B'DE to furnish correct reports.	
	Capt RENDALL Supply Officer proceeded on leave to England –	
	Clerk Ambica Charan absent from work.	

1247 W 3299 200,000 (E) 8/14 J.B.C. & A. Forms/C. 2118/11.

Instructions regarding War Diaries and Intelligence Summaries are contained in F. S. Regs., Part II. and the Staff Manual respectively. Title pages will be prepared in manuscript.

WAR DIARY or INTELLIGENCE SUMMARY

(Erase heading not required.)

Army Form C. 2118.

Hour, Date, Place	Summary of Events and Information	Remarks and references to Appendices
Jan 13th MANETZ – 11.50 am 12.45 pm 4 pm. 9 am.	Routine work – Adjt. proceeded to MONT DE LAMBRES to see BTO SECUNDERABAD B'de with reference to Horse Transport Classification in that Brigade. Then proceeded to BETHUNE with reference to supplies for MEERUT Brigade. Returned to AIRE to obtain additional supplies for 2nd Indians and 48 mules – Clerk Ambica Charan sent to Hospital. The system employed for forwarding supplies for Troops in the trenches was as follows. The numbers by units were obtained under heads British & Indian for men & also the numbers of animals sent. Supplies for these were sent to Refilling Point from Rail head [illegible] and the ~~[illegible]~~ total quantity [illegible] rations sent to unit Head Quarters – A supply of coal & charcoal was also despatched and arrangements were made to provide Tea & Rum for units on return from trenches at the Refilling Point –	[illegible]
Jan 14th	Orders received that from 18th Oats and Sugar would be drawn from Reserve Parks – ADS&T 1st Division arrived with ADS&T & then O.C. Supply Columns 1st & 2nd Divisions were visited. These officers proceeded to reconnoitre the roads leading to the various stations of their Reserve Parks and to arrange ~~that~~ with O.C.'s reserve Parks with reference to the drawing of these supplies – Orders were also received for a general reconnaissance of the country NORTH and WEST of the line BETUNE-HESDIN-CRECY-ABBEVILLE in connection with the fodder supply as it is proposed to draw with the amount of forage being sent up by rail – The 2nd Divisional Area was divided up into four areas and these given one to each of the Requisitioning officers for purposes of reconnoitring	

1247 W 3299 200,000 (E) 8/14 J.B.C. & A. Forms/C. 2118/11.

Instructions regarding War Diaries and Intelligence Summaries are contained in F. S. Regs., Part II. and the Staff Manual respectively. Title pages will be prepared in manuscript.

WAR DIARY
or
~~INTELLIGENCE~~ SUMMARY
(Erase heading not required.)

Army Form C. 2118.

Hour, Date, Place	Summary of Events and Information	Remarks and references to Appendices
Jan 15th Manetz –	Report called for as to how far A.T. Carts can be employed for drawing supplies from Railhead in lieu of Motor Lorries – A.D.S.&T. proceeds to consult A.D.S.&T. 1st Division on the subject	ac
Jan 16th "	O.C. M.T. reported that the full quantities of oats were not available for issue in Reserve Parks. O.C. 1st Divl M.T. visits G.H.Q. and reported the fact. A.D.S.T. proceeds to AIRE to investigate complaints of shortage [illegible] in rations received from 36th C.I.H.	
Jan 17th MANETZ	Capt Kendall returned from leave. Orders received that the reserve park were to be drawn on in one day and any bad oats were returned to be discussed. Orders received for parade of Division on 18th	ac
Jan 18th MANETZ	Division paraded at ERNY. Transport on road ENQUIN–CERNY–LIEZRES – Head at ENQUIN. in order DIVISIONAL TROOPS – MEERUT BRIGADE – MHOW BRIGADE – SECUNDERABAD BRIGADE – Transport in line by 11 a.m. Very bad weather – rain and snow – A.D.S.&T. with transport. First Report from SECUNDERABAD BRIGADE re fodder supplies found on reconnaissance of area allotted received	ac ac

Instructions regarding War Diaries and Intelligence Summaries are contained in F. S. Regs., Part II. and the Staff Manual respectively. Title pages will be prepared in manuscript.

WAR DIARY
or
INTELLIGENCE SUMMARY
(Erase heading not required.)

Army Form C. 2118.

Hour, Date, Place	Summary of Events and Information	Remarks and references to Appendices
Jan 19th MAMETZ	AD S+T proceeded on leave –	
	Report received on amount of Forage available from MHOW and MEERUT BRIGADES	ac
Jan 20th MAMETZ.		
Jan 21st MAMETZ.	Babu Clerk Ambica Charan Ghose rejoined from Lahore Clearing Hospital	ac
Jan 25th MAMETZ	Report received from MEERUT Cavalry Brigade re Supply of Fodder available [illegible]	
	Information received that four riding ponies for Veterinary assistants [illegible]	
	Intimation received from Cavalry Corps in the event of a thaw following a heavy frost, certain roads would be closed to mechanical and other heavy traffic –	ac
Jan 26th "	Clerk Ambica Charan Ghose returned to Base –	
	Lt Col E.G. Vaughan DSO returned from leave –	
Jan 27th "	Orders received that full quantity of 10 lbs of Hay per animal would be sent up and that the question of obtaining fodder in area under investigation would be closed –	
Jan	The number of Heavy Horses required to complete Transport of Division on Revised Scale was submitted –	ac
Jan 28th	Consequent on notification of re-organization the following postings were received	
	Lt Col A.F. Thomason to be O.C. A.S.C. 2nd Ind Cav Div.	
	Lt Col E.G. Vaughan DSO to be Senior Supply Officer 2nd Ind Cav Div –	
Jany 31st	Temporary Commission recommended for temporary Sergeant C.W.H. Scott 51st Coy A.S.C	ac
	Pte A.T. Carli ordered to be handed over from Secunderabad Brigade to Jodhpur Lancers for ammunition –	

[Signature] Lieut Col
OC ASC 2nd Ind. Cavy Div.

1247 W 3299 200,000 (E) 8/14 J.B.C. & A. Forms/C. 2118/11.

Serial No. 123

121/4719

WAR DIARY

of

A. S. C. 2nd Indian Cavalry Division

From 1st February 1915 To 28th February 1915

KM
6/3.

Army Form C. 2118.

WAR DIARY
~~or~~
~~INTELLIGENCE~~ SUMMARY
(Erase heading not required.)

Instructions regarding War Diaries and Intelligence Summaries are contained in F. S. Regs., Part II. and the Staff Manual respectively. Title pages will be prepared in manuscript.

Hour, Date, Place	Summary of Events and Information	Remarks and references to Appendices
MAMETZ ~~January~~ February 1st	Indian Cavalry Corps notified that Barriers would be placed across the roads with effect from this date owing to thaw. On receipt of this information Supply officers and OC M.T. Column were warned and instructions previously issued were carried out.	ac
February 2nd	Indian Cavalry Corps ~~ay~~ sanctioned one A.T Cart being allotted to No 40 Field Post office (Divl H.Q) from number with Secunderabad Brigade ammunition Column; when A.T. Carts with the latter are replaced by G.S. wagons. "A" & "B" Echelon transport defined in Corps Order No 21/14. d. 31st Jany.	ac
February 3rd	Capt A.M McDonnell A.S.C. ordered to England. Proposal received to increase transport of Cavalry Field Ambulances by one A.T Cart per section - i.e. 3 per field Ambulance.	ac
February 4th		
February 5th	Captain A.M. McDonnell left for England. Large Reserves of Oats being accumulated at Railhead owing to units underdrawing their rations. If units find Rations too large, units to warn Supply officers, Railhead so that amount coming up may be reduced. GOC Cavalry Corps inspected Supply Column and Ammunition Park	ac
	Indian Cavy Corps intimated that first orders for removal of barriers on roads were issued yesterday. Supply Officers & OC MT Column informed accordingly.	
Feb: 6th	Lt Col R. Burlton S.T.C assumed the appointment of O.C. A.S.C 2nd Cavl Div. from A.D.S&T. Meerut Divn which appointment was abolished. Lt-Col E.J. Vaughan became Senior Supply Officer 2nd Cavl Divn from this date.	

R E Vaughan
Lieut Col
OC ASC 2nd Ind. Cavy Divn

1247 W 3299 200,000 (E) 8/14 J.B.C. & A. Forms/C. 2118/11.

Instructions regarding War Diaries and Intelligence Summaries are contained in F. S. Regs., Part II. and the Staff Manual respectively. Title pages will be prepared in manuscript.

WAR DIARY

or

INTELLIGENCE SUMMARY

(Erase heading not required.)

Army Form C. 2118.

1915 Hour, Date, Place		Summary of Events and Information	Remarks and references to Appendices
MAMETZ	Feb. 7th	1. Capt. A. S. Crawford Adjt. to O.C. A.S.C. proceeds to England on 7 days leave. Major W. StG. Chamier, RO Meerut Brigade proceeds to England on 7 days leave. 2. Intimation received that Advanced Mule Transport Depot moves from Orleans to ROUEN to-day. 3. Sale of any article of Army Rations prohibited in Army R.O. 609 d/. 4 Feb. owing to such articles having been seen exposed for sale in shop windows.	Feb 9th Major A.W. Fox proceeded on leave
	" 10th	Proposal to allot one A.T. Cart to each Brigade & to Div'l Troops for Veterinary Stores. Capt. Cu[illegible] proceeded on leave.	Q.2348 I.C.C d 10-2-15
MAMETZ	" 11th	Lt Col A.R. Burlton, O.C. A.S.C. proceeded to England on 4 days leave.	I.C. Chetter Q.2396 d 11/2/15
	" 12th	Question of feeding B Echelon Transport when divisions are in movement to be considered.	
	" 13th	Capt A.S. Crawford rejoined from leave. Major W. StG. Chamier rejoined from leave.	ac
	14th	Lt. Col A.R. Burlton rejoined from leave. Weather indifferent	
	" 15th	Major A.W. Fox returned from leave. Lieut (Hony) T. Whittaker proceeded on leave. Weather bad.	ac
	" 16th	Fine weather.	ac

Instructions regarding War Diaries and Intelligence Summaries are contained in F. S. Regs., Part II. and the Staff Manual respectively. Title pages will be prepared in manuscript.

WAR DIARY
or
INTELLIGENCE SUMMARY
(Erase heading not required.)

Army Form C. 2118.

Hour, Date, Place	Summary of Events and Information	Remarks and references to Appendices
Feb 17th MAMETZ	Inspection of Transport MHOW CAV. BGDE postponed on account of inclement weather. Weather very bad all day - rain and high wind 2nd Leave opened. Capt C W HEXT returned from leave. Capt OH HARRISON. R.O. SEC'BAD BDE proceeded on leave	
18th "	O.C A.S.C inspected Transport SECUNDERABAD. CAV. BGDE at 12 noon near TREIZENNES. Leave temporarily closed. Weather fine till about 5 pm when light rain fell.	ac.
19th "	Weather indifferent	ac
20th "	OC A.S.C inspected depot delivery of rations in the Meerut Brigade. Captain JCS RENDALL Lieut. C.I. CLARK proceeded on leave. Lt. JA BOSWORTH returned from leave. Weather good	ac.
21st	Weather fine. Cav. Corps sanction increase of 3 A T Carts to each Cav. Field Ambulance and 2 to Jodhpur Field Ambulance.	a.c.
22nd	Lt (Asst. Commissary) T. WHITAKER returned from leave. Weather fair foggy in the evening. Gov. of India Army Department sanction consolidated rates of pay to Departmental Officers (H.R) and Warrant Officers performing duties of combatant officers.	ac ac

1247 W 3299 200,000 (E) 8/14 J.B.C. & A. Forms/C. 2118/11.

Instructions regarding War Diaries and Intelligence Summaries are contained in F. S. Regs., Part II. and the Staff Manual respectively. Title pages will be prepared in manuscript.

WAR DIARY or INTELLIGENCE SUMMARY

(Erase heading not required.)

Army Form C. 2118.

Hour, Date, Place	Summary of Events and Information	Remarks and references to Appendices
23rd Febry MAMETZ –	Weather good – dry and cold ~~[illegible]~~	
2.30 p.m.	O.C. A.S.C inspected Horse Transport (Mule) 2nd Ind. Cav. Div! Headquarters – Capt J R HARRISON returned from leave –	AC
24th Febry –	Frost during night of 23rd–24th. Snowstorm on morning of 24th clearing up about 3 p.m. Lieut Col E G Vaughan D.S.O proceeded to England on leave	AC
25th February –	Heavy snow during night 24–25th. Thaw during day – Fine. 4 Pack Ponies received from Railhead – as unit unknown for which allotted temporarily handed over to T.O. Divisional Troops. Capt H.C Hall proceeded on leave –	AC
26th Feb. –	Fine day after frost during previous night. 3 mules Carts complete each handed over to 104th, 119th and 1st Cav Field Ambulances respectively and 2 mule Carts complete to Jodhpur Lancers Field Ambulance – authority D.A.Q.M.G. ICC Q.V.174 21-2-15. mule Carts received from Sec'bad Bgde Ammunition Column –	AC
27th Feb. –	Cold day inclined to snow with a high wind – Majors W. St. G. Chamier & L.W. Fox proceeded on leave –	AC
28th Febry –	Fine day with high wind – Slight rain during night of 28th Feb–1st March. Lt Col E G Vaughan, Major Chamier & Fox & Capt Hall returned from leave	AC

[signature] O.C. [illegible]

123

121/5114

WAR DIARY

OF

Supply + Transport
~~Army Service Corps~~, 2nd Indian Cavalry Division

From 1st March 1915 To 31st March 1915

Instructions regarding War Diaries and Intelligence Summaries are contained in F. S. Regs., Part II. and the Staff Manual respectively. Title pages will be prepared in manuscript.

WAR DIARY
or
INTELLIGENCE SUMMARY
(Erase heading not required.)

Army Form C. 2118.

Hour, Date, Place	Summary of Events and Information	Remarks and references to Appendices
MAMETZ MARCH 1st	O.C. A.S.C. inspected Horse and Mule Transport MHOW CAVALRY BRIGADE at 9.30 a.m. on CRECQUES-THEROUANNE ROAD.	
	State of Transport attached to 2nd LANCERS and 38th CENTRAL INDIA HORSE was most unsatisfactory.	
	Casualties in TRANSPORT for week ending 28th Feby as under:	
	(Mules. / Drivers. / Horses A.D. / A.S.C. Drivers.) MHOW CAV BGDE 1 / 1; MEERUT CAV BGDE 2 / 1 / 1 / 1; SEC'BAD CAV BGDE nil.	
	Weather fine morning clouding over towards noon. Snow commenced about 3.30 p.m.	
MARCH 2nd	Weather fine and sunny in the morning, clouded over somewhat in afternoon. Wind N.E. stronger in afternoon than morning.	ac
	All Horse Artillery Batteries and Gun Sections of Ammn. Columns left to join 4th Corps.	
	For rationing these units lorries were detached from Supply Column to join Supply Column 8th Division. Rations for men to be drawn from Railhead at AIRE, rations for animals from Railhead 4th Corps.	
7 p.m.	Orders received to form a section of a Divisional Train for the 3 Batteries and Ammunition Column. 14 G.S. wagons were allotted as follows: Each Battery 3. Combined Ammunition Column 4. Spare 1.	
	These were withdrawn from units as follows:	
	~~[illegible]~~ MEERUT BRIGADE each Cav. Regt 3 = 9	
	104th + 119th Cav. Field Ambulances = 5 Total 14.	
	Capt. H. F. Hall was ~~sent~~ ordered to proceed in charge of these wagons.	ac

Instructions regarding War Diaries and Intelligence Summaries are contained in F. S. Regs., Part II. and the Staff Manual respectively. Title pages will be prepared in manuscript.

WAR DIARY
or
INTELLIGENCE SUMMARY
(Erase heading not required.)

Army Form C. 2118.

Hour, Date, Place	Summary of Events and Information	Remarks and references to Appendices
NAMETZ 3rd March – 3 30 am	Capt. H.E. Hall left in charge of Wagons G.S. as detailed Owing to absence of Batteries it was found impossible to make change of Light and Heavy Draught Horses as originally ordered – Weather Rain in early morning – dull and overcast all through the day –	
NAMETZ 4th March –	Intimation received of despatch of 50 Heavy Draught Horses from ROUEN and necessary orders issued for exchange in Division – Weather High wind – dull day with an overcast sky. No rain –	
5th March 220am.	Heavy horses arrived complete with harness and were detrained – These horses were taken over by Secunderabad Cavalry Brigade – Following exchanges of Horses took place –	

(a) Heavy Draught –

No	From –	To
4	104 Cav F A	141 Cav F A
4	119 Cav F A	141 Cav F A
12.	Mhow Cav. Bde –	6 to 141 Cav F A. 2 to 13th Hussars – 2 to 3rd Horse 2 to 18th Lancers –

Horses were handed over with Harness except in the case of 2 Horses from 38th C I H. to 141 C F A – Orders were given for harness to be supplied by the unit handing over –

Following exchanges of L.D. Horses made –

No.	From	To
16	Sec'bad Cavalry Brigade (50)	104 C F A
16		104 C F A
6		Mhow Cav. Bde H Q.
6		6th Inniskilling Dragoons
6		38th C.I. Horse –

1247 W 3299 200,000 (E) 8/14 J.B.C. & A. Forms/C. 2118/11.

Army Form C. 2118.

Instructions regarding War Diaries and Intelligence Summaries are contained in F. S. Regs., Part II. and the Staff Manual respectively. Title pages will be prepared in manuscript.

WAR DIARY
or
INTELLIGENCE SUMMARY
(Erase heading not required.)

Hour, Date, Place	Summary of Events and Information	Remarks and references to Appendices
MAMETZ. 5th March	Weather – dull and damp – no rain – high wind WEST – mild –	AC
6th March	Weather – very bad and wet rain all the morning – in afternoon no rain until 5 pm when a very heavy shower occurred – 5 Horses from Secbad Bgde and 22 from 1st Cav D.A. handed over to Indian Corps at BUSNES	AC
7th March	Weather – dull and overcast in the morning with slight rain – finer in afternoon and heavy rain at night – High wind	
10.45 pm	Capt. H F Hall arrived with 14 G.S. Wagons which had temporarily been detached to 8th Division –	
	Major W. St. G Chauncey transferred to LAHORE Reserve Park	
	Major W. Synge posted Bde Supply Officer MEERUT BGDE in his place –	
	Capt R.F. Grant appointed Requisitioning Officer MHOW BGDE.	
	Lieut RF SMITH and 2nd Lt S L E SKEEN appointed Bgde Transport Officers	AC
8th March	Capt. R.F. Grant reported his arrival	
	Major W. Synge reported his arrival –	
	Weather – high wind – very cold – frost during night 8th–9th.	
9th March	Lt RF SMITH + 2/Lt SKEEN reported their arrival – former posted MHOW BGDE and latter to MEERUT BGDE	
	5 Horses obtained from XX Deccan Horse in lieu of 5 Transport Riding Ponies cast, previously inspected by O.C. A.S.C. –	
	7 mules unsuitable for Pack Work with Cavalry from MEERUT BGDE inspected by O.C. A.S.C., and orders were given to put them up for casting –	AC

1247 W 3299 200,000 (E) 8/14 J.B.C. & A. Forms/C. 2118/11.

1

Instructions regarding War Diaries and Intelligence Summaries are contained in F. S. Regs., Part II. and the Staff Manual respectively. Title pages will be prepared in manuscript.

WAR DIARY
or
~~INTELLIGENCE~~ SUMMARY.
(*Erase heading not required.*)

Army Form C. 2118.

Hour, Date, Place	Summary of Events and Information	Remarks and references to Appendices
MAMETZ 10th March 3.30 am	Division received orders to hold itself in readiness to move at an hours notice from 3 am. O.C A.S.C instructed to make all necessary arrangements.	
6 am	O.C issued instructions to S. Co and Transport officer, Divisional Troops.	
	Weather – dry and fairly mild – frost during previous night.	
9 p.m.	Orders received for Division to march. Transport under command of O.C A.S.C. ordered to leave MAMETZ at 4 am preceded by Field Squadron RE and MHOW CAVALRY FIELD AMBULANCE. MHOW BRIGADE TRANSPORT to move in rear of Divl Troops Transport and to join column at X Roads near BASSE BOULOGNE. MEERUT BRIGADE TRANSPORT to join column at ESTREE BLANCHE following in rear of DIVL Troops Transport and ahead of MHOW BRIGADE TRANSPORT.	AG
11th March 4 am	O.C. A.S.C proceeded to cross roads at BASSE BOULOGNE. FIELD SQUADRON passed at MARTHES. On arrival at X roads it was found that Transport of 38th C I H had moved along road to S of X roads. Ahead of them 2nd Lancers were on road. The whole of Divl Troops Transport and Field Squadron had therefore to pass these units Transport.	AG
4.45 am	Transport Divl Troops left MAMETZ.	
	Transport delayed at ESTREE BLANCHE by troops. MEERUT CAVY BDE	
6 am	Transport interposed in column at correct place.	
8 am	At AMETTES column of Transport 1st Indian Cavalry Division crossed head of 2nd Division Transport.	

Instructions regarding War Diaries and Intelligence Summaries are contained in F. S. Regs., Part II. and the Staff Manual respectively. Title pages will be prepared in manuscript.

WAR DIARY
or
INTELLIGENCE SUMMARY.
(Erase heading not required.)

Army Form C. 2118.

Hour, Date, Place	Summary of Events and Information	Remarks and references to Appendices
11th March – 8.30 am	Field Squadron and MHOW CAVALRY BGDE F.A. left column at x roads N. of CAUCHY-A-LA-TOUR to proceed to HAUT RIEUX and BURBURE respectively – Remainder of column proceeded via AUCHEL to LOZINGHEM.	
10. am.	Head of Column arrived at LOZINGHEM.	
	Weather – night very dark no moon – mild – Day. mild and misty. no rain.	ac
12th March. LOZINGHEM.	Rain in morning – mild day overcast with tendency to rain – Division under orders to move at one hours notice.	ac
13th March.	Weather fine and sunny.	
	Division under two hours notice to move with 'A' Echelon only.	
	B Echelon to remain behind at LOZINGHEM	
	Question of separate rationing of 'B' Echelon was considered and S.S.O. instructed to collect from Brigades numbers of men (B.E) and animals in B Echelon and arrange for their rations to be loaded on separate lorries.	ac
14th March	Weather fine and clear.	
3.30 pm	Division received orders to move. D.C. ASC to NORRENT-FONTES.	
9.30 pm	Divisional Troops Transport assembled in readiness to move off	
10 p.m	Divisional Troops Transport under Capt Hall left LOZINGHEM being delayed by Transport of SECUNDERABAD BRIGADE not being clear of LOZINGHEM	
11 p.m.	Transport Column joined DIVL. TROOPS at HAUT-RIEUX and proceeded via LILLERS and HAM-EN-ARTOIS – at turning about 1 Kilometre N of HAM column blocked by two wagons of Field Squadron, R.E. which went into ditch at cross roads about 1 mile due South of L in Molinghem – on clearing one of these wagons which cleared the	ac

(9 29 6) W4141—463 100,000 9/14 H W V Forms/C. 2118/10

Instructions regarding War Diaries and Intelligence Summaries are contained in F. S. Regs., Part II. and the Staff Manual respectively. Title pages will be prepared in manuscript.

WAR DIARY
or
INTELLIGENCE SUMMARY.
(*Erase heading not required.*)

Army Form C. 2118.

Hour, Date, Place	Summary of Events and Information	Remarks and references to Appendices
MARCH 15th	the road, Store wagon of AMBULANCE REPAIR UNIT went into ditch on other side of road. The road was finally sufficiently cleared by pushing one G.S. wagon fully into ditch to enable rest of transport to pass.	
NORRENT FONTES 6.30 am	Transport Div! Troops arrived.	
	Day misty with a slight drizzle.	AC
MARCH 16th	Weather fine and clear - mild -	
	Division under two hours notice to move.	AC
MARCH 17th	Weather fine and clear - mild	
	Division under four hours notice to move	
	Divisional Headquarters received orders to move to ROQUETOIRE by 12 noon on 18th. MHOW and MEERUT BRIGADES ordered to change their billets	
5 pm	Divisional Troops Transport and Signal Squadron ordered to move at 9 a.m. on 18th and be clear of NORRENTES FONTES by 9.30 am ~~to move~~ under command of Capt HALL	AC
MARCH 18th	Divisional Troops Transport under Capt HALL left NORRENT-FONTES at 9 am and marched via WITTERNESSE - BLESSY - MAMETZ to ROQUETOIRE arriving at 11.45 a.m.	
	Weather very cold and overcast - no rain.	
ROQUETOIRE MARCH 19th	Weather - Snow during night and alternate snow & sleet showers on and off during day - very cold.	
	2/Lt H.G. DUNNING reported his arrival on appointment as Requisitioning Officer SECUNDERABAD Brigade.	
	Division under six hours notice to move	

Army Form C. 2118.

Instructions regarding War Diaries and Intelligence Summaries are contained in F. S. Regs., Part II. and the Staff Manual respectively. Title pages will be prepared in manuscript.

WAR DIARY
or
~~INTELLIGENCE SUMMARY.~~
(Erase heading not required.)

Hour, Date, Place	Summary of Events and Information	Remarks and references to Appendices
ROQUETOIRE. MARCH 20th	Frost during night of 19th–20th. Day cold and fine –	
" MARCH 21st	Very fine day – sunny –	ac.
	Casualties in Horse + Mule Transport week ending 21st March –	

	Horses H.D.	Horses L.D.	A.S.C. Drivers	Mules Draught	Mules Pack	S.T. Cart
Divisional Headquarters –	1	–	–	–	–	2
Secunderabad Brigade	–	–	–	1	–	–
Mhow Brigade	–	–	–	4	1	4.
Meerut Brigade.	–	–	–	–	2	–

Hour, Date, Place	Summary of Events and Information	Remarks and references to Appendices
		ac
" MARCH 22nd	Weather – dull and overcast with occasional light showers – mild –	ac
" 23rd	Weather dull and overcast – mild –	ac
" 24th	Weather dull and cold, slight rain during day –	
" 25th	Weather – dull and cold – rain in the afternoon and evening –	
" 26th	Weather – Fine in morning, but dull + cold in afternoon. O.C. A.S.C. inspected Ammunition Park under Major H. B. Crawford A.S.C. at AIRE at 11 a.m.	
	Orders received that "no Hay, cattle or horses are to be requisitioned or purchased in the area occupied by the British Forces in France.	GRO No 741 d. 26-3-15
" 27th	Weather fine + cold – cold wind –	ac
" 28th	Lieut P Weir S.O. Railhead transferred as S.O. 2nd Cav Bde 1st Cav Divl A.S.C.	ac
	Weather fine + cold.	
" 29th	Weather fine. Cold wind –	
	O.C. A.S.C. inspected Transport MHOW CAVALRY BGDE at ECQUES at 10 am – Turn out satisfactory	

Instructions regarding War Diaries and Intelligence Summaries are contained in F. S. Regs., Part II. and the Staff Manual respectively. Title pages will be prepared in manuscript.

WAR DIARY
or
~~INTELLIGENCE SUMMARY.~~
(Erase heading not required.)

Army Form C. 2118.

Hour, Date, Place	Summary of Events and Information	Remarks and references to Appendices
ROCQUETOIRE MARCH 29th	Capt C BROWN + Hony Lieut J.A. BLOOMFIELD, S.T. Corps ordered to proceed to England forthwith and report in writing to War Office –	Authority AG GHQ No A/3016 d 27-3-15
	Weather fine + cold – very cold wind.	AC
MARCH 30th	O.C. A.S.C proceeded on seven days leave to England on urgent private affairs	
	Weather fine + cold	
MARCH 31st	Weather fine + cold.	
	Under orders from Indian Cavalry Corps [illegible] spare lorry detailed for temporary duty at ST VENANT in connection with defence works –	AC
		[illegible] Lieut Col. O.C. A.S.C. 2nd Ind. Cav. Div.

(73989) W4141—463. 400,000. 9/14. H.&J.Ltd. Forms/C. 2118/10.

121/5504

Serial No. 123

WAR DIARY

OF

Army Service Corps, 2nd Indian Cavalry Division.

From 1st April 1915 To 30th April 1915

mel 8/5

Instructions regarding War Diaries and Intelligence Summaries are contained in F. S. Regs., Part II. and the Staff Manual respectively. Title pages will be prepared in manuscript.

WAR DIARY
or
INTELLIGENCE SUMMARY.
(*Erase heading not required.*)

Army Form C. 2118.

Hour, Date, Place	Summary of Events and Information	Remarks and references to Appendices
ROCQUETOIRE. APRIL 1st	Weather very fine – warm and sunny – frost during night –	
3 p.m.	Lieuts. WILSON & NESBITT. S.T. Corps. I.A.R. of O. reported their arrival and following postings were ordered, consequent on posting of Hony CAPT. S. BROWN and Hony Lt J A BLOOMFIELD.	I.C.C. Telegram Q.V. 229 d 1/4/15 –
	CAPT R.F. EWART S.T. Corps from R.O. Mhow Cav Bde to Supply Officer Railhead	
	Hony Lt T WHITAKER S.T.C. from R.O. MEERUT Cav Bde to " " "	
	2/Lt NESBITT S.T.C. to R.O. Mhow Cav Bde.	
	2/Lt WILSON S.T.C. to R.O. MEERUT Cav Bde –	ac
" 2nd	Weather fine & sunny –	
	Capt. R.F. EWART ordered to report to A.D. S.T. I.C.C. for special duty with mule transport	I.C.C. Telegram Q.V. 231 d. 1/4/15.
	Lieut. H.G. Dunning I.A.R. of O. from R.O. Sec. Cav Bde to Supply officer Railhead	
	Orders received for entrainment of Reg Carts (A.T. mule) at BERGUETTE on morning of 5th. Carts to be present at BERGUETTE by 3 p.m. on 4th inst. –	ac
" 3rd	Weather – rain all day –	
" " 4th	Weather – rain on and off during day –	ac
	162 draught mules, 51 A.T. Carts and 87 Transport Ranks handed over at BERGUETTE STATION by 3 p.m. –	
	Capt. E.C. PINDER, ASC ordered to report to D. of T. GHQ as soon as possible. Hony Lieut. J.A. BLOOMFIELD departs for England.	I.C.C. Telegram Q.4027 d 4/4/15 –
" 5th	Weather – light rain during morning till about 11 a.m. – Heavy rain from 2 p.m. onwards –	ac
5 p.m.	All billets WEST of road EBLINGHEM – WARDRECQUES – THEROUANNE – BOMY – BEAUMETZ-LEZ-AIRE ordered to be evacuated, and troops to close up into remainder of Area – All billets on road as well ordered to be evacuated. – 7th D.G. and N Bty RHA SEC BAD BDE ordered evacuate THEROUANNE and MHOW BRIGADE ordered into area MAZINGHEM – MOLINGHEM – NORRENT FONTES – All Billets ordered to be cleared by 12 noon on 6-4-15	
	Lt Col A.R. BURLTON returned from leave – Hony Capt S. BROWN S.T.C. left for England	ac

Army Form C. 2118.

Instructions regarding War Diaries and Intelligence Summaries are contained in F. S. Regs., Part II. and the Staff Manual respectively. Title pages will be prepared in manuscript.

WAR DIARY
or
INTELLIGENCE SUMMARY.

(*Erase heading not required.*)

Hour, Date, Place	Summary of Events and Information	Remarks and references to Appendices
ROCQUETOIRE April 6th	Weather - fairly fine with a tendency to rain - CAPT. C.E. PINDER left H.Q.	ac.
April 7th	Weather - fine in morning, showery in afternoon - O.C. A.S.C. inspected Transport SECUNDERABAD BRIGADE at BASSE BOULOGNE at 9.30 am Turnout fairly satisfactory Billeting claims at REBECQ, MAMETZ, NORRENT FONTES & LOZINGHEM settled.	ac.
April 8th	Fine day on the whole -	ac
April 9th	Weather changeable - fine and raining alternately - two sharp showers one in morning and one in afternoon O.C. A.S.C. inspected all Transport MEERUT CAVALRY BRIGADE at 10.30 am on road leading EAST from ROCQUETOIRE EAST. Turnout satisfactory -	ac
" 10th	Fine day -	
" 11th	Fine day - Capt. R.A. Ewart returned from duty under A.D. S.T. reported to MHOW BDE. Intimation received of early arrival of ORDNANCE MULES to replace Pack Mules with Cavalry Regts -	ac
" 12th	Weather - dull - tendency to rain - O.C. A.S.C. inspected transport of Divl. Troops - i.e. 3 Field Ambulances and Head Quarters - The turn out of the Head Quarter Transport was reported as particularly good - These remarks, together with the expression of the appreciation of the G.O.C., were communicated by order to Capt Hall T.O. Divl Troops,	ac
" 13th	All Units returned to billets evacuated on the 5th inst Weather - dull - rain both in morning and evening - Capt R.A. Ewart transferred as Supply officer Secunderabad Bde & Capt H.H. HARRISON appointed REQUISITIONING OFFICER That Bde -	ac

Instructions regarding War Diaries and Intelligence Summaries are contained in F. S. Regs., Part II. and the Staff Manual respectively. Title pages will be prepared in manuscript.

WAR DIARY
or
~~INTELLIGENCE SUMMARY~~.
(Erase heading not required.)

Army Form C. 2118.

Hour, Date, Place	Summary of Events and Information	Remarks and references to Appendices
ROCQUETOIRE. APRIL 13th	Capt EWART took over his duties on the forenoon of this day.	
	Intimation received that 140 Ordnance Mules were to be despatched on 14th inst from ROUEN.	
4 p.m.	Intimation received that only 110 Ordnance Mules would be despatched. These were allotted as follows 66 Meerut Brigade 22 to each Regt. 44 Mhow Brigade 22 for two Regts only.	
	Units again evacuated billets ON and WEST of road EBLINGHEM - WARDRECQUES - THEROUANNE	ac
April 14th	Weather dull and cold. Excellent day for some weeks.	ac
April 15th	Weather very fine and warm.	
	110 Ordnance Mules arrived at Rail Head to replace Pack Mules with Cavalry Regiments. They were distributed as follows:-	
	MEEROT CAV. BDE :- 13th Hussars 22. 3rd Skinner's Horse 22 18th Lancers 22	
	MHOW CAV. BDE. 6th (Inniskilling) Dragoons 22 38th C.I. Horse 22.	
	All arrived without accident and were handed over to units at Railhead	
April 16th	Weather fine and warm.	ac
April 17th	Weather fine and warm.	
April 18th	Weather fine and warm.	ac
	Capt. P. MORTIMER S.T.C. arrived from MEERUT DIVISIONAL TRAIN + reported for duty. He was appointed Transport Officer MEERUT CAV. BDE vice 2Lieut E.L.E SKEENE posted to MEERUT. Dvl Train.	ac
	2Lt. E.L.E SKEENE left the Division on this date.	
	Notification received of arrival on 19th of 88 Ordnance Mules to ~~ac~~ equip SECUNDERABAD Brigade and remaining Regiment (2nd Lancers) of MHOW BDE.	ac

(73989) W4141—463. 400,000. 9/14. H.&J.Ltd. Forms/C. 2118/10.

Army Form C. 2118.

Instructions regarding War Diaries and Intelligence Summaries are contained in F. S. Regs., Part II. and the Staff Manual respectively. Title pages will be prepared in manuscript.

WAR DIARY
or
~~INTELLIGENCE SUMMARY.~~

(Erase heading not required.)

Hour, Date, Place			Summary of Events and Information	Remarks and references to Appendices
ROCQUETOIRE	April 19th		Weather fine and bright. 88 Ordnance mules arrived at Railhead at and detailed to units.	C
do — do	April 20th		Weather fine	
do	April 21st		Weather fine.	
do	April 22nd		Weather fine	
do	April 23rd		Weather fine. Orders received to entrain PACK MULES at AIRE at 4. p.m on 24th.	C
do — do	April 24th		Weather fine during day with cold wind.	
		9 am	Orders received for division to be in readiness to move at 2 hours notice.	
		3. p.m	~~mules~~ 206 Pack mules, 1 Pack Pony, 1 Riding Pony and S.T. personnel arrived at AIRE and handed over to Conducting officer for transit to Base	
		3.15 pm	Orders received to move. B Echelon under Lt. Col BURLTON to rendezvous at WARDRECQUES STATION at 7 p.m.	
		6 p.m.	B. ECHELON DIVISIONAL TROOPS left ROCQUETOIRE. owing to enforced halts to allow SECUNDERABAD BRIGADE and DIVISIONAL AMMUNITION COLUMN to pass, rendezvous was not reached until 8 p.m. March continued via EBLINGHEM STATION – LE NIEPPE – EY HOUCK. Delay at X roads at EY HOUCK caused by AMMUNITION COLUMN.	
		12 mn	Heavy rain commenced to fall. owing to delay of column, Head Quarters	
	April 25th		transport moved on to cross roads ½ mile S of BAVINCHOVE. thence WESTWARDS parallel to railway as far as (crossing under) RAILWAY ARCH near ~~[illegible]~~ ZUYTPEENE. Here a	
		1.30 am	delay of about two and a half hours occurred owing to 3 wagons of AMMUNITION column becoming ditched. After clearing obstructions Transport was	
WEMAERS-CAPPEL		4 30 am	enabled to move on arriving at WEMAERS-CAPPEL about 4 30. a.m. Heavy rain continued until about 4 a.m. Division in readiness to move at one hours notice until 9 p.m	
do — do	April 26th		CAPT A C BIRD S.T.C reported his arrival & was appointed Requisitioning Officer Divisional Troops. Fine day on the whole – dull in morning and very cold at night	AC
			Division under 1 hours notice to move from 5 am to 12 midnight	AC

Instructions regarding War Diaries and Intelligence Summaries are contained in F. S. Regs., Part II. and the Staff Manual respectively. Title pages will be prepared in manuscript.

WAR DIARY
or
INTELLIGENCE SUMMARY.
(*Erase heading not required.*)

Army Form C. 2118.

Hour, Date, Place	Summary of Events and Information	Remarks and references to Appendices
WAEMAERS. CAPPEL Apr. 27th	Weather very fine and warm	
	Division under one hours notice to move_	a.c.
Apr. 28th	Weather very fine and warm	
11.30 am.	Division with A Echelon only ordered to move to HOUTKERQUE_ B' ECHELON to remain behind and concentrated. B ECHELON MEERUT BRIGADE moved to WAEMAERS-CAPPEL and B ECHELON SEC'BAD BRIGADE to ZUYTPEENE_ movements completed by 4. p.m.	
Apr. 29th	Weather very fine and warm.	a.c.
5 pm	Orders received for B' ECHELON to march at 6 am to rejoin Division_	
Apr 30th	Weather_ a misty morning_ mist continued until about 8.30 am. Remainder of day very fine and warm.	a.c.
HOUTKERQUE 6.30 am	B EECHELON marched from WAEMARS CAPPEL via L'ANGE and WINNEZEELE. Head arrived at HOUTKERQUE at 10. am. Divisional Troops arrived at 10.30 am.	
10.30 am	B ECHELON of Brigades proceeded to join their units_ There were no Casualties on the march	a.c.

[signature]

Lieut Colonel. S.T. Corps
O.C. A.S.C.
2nd Ind Cav Div_

(73989) W4141—463. 400,000. 9/14. H.&J.Ltd. Forms/C. 2118/10.

Serial No 123.

121/5799

WAR DIARY

OF

Army Service Corps 2nd Indian Cavalry Division.

FROM 1st May 1915 TO 31st May 1915

Instructions regarding War Diaries and Intelligence Summaries are contained in F. S. Regs., Part II. and the Staff Manual respectively. Title pages will be prepared in manuscript.

WAR DIARY
or
~~INTELLIGENCE SUMMARY.~~

(*Erase heading not required.*)

Army Form C. 2118.

Hour, Date, Place	Summary of Events and Information	Remarks and references to Appendices
HOUTKERQUE MAY 1st	Fine day - bright sunshine -	
11 pm	Orders received for Division to return to previous billeting area -	a.c.
MAY 2nd	Dull morning with a tendency to rain - fine later -	
	B Echelon marched with their own brigades to WAEMERS-CAPPEL area.	
	Transport of Divisional Troops left at 8.30 a.m. and marched via	
WAEMERS-CAPPEL	to WAEMERS-CAPPEL arriving at about 12 noon.	a.c.
MAY 3rd	Weather very fine -	
	Divisional Head Quarters moved to CHATEAU near LE COUVENT	
MAY 4th	Weather sultry until about 5 p.m. when thunderstorm broke - rain lasted about one hour.	
6 pm	Orders received that Division would march at 8-30 p.m. to new billeting area S.W. of AIRE	
9.30 pm	Divl. Troops Transport left at 9.30 p.m. marching via STAPLE - WALLON CAPPEL - BOSENGHEM - LA ROUPIE - LE HAMEL to DENNEBROECQ.	a.c.
DENNEBROECQ. May 5th 2.30 pm	Divisional Troops Transport arrived - There were no Casualties but frequent delays and checks.	
	Weather fine -	a.c.
MAY 6th	Weather fine -	
May 7th	Weather fine in morning, but turned to rain in afternoon + evening	
	OC A.S.C visited Head Quarters I.C.C. in connection with changes in transport	a.c.
May 8th	Weather fine	
7.45 pm.	Division ordered to be in readiness to move at 2 hours notice from 5. a.m. on 9th. On receipt of order to move B Echelon to be brigaded and Baggage to be	

Army Form C. 2118.

Instructions regarding War Diaries and Intelligence Summaries are contained in F. S. Regs., Part II. and the Staff Manual respectively. Title pages will be prepared in manuscript.

WAR DIARY
or
INTELLIGENCE SUMMARY.
(Erase heading not required.)

Hour, Date, Place		Summary of Events and Information	Remarks and references to Appendices
DENNEBROECQ.	MAY 8th	dumped at Brigade Centres.	
	9.30 pm.	Order received that Baggage would be dumped at COYECQUE for Divl H.Q. Baggage wagons would then proceed to AIRE and be loaded with two days supplies at a special scale. When Division is at short notice to move Baggage wagons to be kept loaded up.	
	MAY 9th	Weather fine and warm during day. Cold at night. Baggage wagons loaded up in readiness to move.	ac
	MAY 10th	Weather fine and warm } Inspection of Divisional Supply Column by Major Hutchinson ASC GHQ a very satisfactory report.	ac
	MAY 11th	Weather fine and warm }	
	MAY 12th	Weather fine and warm	
	7 pm	Division under four hours notice to move.	ac
	MAY 13th	Weather - rained almost without ceasing the whole day.	
	MAY 14th	Weather. Cloudy with occasional rain in morning, turning fine in the afternoon & evening	ac
	MAY 15th	Weather fine and warm.	ac
	16th	9 am Division under two hours notice to move. Weather fine.	
	17th	Dull day with frequent showers - wet night	
	4.30 pm	B Echelon Transport moved at 4.30 pm to COYECQUE where all baggage was	
COYECQUE		stored - B Echelon remained at COYECQUE	
		Capt H.C. Hall ordered to report to A.D.S.&T. for service with Transport overseas	
	18th	Dull misty day with frequent showers - a wet night	
		Capt H.C. Hall left in forenoon - Capt A.E. Crawford assumed duties of Transport Officer, Divl. Troops in addition to his own duties.	
BOMY	19th	Dull day with showers - clearing up towards evening	
		B Echelon Divl Troops moved at 5 a.m. from COYECQUE to BOMY arriving at 6 p.m.	
	20th	Fine morning turning dull & misty in evening	
		Division under four hours notice	
		Draught horses with drivers and brakesmen G.S. wagons arrived at AIRE by two trains 1st train arrived 4.30 pm - units took over new transport on following scale:-	

Instructions regarding War Diaries and Intelligence Summaries are contained in F. S. Regs., Part II. and the Staff Manual respectively. Title pages will be prepared in manuscript.

Army Form C. 2118.

WAR DIARY
or
INTELLIGENCE SUMMARY.
(Erase heading not required.)

Hour, Date, Place	Summary of Events and Information	Remarks and references to Appendices

BOMY MAY 20th

Unit	Limbered G Swagons	Mules Draught	Horse Draught	Regt. Drivers	A.S.C. Drivers	A.S.C. Artificers	A.S.C. NCO's	Regt NCO's	Riding Horses
British Cav. Regt	5	20		11	–	1		1	1
Indian Cav Regt	5	20		–	11	1	1	–	1
Battery RHA	1	–	2	–	–	–	–	1	–
Cav Field Amb.	3	13	–	–	7	4	1	–	1
Mob Vet Sec.	1	4	–	–	2	–	–	–	–
Bde Head Quarters	1	4	–	–	2	–	–	–	–
Divl Head Quarters	1	4	–	–	2	–			

One mule was severely injured, and destroyed under the orders of the O.C. A.S.C.
Two A.S.C. Drivers were injured by runaway mules & carts. — ac

" MAY 21st

Fine day on the whole – one or two slight showers
D.A. & Q.M.G. I.C.C. inspected Divl Supply Column
Balance of Mule Transport left and handed over to Railhead Supply officer at AIRE.
Total strength (excluding that of Cav. Field Ambulances)

W.O.	N.O.	K.D.C.N.	L.D. & O.	Mules Draught.	Artificers	Carts.	Ponies
1	1	4	32	57	6	26	4

ac

MAY 22nd — Fine day

May 23rd — Fine sunny day. O.C. A.S.C. visited Corps Head Quarters. — ac

May 24th — Fine sunny day

May 25th, May 26th — Weather cold and dull with high wind — ac

May 27th — Weather dull & cold.

May 28th — Weather fairly fine – Light Draught Animals to replace Heavy Draught Horses with S wagons — ac

(73989) W4141—463. 400,000. 9/14. H.&J.Ltd. Forms/C. 2118/10.

Army Form C. 2118.

Instructions regarding War Diaries and Intelligence Summaries are contained in F. S. Regs., Part II. and the Staff Manual respectively. Title pages will be prepared in manuscript.

WAR DIARY
or
~~INTELLIGENCE SUMMARY.~~
(Erase heading not required.)

Hour, Date, Place	Summary of Events and Information	Remarks and references to Appendices
BOMY May 28th	with Divisional Head Quarters & Brigade Head Quarters 5 Cav Regts of SECUNDERABAD Brigade + Field Ambulances on following Scale	
		Mules / Drivers ASC	
	Divl Head Quarters – 18 10	
	1 Brigade Head Quarters 9. 5.	
	1 Field Ambulance 13. 7.	
	1 Cavalry Regiment 22.	
	Total mules = 150 with 46 drivers –	
	These arrived at Railhead at 3.30 pm. when expected at 6.30 pm. They were taken over & those for Divl Head Quarters arrived about midnight without casualties.	ac.
May 29th	Lt Col A.R. Boulton on leave to England – Lt Col E. G. Vaughan DSO acting as O.C. A.S.C. in addition to his own duties. Fine weather –	ac
May 30th	132 Draught mules due to arrive at Railhead at 8.30 am arrived at 11.30 am. These were distributed to the Cavalry Regts of of MHOW & MEERUT Brigades –	
	57 Heavy Draught Horses & 65(a) A.S.C Drivers were handed over to A.D. S.T. 3 C.C at Railhead at 12.30 pm. – These were from units which had received Mules on the 28th May – Fine weather –	(a) includes 36 A.S.C Drivers of Conducting Party which brought up mules on 28-V-15 – ac

(73989) W4141—463. 400,000. 9/14. H.&J.Ltd. Forms/C. 2118/10.

Instructions regarding War Diaries and Intelligence Summaries are contained in F. S. Regs., Part II. and the Staff Manual respectively. Title pages will be prepared in manuscript.

WAR DIARY

or

~~INTELLIGENCE SUMMARY.~~

(Erase heading not required.)

Army Form C. 2118.

Hour, Date, Place	Summary of Events and Information	Remarks and references to Appendices
BOMY MAY 31st	Weather - fine & warm - The remaining Heavy Draught Horses (12 per Regiment) from each of the three Regiments of the Lahore & Meerut Cavalry Brigades replaced by mules on May 30th were sent to Railhead i/c of the B T O [illegible] Meerut Cavalry Brigade - E. G. [illegible] Lieut Colonel for O.C. R.C. 2nd I.C.D.	a.e.

(73989) W4141—463. 400,000. 9/14. H.&J.Ltd. Forms/C. 2118/10.

Serial No. 123.

121/6128

WAR DIARY

OF

A.S.C. 2nd Indian Cavalry Division.

From 1st June 1915 To 30th June 1915.

2nd/5

6

June 1915 –

Instructions regarding War Diaries and Intelligence Summaries are contained in F. S. Regs., Part II. and the Staff Manual respectively. Title pages will be prepared in manuscript.

WAR DIARY

~~or~~

~~INTELLIGENCE SUMMARY.~~

(Erase heading not required.)

Army Form C. 2118.

Hour, Date, Place		Summary of Events and Information	Remarks and references to Appendices
BONY	June 1st	Fine weather –	ac.
	" 2nd	Fine weather –	ac.
	" 3rd	Fine weather –	ac.
	" 4th	Weather – dull morning followed by a fine afternoon Lieut Col A.R. Burlton VC ASC returned from leave	ac
	" 5th	Weather fine and warm – A Section Supply Column moved from BERGUETTE to MARTHES	ac
	" 6th	Weather fine and warm	ac
	" 7th	Weather fine and very hot	ac
	" 8th	Weather very hot and sultry morning which was followed by a thunderstorm commencing about 2.30pm. G.O.C. inspected Divisional Troops and Transport at 10.30 am at fork in roads near point 140 between ERNY ST JULIEN and COYECQUES – Transport returned via Cross roads near COYECQUES + PETIGNY	ac
	" 9th	Weather – rained nearly all day	
	" 10th	Weather – rainy	
	" 11th	Weather – fine –	
	" 12th	Weather – fine –	
	" 13th	Weather – fine	
	" 14th	" fine	
	" 15th	" fine	
	[illegible]	GOC ICC inspected near RILEY all remounts received since 1st March this included all Draught [illegible] recently received	
	16th	Weather fine	ac

Army Form C. 2118.

Instructions regarding War Diaries and Intelligence Summaries are contained in F. S. Regs., Part II. and the Staff Manual respectively. Title pages will be prepared in manuscript.

WAR DIARY
or
~~INTELLIGENCE SUMMARY.~~
(Erase heading not required.)

Hour, Date, Place	Summary of Events and Information	Remarks and references to Appendices
BONY June 17th	weather fine – OC. A.S.C inspected roads ~~at~~ near Barges on canal at AIRE and approaches there to ~~for~~ through AIRE in accordance with DCC. No Q 6340 d. 16th June 1915	ac
June 18th	weather fine	ac
June 19th	Weather fine	ac
June 20th	weather fine	ac
June 21st	Weather fine – Capt. A.S. Crawford on leave for 7 days to England	ac
June 22nd to June 25th	Fine weather	ac
June 26th	weather very wet.	ac
June 27th	Weather very wet – Capt. A.S. Crawford returned from leave –	ac
June 28th	Weather wet – Lieut Col. [illegible] O.C.O. proceeded on leave to England. Lt Col A.R. Burton performing duties of O.C. in addition to his own. O.C. A.S.C inspected "A" Section, Divisional Supply Column at Fontes at 10. a.m. Turnout satisfactory.	
4.30 pm	A digging party Strength Field Squadron British 70 Indian 70, Meerut Cavalry Bde British 140 Indian 460 proceeded to defensive zone to construct trenches under the orders of the 1st Army.	ac
June 29th	weather dull with slight showers –	
9.30 am	OC A.S.C inspected 'A' & 'B' Echelon Transport of Meerut Cav. Bde at WITTERNESSE. Evening very wet. heavy rain fell from about 5 pm	ac
June 30th	weather – variable in morning – fine in evening –	ac

[illegible]
Lieut Colonel
O.C. A.S.C
[illegible] Cav. Bde

Serial No. 123.

121/6502

WAR DIARY OF

Army Service Corps, 2nd Indian Cavalry Division.

FROM 1st July 1915 TO 31st July 1915

Instructions regarding War Diaries and Intelligence Summaries are contained in F. S. Regs., Part II. and the Staff Manual respectively. Title pages will be prepared in manuscript.

WAR DIARY
or
INTELLIGENCE SUMMARY.
(*Erase heading not required.*)

July

Army Form C. 2118.

Hour, Date, Place	Summary of Events and Information	Remarks and references to Appendices
BONY. JULY 1st	Weather dull & changeable –	ac
2nd	Weather dull in morning fine later –	ac
	600 men of Mhow Brigade proceeded to join 1st Army in relief of digging party of 600 men of Meerut Brigade who returned to billets	
3rd	Weather dull & overcast –	ac
4th	Weather very fine & hot	ac
5th	Weather dull in morning and evening with tendency to rain – fine evening	ac
6th	Weather hot & fine in morning, clouding over towards evening with occasional showers	
10 am	O.C. A.S.C. inspected Horse Transport of 102nd (MHOW) Field Ambulance at ROBECQ –	ac
	900 men of Secunderabad Brigade proceeded digging in relief of men of MHOW Brigade	
7th	Weather – windy day with occasional showers in afternoon & evening	
10 am	O.C. A.S.C. inspected Ammunition Park at AIRE – The men were first seen at Company Drill and afterwards lorries were inspected	ac
8th	Weather dull and overcast.	
9th	Weather – dull in morning – cloudy and overcast in afternoon & evening	
6.30 am	Inspected Horse Transport of 131st (Secunderabad) Indian Cavalry Field Ambulance at GREUPPE.	ac
10th	Weather fine & sunny.	
10 am	O.C. A.S.C. inspected all Horse Transport of MHOW Cavalry Brigade at NEDONCHELLE.	
	900 men of MEERUT Bde proceeded digging in relief of men of the Secunderabad Bde –	ac
11th	Dull day, cloudy with a tendency to rain	ac

Army Form C. 2118.

Instructions regarding War Diaries and Intelligence Summaries are contained in F. S. Regs., Part II. and the Staff Manual respectively. Title pages will be prepared in manuscript.

WAR DIARY
or
INTELLIGENCE SUMMARY.
(Erase heading not required.)

Hour, Date, Place	Summary of Events and Information	Remarks and references to Appendices
BOMY July 12th	Weather - cloudy in morning with a fair wind - fine later	
	OC ASC inspected Horse Transport of Secunderabad Brigade at WANDONNE at 10 30 am	
July 13th	Fine day on the whole -	ae
	OC ASC inspected Horse Transport 119 C.F.A. near PETIGNY at 10 am.	ae
July 14th	Dull day with very heavy rain during night of 14-15th July	ae
15th	Fine day	
10 am	OC ASC inspected Horse Transport of Divl Head Quarters + Divl ASC at Bomy and. One pair of mules were tested in a full water cart and found insufficient	ae
16th	A dull morning followed by a wet afternoon	
11 30 am	DADHMG LCC inspected Ammunition Park 2nd ICD at Aire	ae
17th	Weather fair - Digging parties ordered to consist of 450 men of each Bde -	ae
18th	Weather fair Portion of digging party proceeded + portion of Meerut Bde party returned	ae
19th	Weather fair	ae
20th	Weather fair Remainder of digging parties proceeded to digging area	ae
21st 10 am	OC A.S.C inspected 83 Coy M.T. A.S.C (Divl Supply Column at AIRE	ae
	Weather fair	
22nd	Weather fine in morning + rained in evening - Heavy rain during night 22nd - 23rd	ae

Army Form C. 2118.

Instructions regarding War Diaries and Intelligence Summaries are contained in F. S. Regs., Part II. and the Staff Manual respectively. Title pages will be prepared in manuscript.

WAR DIARY
or
~~INTELLIGENCE SUMMARY.~~
(Erase heading not required.)

Hour, Date, Place	Summary of Events and Information	Remarks and references to Appendices
BOMY July 23rd	Weather changeable – various showers during day rain during night	AC
July 24th	Weather fine on the whole – one or two slight showers –	
10.30 a.m.	G.O.C. I.C.C. inspected Transport SECUNDERABAD Bde at GLEM	AC
July 25th.	Weather fine –	
July 26th	Weather fairly fine –	a
July 27th.	Weather fine –	a a
10 a.m.	G.O.C. I.C.C. inspected [illegible] Transport. MHOW Bde at Auchy.	
	Following transfers ordered with effect from 28th inst.	
	Capt A.C. Bond from R.O. Divl. Troops to Supply Officer, Divl. Supply Column	
	Lieut A.A. [illegible] from Supply Officer, Divl. Supply Column to R.O. Sec'bad Bde.	
	Capt A.C. Harrison from R.O. Sec'bad Bde to R.O. Divl. Troops	AC
July 28th	Weather showery in morning, fine later –	
July 29th	Weather fine	a
July 30th	Weather fine	a
1 p.m.	Orders received for Division to move to 3rd Army Area on Aug 1st	ac
July 31st	Fine weather –	AC

[signature] Lieut Colonel
O.C. A.S.C. 2nd Ind. Cav. Div. –

Serial No: 123.

121/6948

WAR DIARY OF

Army Service Corps, 2nd Indian Cavalry Division

FROM 1st August 1915 TO 31st August 1915

12

Instructions regarding War Diaries and Intelligence Summaries are contained in F. S. Regs., Part II. and the Staff Manual respectively. Title pages will be prepared in manuscript.

WAR DIARY
or
~~INTELLIGENCE SUMMARY.~~
(*Erase heading not required.*)

Army Form C. 2118.

Hour, Date, Place	Summary of Events and Information	Remarks and references to Appendices
BONY August 1st.	Divisional Troops marched in rear of MEEROT CAV. Bde from BONY to ROYON via BEAUMETZ-LEZ-AIRE, FRUGES, CREQUY.	
10 a.m.	B ECHELON left BONY at 10 a.m. passing starting point at BEAUMETZ at 11.15 a.m. thence moving in rear of Ammunition Column	
ROYON 5.30 p.m.	until arrival at ROYON at 5.30 p.m.	
	Weather hot and fine — No casualties —	
August 2nd	Divisional Troops marched in rear of MEEROT CAV. BDE from ROYON to GORENFLOS via BEAURAINVILLE - DOURIEZ - CRECY - DOMVAST - ST. RIQUIER.	
8. a.m.	B Echelon, Divl H.Q. left ROYON at 8 a.m. passing starting point at LOISON at 9. a.m. moving in rear of Field Squadron.	
	At BEAURAINVILLE it was found that road via LA NEUVILLE to GOUY was too bad for Transport to pass, so DIVL. TROOPS marched via	
12 noon.	CAMPAGNE-LEZ-HESDIN and ST REMY aux BOIS to DOURIEZ arriving at 12 noon.	
1.30 p.m.	After halting for 1½ hours column marched via LIGESCOURT & CRECY (4.30 p.m.),	
GORENFLOS. 7.30 p.m.	ST RIQUIER (6 p.m.) to GORENFLOS which was reached at 7.30. p.m.	
	Weather dull in morning but fine on the whole — heavy shower about 4 p.m. and rain again ~~fell~~ commences to fall at 7 p.m.	
August 3rd.	DIVISIONAL TROOPS marched in rear of MEERUT CAV. BDE from GORENFLOS to BELLOY SUR SOMME by ROUTE NATIONALE No 35 through MOUFLERS-LA FOLIE and FLIXECOURT.	
9.30 a.m.	B Echelon Divl Troops left GORENFLOS at 9.30 a.m. passing starting point at MOUFLERS-LA FOLIE at 11 a.m. and arrived at BELLOY SUR SOMME	
BELLOY-SUR-SOMME 1 p.m.	at 1 p.m.	

Instructions regarding War Diaries and Intelligence Summaries are contained in F. S. Regs., Part II. and the Staff Manual respectively. Title pages will be prepared in manuscript.

WAR DIARY
or
INTELLIGENCE SUMMARY.
(*Erase heading not required.*)

Army Form C. 2118.

Hour, Date, Place	Summary of Events and Information	Remarks and references to Appendices
BELLOY-SUR-SOMME August 3rd	Weather. Rain commenced to fall early in morning and continued to about 10.15 a.m. Very heavy rain again fell about 11.30 a.m. but stopped before noon remainder of day fairly fine.	OC
August 4th	Wet morning and dull evening	OC
5th	Cloudy day with rain.	OC
6th	Wet morning finer in evening	OC
7th	Fine and hot.	
8th	Fine and hot.	OC
9th	Weather very close all day followed by a thunderstorm in evening	OC
8 p.m.	900 men MEERUT CAV. Bde with Signal Squadron and portion of Field Squadron proceeded to BAIZIEUX by motor bus. S.A.A. Section Ammunition Column & portion of 119th Cav. Field Ambulance proceeded to CONTAY. 'A' Echelon Transport plus 2 G.S. Wagons B Echelon per Regt proceeded by day	
10th	Weather fine and hot.	OC
8 pm	900 men SECBAD CAV. Bde with portion of Field Squadron proceeded by motor bus to FRANVILLERS. 'A' Echelon Transport plus 2 G.S. Wagons B Echelon per Regt proceeded by day	
11th	Weather fine.	OC
	900 men MHOW CAV. Bde with portion of Field Squadron proceeded by motor bus to FRANVILLERS 'A' Echelon Transport plus 2 G.S. Wagons B Echelon per Regt proceeded by day	
12th	Weather fairly fine.	OC
	Meerut and Secbad Bdes moved to MARTINSART and to ~~[illegible]~~ for the supply of rations to these units a 'Train' consisting of 2 G.S. Wagons per Regt was formed under Capt. HEXT to work between HEDAUVILLE and MARTINSART	OC
13th	Weather dull with occasional slight showers.	

(73989) W4141—463. 400,000. 9/14. H.&J.Ltd. Forms/C. 2118/10.

Instructions regarding War Diaries and Intelligence Summaries are contained in F. S. Regs., Part II. and the Staff Manual respectively. Title pages will be prepared in manuscript.

WAR DIARY
or
~~INTELLIGENCE SUMMARY.~~
(Erase heading not required.)

Army Form C. 2118.

Hour, Date, Place	Summary of Events and Information	Remarks and references to Appendices
BELLOY-sur-SOMME		
August 13th	MHOW and SIALKOT Bde. moved from CONTAY and FRANVILLERS respectively to MARTINSART and supplied 15 wagons at 3 per regt ~~for~~ in order to complete the Divisional Train ~~at~~ under Capt. Head.	
	3. RHA Battery moved to CONTAY.	
	All horses and transport not required moved to a Camp in VADENCOURT Wood under CAPT MORTIMER.	
	Divl Ammunition Park moved to VILLERS-BOCAGE being attached to 51st Ammunition Park and rationed by them.	
August 14th	Weather fine –	ac
	Gun Sections Ammunition Column moved to CONTAY.	
	Tempy 2/Lt. L.E.C. PRICE, ASC ~~arrived~~ reported his arrival and posted as Transport Officer MHOW Cav. Bde vice Capt R.J. SMITH.	ac
August 15th	Weather fine.	
	~~...~~ Capt. W.P.R. Wheatley S.I.T.C joined Ammunition Park.	ac
August 16th	O.C. A.S.C inspected Divisional Train at MARTINSART and also Transport Camp at VADENCOURT Wood.	
	T/CAPT R.J. SMITH A.S.C proceeded to England.	ac
August 17th	Weather fine.	
	O.C. A.S.C inspected Divisional Supply Column at LONGPRÉ	ac
18th	Weather fine.	ac
19th	Weather fine	ac
20	Weather fine	ac
21st	Weather fine	ac

Instructions regarding War Diaries and Intelligence Summaries are contained in F. S. Regs., Part II. and the Staff Manual respectively. Title pages will be prepared in manuscript.

WAR DIARY
or
~~INTELLIGENCE SUMMARY~~.
(*Erase heading not required.*)

Army Form C. 2118.

Hour, Date, Place		Summary of Events and Information	Remarks and references to Appendices
BELLOY	Aug 22nd	Weather fine –	
		Conducting parties with 300 horses per Regiment and 1 G.S. Wagon marched independently by Brigades to BEAUCOURT area – Tail of last Brigade to reach BEAUCOURT area by 2 a.m. 23rd	
	Aug 23rd	Weather fine – 119th C.T.A. returned to permanent billets arriving at 12 noon. Conducting party with horses moved to rendezvous near FORCEVILLE head passing starting point at 7.30 pm	
	7.30 pm	Troops relieved from trenches and marched to rendezvous where they met the horses and ~~[illegible]~~ moved to BEAUCOURT area –	
	Aug 24th	Weather fine – Conducting parties returned to permanent billets – horses for troops remaining in advanced area.	
	Aug 25th	Weather fine –	
	Aug 26th	Weather fine	
	Aug 27th	Weather fine – very hot –	
	Aug 28th	Weather morning very hot and close – heavy rain commenced falling about 5 pm. Wet night	
	Aug 29th	Weather – raining on and off during day with heavy rain in evening	
	Aug 30th	Weather fine	
	Aug 31st	Weather fine – Conducting parties proceeded to advanced positions during night of Aug 31st – Sept 1st	

[Signature]
Lieut Colonel
O.C. A.S.C.
2nd Ind. Cav. Div.

(73989) W4141—463. 400,000. 9/14. H.&J.Ltd. Forms/C. 2118/10.

Serial No. 123

WAR DIARY

OF

A.S.C., 2nd Indian Cavalry Division.

FROM 1st September 1915 TO 30th September 1915

Instructions regarding War Diaries and Intelligence Summaries are contained in F. S. Regs., Part II. and the Staff Manual respectively. Title pages will be prepared in manuscript.

WAR DIARY
or
~~INTELLIGENCE SUMMARY.~~
(Erase heading not required.)

Army Form C. 2118.

Hour, Date, Place	Summary of Events and Information	Remarks and references to Appendices
BELLOY-SUR-SOMME Sept 1st	Weather – unsettled with heavy rain in evening and during night. Trench parties and conducting parties moved from BEAUCOURT AREA to bivouac near FORCEVILLE and conducting parties returned with horses to BEAUCOURT AREA. All movements during night of Sept 1st/2nd. Strength of Trench parties 250 rifles per Regt.	[illegible]
Sept. 2nd.	Weather – rain fell on and off during day – wet evening and night.	
Night of 2nd–3rd	250 Rifles per Regiment proceeded to Trenches from bivouac near FORCEVILLE. Conducting Parties returned from BEAUCOURT AREA to permanent billets. Capt. C.R. Harrison admitted to Hospital	
Sept 3rd	Weather – heavy rain fell during most of the day.	[illegible]
10 am to 2 30 pm	O.C. A.S.C. proceeded to MARTINSART to inspect Divisional Train and arrangements at Refilling Point	
11 pm	"A" Echelon Transport proceeded to march back to permanent billets, instead of going into camp at VADENCOURT.	
Sept 4th	Weather – morning fine but weather became unsettled later – rainy – "A" Echelon Transport arrived at permanent billets	[illegible]
Sept 5th	Weather fine	[illegible]
Sept 6th	Weather fine	[illegible]
Sept 7th	Weather fine	[illegible]
Sept 8th	Weather fine	[illegible]
Sept 9th	Weather fine	[illegible]
Sept 10th	Weather fine	[illegible]

(73989) W4141—463. 400,000. 9/14. H.&J.Ltd. Forms/C. 2118/10.

Instructions regarding War Diaries and Intelligence Summaries are contained in F. S. Regs., Part II. and the Staff Manual respectively. Title pages will be prepared in manuscript.

WAR DIARY
or
INTELLIGENCE SUMMARY.
(*Erase heading not required.*)

Army Form C. 2118.

Hour, Date, Place	Summary of Events and Information	Remarks and references to Appendices
BELLOY-sur-SOMME	Weather fine	
Sept 11th. 3.15 pm	Orders received to send up a portion of 'A' Echelon Transport to SENLIS.	
4.45 pm	Orders distributed for Transport to Rendezvous at SAINT SAUVEUR at 9 pm on Sept 11th under Lieut. R. Price B.T.O. MHOW CAV. Bde. Owing to non-receipt of orders in sufficient time SEC.BAD. Bde reports their transport could not reach rendezvous in time and moved direct to destination under [illegible] Transport Officer	
9 pm	O.C. A.S.C. proceeded to rendezvous where MHOW Bde Transport was collected. Transport of other Bdes [illegible] – 18th Lancers Transport arrived about 9.20 pm and 38th Horse at 10.15 pm.	[illegible]
Sept 12th.	Weather fine. Led horses proceeded during day to Trench area to bring back troops to BEAUCOURT AREA.	[illegible]
Sept 13th.	Weather unsettled. Showery. During night 13th/14th advanced troops returned to permanent billeting area.	[illegible]
Sept 14th.	Weather unsettled – wet in morning, fine in evening.	
[illegible]	O.C. A.S.C. proceeded to inspect route for use of wagon convoy & [illegible] portion of leading wagons from barge en route to Rendezvous. Orders received that MHOW. Cav. Bde. would be transferred to 1st I. Cav. Div. and AMBALA Bde to 2nd I. Cav. Div. B.S.O. & Supply Establishments not to be interchanged but B.T.O.s to remain [illegible] with their Brigades	[illegible]

(73989) W4141—463. 400,000. 9/14. H.&J.Ltd. Forms/C. 2118/10.

Original

Instructions regarding War Diaries and Intelligence Summaries are contained in F. S. Regs., Part II. and the Staff Manual respectively. Title pages will be prepared in manuscript.

WAR DIARY

or

~~INTELLIGENCE SUMMARY.~~

(*Erase heading not required.*)

Army Form C. 2118.

Hour, Date, Place	Summary of Events and Information	Remarks and references to Appendices
BELLOY. sur- SOMME Sept. 15th	Weather dull + misty	
Sept 16th	Weather dull + misty inclined to rain.	ac
12 noon	2Lieut Pemberton, A.S.C reported his arrival + posted as R.O. [illegible] Cav. Bde	ac
Sept 17th	Weather fine	ac
Sept 18th	Weather fine – O.C. A.S.C. inspected Transport SEC'BAD Bde at 9.30 a.m. at CAUILLON	ac
Sept 19th	Weather fine	
Sept 20th	Weather fine	
Sept 21st	O.C. A.S.C inspected Transport SEC'BAD Cav. Field Ambulance at BOURDON at 10.30 a.m.	ac
Sept 22nd	Weather fine Div. marched to an area about 12 miles North Divisional Troops marched via VIGNACOURT – St LEGER-les-DOMART – DOMART to RIBEAUCOURT.	
RIBEAUCOURT	Bul. 40 Transport left BELLOY at 2 p.m. passing starting point at 2.30 pm and arriving about 6 pm	ac
Sept 23rd	Weather dull and close followed by a wet evening – Rain fell during night 23rd–24th	ac
Sept 24th	Weather dull + close + rained more of the night of 24–25th.	

Original

Instructions regarding War Diaries and Intelligence Summaries are contained in F. S. Regs., Part II. and the Staff Manual respectively. Title pages will be prepared in manuscript.

WAR DIARY
or
INTELLIGENCE SUMMARY.
(Erase heading not required.)

Army Form C. 2118.

Hour, Date, Place	Summary of Events and Information	Remarks and references to Appendices
RIBEAUCOURT Sept 25th	Weather fine. Orders arrived for all B. Echelon of Division & Divisional Troops to march via road BERNEUIL – FIENVILLERS – HEM – RISQUETOUT to DOULLENS so as to arrive at 3 A.M. night of 25th – 26th. On arrival loaded up with two days Iron Rations & then moved off & parked on the AUXI LE CHATEAU – DOULLENS main road in rear of 2nd Division's Wagons. O.C. A.S.C. supervised loading of all B Echelon of 2nd Division & took command of the Train which was divided into two sections under Captain HEXT and Captain MORTIMER. Each section carrying one days rations for the Division.	
	AMBALA BRIGADE detached from the Division for duty with 3rd Army for morning of 26th inst.	
AUXI LE CHATEAU – DOULLENS ROAD Sept 26th	Fine but cold and windy & slight showers towards evening. Division received orders to move at one hours notice which later in the day was extended to 3½ hrs. Orders received	
Sept 27	during morning for B Echelon to return to Brigade Areas & to remain parked there loaded up with two days rations, which would come under charge of Supply Officers of Brigades and Divisional Troops. Marched at 12.30 pm under O C A.S.C	

Instructions regarding War Diaries and Intelligence Summaries are contained in F. S. Regs., Part II. and the Staff Manual respectively. Title pages will be prepared in manuscript.

WAR DIARY
or
INTELLIGENCE SUMMARY.
(Erase heading not required.)

Army Form C. 2118.

Hour, Date, Place	Summary of Events and Information	Remarks and references to Appendices
Sept 27th RIBEAUCOURT	arriving at RIBEAUCOURT at 5pm where B ECHELON was parked and put under a guard. Captain A.E. CRAWFORD left today to join ROYAL ARTILLERY 1st ARMY on Transfer, the duties of Adjutant to O.C. A.S.C being assumed by Captain C.W. Hext S&T Corps	
Sept 28th	Cold & raining hard all the afternoon & evening. At 10-20AM O.C. A.S.C went to CANAPLES and took over the Auxiliary Horse Transport Company A.S.C under the command of Captain G. H BOROUGH and 2nd Lieut G. EAGAR. This Transport has been provided for the carriage of Horse Rugs & when the Division is not in movement will be attached to Head Quarters A.S.C. for general Transport work. Twelve G.S. Wagons & the necessary Horses and Personnel were handed over today to the AMBALA Cavalry Brigade who are at present attached to 3rd ARMY. The remainder went into billets at RIBEAUCOURT.	
" Sept 29th	Cold and raining all day. Very misty & cloudy	
" Sept 30th	Weather fine but cold. Roads by evening had dried up a lot	[signature] Lt Col O/c A.S.C 1 Oct 1915

Serial No. 123

Confidential

121/7601

War Diary

of

Army Service Corps, 2nd Indian Cavalry Division.

FROM 1st October 1915 TO 31st October 1915.

ORIGINAL.

Instructions regarding War Diaries and Intelligence Summaries are contained in F. S. Regs., Part II. and the Staff Manual respectively. Title pages will be prepared in manuscript.

WAR DIARY
or
INTELLIGENCE SUMMARY.
(Erase heading not required.)

Army Form C. 2118.

Hour, Date, Place	Summary of Events and Information	Remarks and references to Appendices
RIBEAUCOURT ~~Sept~~		
Oct 1st	Weather fine. Auxiliary Horse Transport Company left RIBEAUCOURT and moved into Billets at BEAUMETZ one mile from here.	
Oct 2nd	Weather fine but cold wind.	
Oct 3rd	Weather fine. Time for Division to be prepared to move extended from 3½ hrs to 5 hrs.	
Oct 4th	Weather cold & some showers. O.C. A.S.C. proceeded to DOULLENS to arrange about supply of coal for the Division etc.	
Oct 5th	Weather fine but cold. O.C. A.S.C proceeded to Corps Head Quarters and Rail Head. Col E.G. VAUGHAN proceeded on one weeks leave to England from todays date.	
Oct 6th	Weather fine. O.C. A.S.C. attended inspection by the I.G. of Transport Brig-General Boyce A.S.C. of Mechanical Transport Column of 2nd Ind Cavalry Division. Later visited MERUT and SEC'BAD Brigades re supply matters.	
Oct 7th	Weather fine. Major H.A.B. CRAWFORD A.S.C. handed over command of the 2nd Ind Cavalry Ammunition Park to Captain W. WHEATLY S.T.C. on the morning of the 7-10-15 and left for duty with No 2 G.H.Q. Ammunition Park vide Q.M.G. GHQ No A.S.C/7433 dated 6-10-15 to I.C.C. received with I.C.C. No Q1071 dated 7-10-15 and 2nd Ind Cavalry Divn No A/9995 dated 7-10-15.	

(73989) W4141—463. 400,000. 9/14. H.&J.Ltd. Forms/C. 2118/10.

Instructions regarding War Diaries and Intelligence Summaries are contained in F. S. Regs., Part II. and the Staff Manual respectively. Title pages will be prepared in manuscript.

WAR DIARY
or
INTELLIGENCE SUMMARY
(Erase heading not required.)

Army Form C. 2118.

Hour, Date, Place	Summary of Events and Information	Remarks and references to Appendices
RIBEAUCOURT Oct 8th	Weather fine	
Oct 9th	Ditto	
" 10th	Ditto	
11th	Weather fine. Orders received from G.H.Q vide letter No A.S.C.d 7497 dated 10th October 1915 from Q.M.G, G.H.Q. to Indian Cavalry Corps for Lt-Col. A.R. BURLTON and Lt-Col E.G. VAUGHAN. D.S.O. and Major L.W. FOX to proceed to ENGLAND as early as possible and report to the Secretary War Office. To replace these Officers Major W.N. LUSHINGTON. Supply and Transport Corps has been appointed O.C. A.S.C and Captain R.V. HUNT A.S.C and 2nd Lieut H.R. PANCKRIDGE for duty with the 2nd Ind Cavalry Division. Colonel A.R. BURLTON proceeded to ENGLAND today (afternoon) according with orders above	
" 12th	Weather fine.	
" 13th	Weather fine. Captain P. MORTIMER S&T Corps assumed the duties of Brigade Supply Officer AMBALA Brigade temporarily on the afternoon of the 13th inst, vice Major L.W. FOX under orders to proceed to ENGLAND. The DIVISIONAL HEAD QUARTERS changed billets today and marched to FROHEN Le GRAND. The HEAD QUARTER TRANSPORT and Auxiliary Horse Transport Company also moved into billets at the above named place.	
FROHEN LE GRAND Oct 14th	Weather dull + cloudy	

Instructions regarding War Diaries and Intelligence Summaries are contained in F. S. Regs., Part II. and the Staff Manual respectively. Title pages will be prepared in manuscript.

WAR DIARY
or
INTELLIGENCE SUMMARY
(Erase heading not required.)

Army Form C. 2118.

Hour, Date, Place	Summary of Events and Information	Remarks and references to Appendices
FROHEN LE GRAND October 15th	Weather fine	
" " 16th	Weather fine. Major W.N. LUSHINGTON assumed command as O.C. A.S.C. from this afternoon vide ~~G.H.Q.~~ letter A.S.C. d/7497 dated 10th October 1915 from Q.M.G., G.H.Q. to Indian Cavalry Corps. Major L.W. FOX. S+T. CORPS. Brigade Supply Officer AMBALA Cavalry Brigade left for England on the 15th inst.	
" " 17th	Weather fine. O.C. A.S.C proceeded to DOULLENS to report at Corps Head Quarters. Captain R.V. HUNT ARMY SERVICE CORPS reported his arrival and is posted temporary as Transport Officer of The MEERUT Brigade	
" " 18th	O.C. A.S.C proceeded to Rail Head and then to Brigades to arrange for the disposal of the two days iron rations at present in their charge. 2nd Lieut H.R. PANCKRIDGE reported his arrival & is posted temporary as Transport Officer of the SECUNDERABAD BRIGADE.	
" " 19th	Weather fine	
" " 20th	Weather fine. O.C A.S.C proceeded to DOLLENS to arrange for fresh coal supply on arrival in new area where the Division moves to on the 22nd inst.	
" " 21st	Weather fine but cold & windy. Temporary Captains G. G. WEITZMAN and H.L. CLARK, A.S.C. reported their arrival.	
" " 22nd	Division marched on the morning of 22nd inst. into a new billeting area, Brigades and Divisional Troops moving independently. Divisional Troops transport marched at 7.30 AM to OISSEMONT via FROHEN LE PETIT – PROUVILLE – LONGVILLERS – DOMQUEUR – COLQUEREL – SOREL – HALLENCOURT. – CITERNE. arriving at DIVISIONAL H. Quarters at 6 pm. which is in OISSEMONT. No accidents on line of march.	

Instructions regarding War Diaries and Intelligence Summaries are contained in F. S. Regs., Part II. and the Staff Manual respectively. Title pages will be prepared in manuscript.

WAR DIARY
or
INTELLIGENCE SUMMARY
(Erase heading not required.)

Army Form C. 2118.

Hour, Date, Place	Summary of Events and Information	Remarks and references to Appendices
OISSEMONT October 22nd	Weather fine. Captain G. G. WEITZMANN. A.S.C assumed the duties of Brigade Transport Officer of the SECUNDERABAD Brigade on the morning of the 22nd inst. 2nd Lieut. H. R. PANCKRIDGE took over the duties of Requisitioning Officer Divisional Troops on the afternoon of the 23rd inst.	[illegible] for Major OC ASC 2nd Ind Cavalry Div 1/11/15
" 24th	Major MARK-SYNGE S+T CORPS having reported his arrival took over the duties of Senior Supply Officer vice Col. E. C. VAUGHAN transferred. Captain MORTIMER S+T CORPS assumed the duties of Brigade Supply Officer MEERUT Brigade on the morning of the 24th inst. vice MAJOR MARK-SYNGE. Captain T. F. BROOK assumed the duties of Brigade Supply Officer AMBALA Brigade on the morning of the 24th inst. vice Captain P. MORTIMER. Captain H. L. CLARK A.S.C assumed the duties of Brigade Transport Officer AMBALA Brigade on the morning of the 24th inst. vice Captain T. F. BROOK appointed Brigade Supply Officer.	
" 25th	Weather cold & raining.	
" 26th	Weather fine	
" 27th	Weather wet and cold	
" 28th	Weather fine	
" 29th	"	
" 30th	"	
" 31st	Weather wet and cold	

1247 W 3299 200,000 (E) 8/14 J.B.C. & A. Forms/C. 2118/11.

SERIAL NO 123.

Confidential

War Diary

of

O.C. A.S.C., 2nd Indian Cavalry Division.

FROM 1st November 1915 TO 30th November 1915

Instructions regarding War Diaries and Intelligence Summaries are contained in F. S. Regs., Part II. and the Staff Manual respectively. Title pages will be prepared in manuscript.

WAR DIARY
or
INTELLIGENCE SUMMARY
(Erase heading not required.)

Army Form C. 2118.

Hour, Date, Place	Summary of Events and Information	Remarks and references to Appendices
OISEMONT Nov. 1st	Nov 1st Weather fine	
" 2nd	" 2nd Weather wet & stormy	
" 3rd	" 3rd Rain & mist all day	
" 4th	" 4th Weather fine	
" 5th	" 5th Weather fine but misty. O.C. A.S.C. inspected the lines of the Auxiliary Horse Transport & arranged for extra accomodation to be provided for Horses as many are still in the open. Six Army Service Corps Clerks reported themselves on the morning of the 4th inst. who will relieve the present Indian Clerks who are being sent back to MARSEILLES. vide D.D.S & T, Indian Contingent No 139/8 dated 13-10-15.	
" 6th	Nov 6th Weather fine	
7th	" 7th "	
8th	" 8th "	
9th	" 9th Weather fine but working up for rain. O.C. A.S.C inspected the transport of the Divisional Head Quarters at 11 A.M. and afterwards the Auxiliary Horse Transport Company	
" 10th	Nov 10th Raining hard all day	
" 11th	" 11th High wind and occasional heavy showers. O.C. A.S.C inspected the Transport with No 141 Secbad Cavalry Field Ambulance & No 119 MEERUT. Cavalry Field Ambulance at 3 PM at AUMATRE. 2nd Lieutenant C.M. GOLD. A.S.C. having reported his arrival is attached for duty with the Supply Officer Divisional Troops until orders are received as regards his disposal.	

1247 W 3299 200,000 (E) 8/14 J.B.C. & A. Forms/C. 2118/11.

Instructions regarding War Diaries and Intelligence Summaries are contained in F. S. Regs., Part II, and the Staff Manual respectively. Title pages will be prepared in manuscript.

WAR DIARY or INTELLIGENCE SUMMARY

(Erase heading not required.)

Army Form C. 2118.

Hour, Date, Place	Summary of Events and Information	Remarks and references to Appendices
OISEMONT November 12th	Weather stormy & heavy showers. O.C. A.S.C. attended inspection of the Ammunition Park by the Cavalry Corps Commander at 3pm at BIENCOURT. Arrangements have been made for a Divisional Supply of 10 tons of coal to be sent up daily from the BRUAY Mines. This coal is being delivered direct to OISEMONT and not at LOMPRÉ as before.	
" 13th	Weather very stormy & heavy rain. Captain R. F. EWART. S&T Corps proceeded on the evening of the 13th inst to report to the O.C. LAHORE Divisional Train vide G.H.Q. No A.S.C./7927 dated 11-11-15. Captain G. G. ~~WEIZM~~ WEITZMAN. A.S.C. assumed the duties of Brigade Supply Officer SECUNDERABAD BRIGADE temporary in addition to his duties as Brigade Transport Officer.	
" 14th	Captain W.P.R WHEATLEY S&T Corps and Captain T. F. BROOK S.T.C. proceeded on the morning of the 14th inst to report to the O.C LAHORE Divisional Train vide GHQ No A.S.C./7927 dated 11-11-15. Captain H.G.N WHITE I.A.R having reported his arrival assumed the duties of O.C. 2nd Indian Cavalry Division Ammunition Park vice Captain W.P.R. WHEATLEY. 2Lieut. E.A. NESBITT I.A.R assumed the duties of Brigade Supply Officer AMBALA BRIGADE vice Captain T.F. BROOK S.T.C transferred 2Lieut C.M. GOLD A.S.C assumed the duties of Requisitioning Officer AMBALA BRIGADE vice 2Lieut E.A. NESBITT	

1247 W 3299 200,000 (E) 8/14 J.B.C. & A. Forms/C. 2118/11.

Army Form C. 2118.

Instructions regarding War Diaries and Intelligence Summaries are contained in F. S. Regs., Part II. and the Staff Manual respectively. Title pages will be prepared in manuscript.

WAR DIARY
or
INTELLIGENCE SUMMARY
(Erase heading not required.)

Hour, Date, Place	Summary of Events and Information	Remarks and references to Appendices
OISEMONT		
November 15th	Weather mild but snowing. Temporary Captain J. SEALY-BELL A.S.C having reported his arrival, is posted as Brigade Transport Officer SECUNDERABAD Cavalry Brigade vice Tem. Captain C.C. WEITZMAN A.S.C appointed Brigade Supply Officer.	
" 16th	Weather cold & snowing	
" 17th	Weather cold & dull & slight showers during day	
" 18th	Weather cold & dull.	
" 19th	Ditto. Captain J. SEALY-BELL A.S.C yesterday having handed over his duties to Captain WEITZMAN proceeded for duty with the 1st Indian Cavalry Division vide Indian Cavalry Corps wire NO Q 2378 dated the 17th inst.	
" 20th	Weather cold & heavy frost at night.	
" 21st	Cold North Wind & frost.	
" 22nd	Weather cold and thick mist	
" 23rd	Ditto	
" 24th	Weather fine. O.C. A.S.C attended inspection by the Corps Commander of all Remounts received in the Division since September 1st 1915.	
" 25th	Weather fine. The six Indian Clerks S.T.C. belonging to the Division proceeded today en route to the Base at MARSEILLES vide Indian Cavalry Corps wire No. Q 2455 dated 22-11-15.	

1247 W 3299 200,000 (E) 8/14 J.B.C. & A. Forms/C. 2118/11.

Army Form C. 2118.

Instructions regarding War Diaries and Intelligence Summaries are contained in F. S. Regs., Part II. and the Staff Manual respectively. Title pages will be prepared in manuscript.

WAR DIARY or INTELLIGENCE SUMMARY

(Erase heading not required.)

Hour, Date, Place	Summary of Events and Information	Remarks and references to Appendices
OISEMONT November 26th	A scheme has been adopted vide Indian Cavalry Corps letter No GA-606 dated Nov 13th 1915 to form a Dismounted Division of two Brigades out of the Cavalry Corps, to be used in case of emergency in the trenches in support of the 3rd ARMY. The Division is so organised as to permit of a Dismounted Brigade complete with Artillery, Engineer & Administrative Units, being detached if required. The Division is divided into two Brigades of three Regiments each, each Regiment consisting of 900 Rifles, formed out of the three Regiments in each Cavalry Brigade. All arrangements regarding Supplies for the Dismounted Brigade formed out of the 2nd Indian Cavalry Division have been made by the Senior Supply Officer 2nd I.C.D. A special scale of Transport has been allowed for the scheme.	
November 27th	Weather cold and heavy frost during the night. Roads very slippery in the early morning. O.C. A.S.C at 11AM inspected the Transport of the SECUNDERABAD Cavalry Brigade at CAUMONT & then proceeded to DOUDELAINVILLE & inspected that with The POONA HORSE which is detached	
" 28th	Weather cold and heavy frost. Captain J. SEALY-BELL, A.S.C, having been transferred from the 1st Ind. Cavalry Division for duty with the 2nd Ind Cavalry Division vide 2nd I.C.D letter No A.3661 dated 26-11-15 is appointed Brigade Transport Officer SECUNDERABAD Cavalry Brigade and assumed his duties on the afternoon of the 28 inst.	

Instructions regarding War Diaries and Intelligence Summaries are contained in F. S. Regs., Part II. and the Staff Manual respectively. Title pages will be prepared in manuscript.

WAR DIARY
or
INTELLIGENCE SUMMARY
(Erase heading not required.)

Army Form C. 2118.

Hour, Date, Place	Summary of Events and Information	Remarks and references to Appendices
OISEMONT		
November 29th	Weather bad. Heavy thaw during the morning & raining. O.C. A.S.C at 11AM. inspected the Transport of the MEERUT Cavalry Brigade at cross roads South of FORCEVILLE.	
" 30th	Weather fine.	

W.H. Austin [?] Lieut Colonel,
OC ASC 2nd Indian Cavalry Div.
1-12-1915.

SERIAL NO 123.

Confidential

War Diary

of

O.C. Army Service Corps, 2nd Indian Cavalry Division

FROM 1st December 1915. TO 31st December 1915.

Instructions regarding War Diaries and Intelligence Summaries are contained in F. S. Regs., Part II. and the Staff Manual respectively. Title pages will be prepared in manuscript.

WAR DIARY
or
INTELLIGENCE SUMMARY
(Erase heading not required.)

Army Form C. 2118.

Hour, Date, Place	Summary of Events and Information	Remarks and references to Appendices
OISEMONT Dec 1st	Weather wet & cloudy.	
" 2nd	Weather bad & rained hard towards evening. Roads a sea of mud & getting very cut up owing to Motor Lorries.	
" 3rd	Weather bad, misty & heavy showers. O.C. A.S.C proceeded to Cross roads south west of RAMBURES and there inspected the Transport of the AMBALA BRIGADE at 11 A.M.	
" 4th	Weather bad, heavy rain & wind.	
" 5th	Weather mild and fine during the morning. Heavy showers during the afternoon.	
6th	Nothing unusual.	
7th	Inspection of Transport by DA + Q.M.G. Indian Cav Corps, starting with MEERUT Brigade. The difficulty of the supply of wood at 2½ lbs per man (sanctioned scale) is becoming acute. None was available in the Divisional Area, & it has to be obtained from the Forest of EU, a long distance for the Transport [illegible] all except AMBALA Brigade, especially in this bad weather.	

Instructions regarding War Diaries and Intelligence Summaries are contained in F. S. Regs., Part II. and the Staff Manual respectively. Title pages will be prepared in manuscript.

WAR DIARY
or
INTELLIGENCE SUMMARY
(Erase heading not required.)

Army Form C. 2118.

Hour, Date, Place	Summary of Events and Information	Remarks and references to Appendices
OISEMONT		
December 8th	DA+Q.M.G. I.C. Corps inspected Transport of the SECUNDERABAD Brigade.	
Decr. 9th	Inspection of Transport of AMBALA Bde postponed, on account of wet weather. Received orders that Divisional Baths open on 10th at BETTENCOURT, & coal to be supplied at once.	
Decr. 10th	DA+Q.M.G. inspected Transport of the 3 7 Ambulances Divl. Headquarters and Auxiliary Horse Transport. Arrangements completed for men going on leave to receive a ½ ration & hot tea at rail head before leaving.	
Decr. 11th & 12th	Nothing unusual. Weather mild & fairly fine	
Decr. 13th	DA&Q.M.G. inspected Transport of the AMBALA Brigade. Weather frosty & fine.	

1247 W 3299 200,000 (E) 8/14 J.B.C. & A. Forms/C. 2118/11.

Instructions regarding War Diaries and Intelligence Summaries are contained in F. S. Regs., Part II. and the Staff Manual respectively. Title pages will be prepared in manuscript.

WAR DIARY
or
INTELLIGENCE SUMMARY
(Erase heading not required.)

Army Form C. 2118.

Hour, Date, Place	Summary of Events and Information	Remarks and references to Appendices
OISEMONT December ~~[illegible]~~ 14th	Nothing unusual. Orders received for move of part of the Division to a new Area on the 17th. Meerut Brigade moves entire, & small portions of AMBALA & SEC'BAD Brigades.	
December 15th + 16th	Nothing unusual. DA & DQMG. made informal inspection of Supply arrangements.	
17th	Weather fine & slight frost during the night	
18th	Weather fine & nothing unusual	
19th	Ditto.	
20th	Ditto	
21st	Weather wet & raining all day	
22nd	Weather wet & heavy mist & rain	
23	Ditto	
24th	O.C. A.S.C. proceeded to Corps Head Quarters at GAMACHES ~~ARAINES~~ to discuss the question of utilizing the Brigade Transport and wagons of MEERUT Reserve Park in lieu of the Supply Lorries, the object being to save petrol & damage to roads	
25th	Raining & stormy in early morning but cleared up later	

1247 W 3299 200,000 (E) 8/14 J.B.C. & A. Forms/C. 2118/11.

Instructions regarding War Diaries and Intelligence Summaries are contained in F. S. Regs., Part II. and the Staff Manual respectively. Title pages will be prepared in manuscript.

WAR DIARY
or
INTELLIGENCE SUMMARY

(Erase heading not required.)

Army Form C. 2118.

Hour, Date, Place		Summary of Events and Information	Remarks and references to Appendices
OISEMONT			
December	26th	Nothing unusual weather fine	
"	27th	Ditto	
"	28th	Ditto. Lt-Col. W. Lushington O.C. A.S.C. admitted into Hospital today. Major Mark-Synge during his absence will take over the duties of O.C. A.S.C. in addition to his own	
	29th	Weather mild & fine	
	30th 31st	} Nothing unusual to report.	

[illegible] Capt
for Major,
for OC ASC 2nd Indian Cavy Divn.

1247 W 3299 200,000 (E) 8/14 J.B.C. & A. Forms/C. 2118/11.

SERIAL NO 123

Confidential

War Diary

of

A. S. C. Headquarters, 2nd Indian Cavalry Division

FROM 1st January 1918 TO 31st January 1918

ORIGINAL

Instructions regarding War Diaries and Intelligence Summaries are contained in F. S. Regs., Part II. and the Staff Manual respectively. Title pages will be prepared in manuscript.

WAR DIARY
or
INTELLIGENCE SUMMARY
(Erase heading not required.)

Army Form C. 2118.

Hour, Date, Place	Summary of Events and Information	Remarks and references to Appendices
OISEMONT		
January 1st	Weather mild and cloudy nothing unusual to report	
" 2nd	Ditto	
" 3rd	Ditto	
" 4th	Ditto	
" 5th	A scheme has been worked out & is being adopted from Sunday the 10th inst. to utilize 80 Wagons of the MEERUT Reserve Park for carrying the daily rations to the majority of Units within the Divisional Area, who are within a days march from Horse Transport of the proposed Refilling Point. The object being to save the cost of running the Supply Lorries as well also saving the roads within the area. Also to find suitable work for the Meerut Reserve Park during the time the Division is at rest. As it has been found unsuitable for Wagons to load up at Rail Head itself, Supply Lorries will load up as usual there & bring the rations out to a DUMP on the BOUTTENCOURT—LE TRANSLAY road, where they will be loaded up on the Wagons every morning & distributed by them to Head Quarters of Units in the three Brigades. All Units who are situated more than a days march from Refilling Point will continue to be rationed by Lorries in two echelons as before.	

1247 W 3299 200,000 (E) 8/14 J.B.C. & A. Forms/C. 2118/11.

Instructions regarding War Diaries and Intelligence Summaries are contained in F. S. Regs., Part II. and the Staff Manual respectively. Title pages will be prepared in manuscript.

WAR DIARY
or
INTELLIGENCE SUMMARY
(Erase heading not required.)

Army Form C. 2118.

Hour, Date, Place	Summary of Events and Information	Remarks and references to Appendices
OISEMONT January 6th	6th Weather dull & raining	
	7th Weather bad, rain & mist all day	
"	8th Weather fine	
"	9th Weather fine	
"	10th Weather misty & raining on & off all day. The scheme for using the Horse Transport in place of the Supply Lorries for the daily issue of rations was started today, & worked well. O.C. A.S.C. was present at Refilling Point & superintended loading up & sending off of the Wagon Convoys to the various Brigades.	
"	11th 12th 13th 14th 15th 16th Nothing unusual to report. Hay reduced to 6 lbs from Railhead. Total ration reduced to 10 lbs.	
"	17th A scheme has been worked out to utilize the MEERUT Reserve Park Wagons & Brigade Transport in place of Lorries, to deliver daily rations during a thaw after heavy frost. Object being to save the roads as much as possible. All fodder to be obtained locally & in view of this 3 days reserve is being collected at all Divl. Head Quarters. MEERUT Reserve Park after filling up at Rail Head bring the rations up the first stage, where they are taken over by Brigade Transport & taken on to their respective areas.	

1247 W 3299 200,000 (E) 8/14 J.B.C. & A. Forms/C. 2118/11.

Instructions regarding War Diaries and Intelligence Summaries are contained in F. S. Regs., Part II. and the Staff Manual respectively. Title pages will be prepared in manuscript.

WAR DIARY
or
INTELLIGENCE SUMMARY
(Erase heading not required.)

Army Form C. 2118.

Hour, Date, Place	Summary of Events and Information	Remarks and references to Appendices
OISEMONT Jan 18th	Reserve Park Wagons and Brigade Transport working satisfactorily in lieu of lorries. Lieut LAURIE ASC arrived. Posted to Div Troops.	
19th	Scheme for temporarily suspending use of all lorries during a thaw following a frost being arranged	
20th	Committee held on improvised pack gear for rations. Committee decided (1) 7th Hussar method best for British troops (2) Umballa Brigade method of packing rations on ammunition mules and ammunition on horses best for Indian troops.	
21st	Lieut PANCKRIDGE on return from leave to join 1st Ind. Cav Div, vice CAPT NOAKE who will join 2nd IC.D as SSO in place of Major Synge appointed AAQMG. Captain WHITCOMBE arrived to take over command of 2nd Ind. Cav. Ammn Park vice Captain N. WHITE.	
22nd	Nothing unusual to report	
23rd	Capt N WHITE left division after handing over command of Ammn Park to Capt WHITCOMBE	
24th	Fodder procuring very hard to buy	
25th	Various economies proposed for conserving fodder supply, e.g. experiment for training horses to eat beet,	
26	Lieut EAGAR ~~ASC~~ Aux H-T placed under arrest at DIEPPE. Matter under investigation	
27	Billeting area of division about to be restricted. Increased purchases of supplies [illegible] orders by ADST in existing areas.	

1247 W 3299 200,000 (E) 8/14 J.B.C. & A. Forms/C. 2118/11.

Instructions regarding War Diaries and Intelligence Summaries are contained in F. S. Regs., Part II. and the Staff Manual respectively. Title pages will be prepared in manuscript.

WAR DIARY
or
INTELLIGENCE SUMMARY

(Erase heading not required.)

Army Form C. 2118.

Hour, Date, Place	Summary of Events and Information	Remarks and references to Appendices
OISEMONT		
January 28th, 29th, 30th	Nothing unusual to report.	
31st	A Dismounted Party consisting of 450 men of all ranks, drawn from the Indian Cavalry Regiments in the Division proceeded by rail today to join the 7th Corps III ARMY for use in work connected with defences. Transport & the necessary Supply Establishment have been arranged by the O.C. A.S.C.	

Lieut Colonel
OC ASC 2nd Ind Cav Divn

1247 W 3299 200,000 (E) 8/14 J.B.C. & A. Forms/C. 2118/11.

SERIAL NO 123.

Confidential

War Diary

of

O.C. Army Service Corps 2nd Indian Cavalry Division

FROM 1st February 1916 TO 29th February 1916

Instructions regarding War Diaries and Intelligence Summaries are contained in F. S. Regs., Part II. and the Staff Manual respectively. Title pages will be prepared in manuscript.

WAR DIARY
or
INTELLIGENCE SUMMARY
(Erase heading not required.)

Army Form C. 2118.

Hour, Date, Place	Summary of Events and Information	Remarks and references to Appendices
OISEMONT February 1st	Lieutenant A.S. LAORIE is appointed Requisitioning Officer Divisional Troops 2nd I.C.D with effect from the 26th January vice 2nd Lieut H.R. PANKRIDGE transferred.	
	Major M. SYNGE Supply & Transport Corps is granted the temporary rank of Lieutenant-Colonel while Commanding the 2nd Indian Cavalry Divisional Army Service Corps. Dated 2nd January 1916 vice Lt. Colonel W.N. LUSHINGTON. S&T Corps invalided - vide Q.M.G. G.H.Q No A.S.C. 8694 dated 18-1-16.	
" 2nd	Weather fine, nothing unusual to report.	
" 3rd	Captain A.S. NOAKE. S&T Corps having reported his arrival assumed the duties of Senior Supply Officer 2nd Indian Cavalry Division for the operation of the 2nd inst - vice Major M. SYNGE appointed O.C A.S.C. vide I.C.C. No Q-4403 dated 20-1-16.	
" 4th	O.C. A.S.C inspected Transport lines of MEERUT Cavalry Field Ambulance at AUMATRE.	
4th	Weather fine but strong wind. O.C. A.S.C inspected Transport Lines of MHOW Field Ambulance at BIENCOURT.	
5th	Weather fine, nothing unusual to report.	

1247 W 3299 200,000 (E) 8/14 J.B.C. & A. Forms/C. 2118/11.

Instructions regarding War Diaries and Intelligence Summaries are contained in F. S. Regs., Part II. and the Staff Manual respectively. Title pages will be prepared in manuscript.

WAR DIARY
or
INTELLIGENCE SUMMARY
(Erase heading not required.)

Army Form C. 2118.

Hour, Date, Place		Summary of Events and Information	Remarks and references to Appendices
OISEMONT			
February	6th	Nothing unusual to report.	
"	7th	O.C. A.S.C inspected the Transport Lines of the SECUNDERABAD Cavalry Field Ambulance at AUMATRE.	
	~~8th~~	Temporary Lieutenant A.S. LAURIE. A.S.C reported his departure today having been transferred to the Royal Engineers vide G.H.Q. No A.S.C. 8920 dated 2-2-16.	
"	8th	Transport inspection of 13th Hussars at VISMES at 10.30 AM.	
"	9th	Fall of snow during the night but heavy thaw set in during morning. Transport Inspection of 34th POONA HORSE at GREBAULT at 10 A.M.	
"	10th } 11th }	Nothing unusual to report.	
"	12th	Transport inspection of 8th Hussars at RAMBURES at 11AM. Lieut. B.M.C. TYLER I.A.R. reported his arrival here on afternoon of 12-2-16 from Marseilles and is appointed R.O.D.T (vide Q.M.G. G.H.Q No. A.S.C/5008 dated 4-2-16) vice Lieut. A.S. LAURIE (transferred to R.E)	
"	13th	Weather wet & stormy & raining hard all day.	
"	14th	2nd Lieut EAGAR. A.S.C. Auxiliary Horse Transport Company was tried today by General Court-Martial & acquitted	
"	15th	Transport Inspection of 18th Lancers at ~~FON~~ MAISNAIRES at 11AM.	
"	16th	Transport Inspection of 20th DECCAN HORSE at TOURS at 11AM.	

1247 W 3299 200,000 (E) 8/14 J.B.C. & A. Forms/C. 2118/11.

Instructions regarding War Diaries and Intelligence Summaries are contained in F. S. Regs., Part II. and the Staff Manual respectively. Title pages will be prepared in manuscript.

WAR DIARY
or
INTELLIGENCE SUMMARY
(Erase heading not required.)

Army Form C. 2118.

Hour, Date, Place	Summary of Events and Information	Remarks and references to Appendices
OISEMONT February 17th	Two British Working Parties drawn from the Division, proceeded from Railhead today to join the 7th Corps III ARMY for use on work connected with defences. Transport and the necessary supply arrangements have been arranged by O.C. A.S.C.	
" 18th	The three R.H.A. Batteries left by rail today of the Division to be attached for duty to the 1st ARMY. Two days rations for men & animals were issued for the journey at Railhead. One Wagon of the Auxiliary Horse Transport was handed over to each Battery for carriage of Horse Rugs.	
" 19th	Transport Inspection of 9th HODSON'S HORSE at MOUFLIERES at 12PM.	
" 20th	Nothing unusual to report.	
" 21st	Inspection by the Inspector General of Transport of the 2nd I.C. Divn. Supply Column and Ammunition Park, at 12pm. Transport drawn for the new Machine Gun Sections with Brigades from Remount Depot at ABBEVILLE today.	
" 22nd	Weather cold & fall of snow during the night. Transport Inspection of 3rd Horse near AIGNEVILLE at 10-20AM.	
23rd	Weather cold and snowing.	
24th	Frost during the night and heavy fall of snow towards evening	
25th	Heavy Frost during the night & continued to snow on & off all day	

1247 W 3299 200,000 (E) 8/14 J.B.C. & A. Forms/C. 2118/11.

Instructions regarding War Diaries and Intelligence Summaries are contained in F. S. Regs., Part II. and the Staff Manual respectively. Title pages will be prepared in manuscript.

WAR DIARY
or
INTELLIGENCE SUMMARY
(Erase heading not required.)

Army Form C. 2118.

Hour, Date, Place	Summary of Events and Information	Remarks and references to Appendices
OISEMONT		
February 26th	Heavy fall of snow during night & heavy frost	
" 27th	Roads very bad owing to snow & frost but thaw set in during the afternoon.	
" 28th	In order to save the roads as much as possible during a thaw, by using Horse Transport in lieu of Motor Lorries, the Thaw Scheme was started this morning & worked well. O.C. A.S.C proceeded to Railhead & superintended loading of MEERUT Reserve Park Wagons from the Supply train. He then proceeded to the three Brigade Meeting Points, where the full wagons were exchanged for empty & latter went to the various units of the Brigades.	
" 29th	Nothing unusual to report	[illegible] Lieut Col. O.C. A.S.C. [illegible] Cav Div 2/3/1916.

1247 W 3299 200,000 (E) 8/14 J.B.C. & A. Forms/C. 2118/11.

SERIAL NO 123.

Confidential

War Diary

of

O.C., A. S. Corps, 2nd Indian Cavalry Division

FROM 1st March 1916 TO 31st March 1916.

Instructions regarding War Diaries and Intelligence Summaries are contained in F. S. Regs., Part II. and the Staff Manual respectively. Title pages will be prepared in manuscript.

WAR DIARY
or
INTELLIGENCE SUMMARY
(Erase heading not required.)

Army Form C. 2118.

Hour, Date, Place		Summary of Events and Information	Remarks and references to Appendices
OISEMONT			
March	1st	Nothing unusual to report.	
"	2nd	THAW. Scheme was stopped after delivery of rations today	
	3rd	Weather dull & towards evening stormy & heavy showers. Rations distributed by Motor Lorries as usual.	
"	4th } 5th }	Nothing unusual to report	
"	6th	Captain H.J. CLARKE. A.S.C. reported his departure on transfer to ENGLAND vide 2nd J.C.D. No A/133 dated the 4th March 1916. The system of delivering rations by a Divisional Train formed by the 46th Reserve Park, which reloaded from the Supply Column, after being in force two months, was given up on 6-3-16 owing to the abolition of this Reserve Park. According to the system followed rations were picked up by units at railhead and transferred next morning to Unit dumps & then loaded on wagons specially told off to these dumps, units providing conducting parties to accompany the wagons to billets. The Supply Column superintended the loading both at railhead and at refilling point, providing loaders at each place. The Reserve Park did not participate in the accounting transactions, as the Supply Column took its receipts direct from Brigade Supply Officers on A.F.W.3316. There was some fear at first that the arrangement might lead to discrepancies or losses en route, but no such case of the kind occurred, as the system worked most smoothly.	

1247 W 3299 200,000 (E) 8/14 J.B.C. & A. Forms/C. 2118/11.

Instructions regarding War Diaries and Intelligence Summaries are contained in F. S. Regs., Part II. and the Staff Manual respectively. Title pages will be prepared in manuscript.

WAR DIARY
or
INTELLIGENCE SUMMARY
(Erase heading not required.)

Army Form C. 2118.

Hour, Date, Place	Summary of Events and Information	Remarks and references to Appendices
OISEMONT		
March 7th, " 8th	Nothing unusual to report	
" 9th	Inspection of 2nd Indian Cavalry Supply Column by G.O.C at SENAPONT.	
" 10th	Weather cold & heavy fall of snow during the night. Inspection by O.C. A.S.C of Auxiliary Horse Transport Company.	
" 11th	Captain P. St. J. R. WOODHOUSE Supply & Transport Corps is posted for duty with the 2nd Indian Cavalry Division vide Q.M.G. G.H.Q wire No Q.P. 806 dated 9th March, & having reported his arrival is appointed Brigade Transport Officer AMBALA Cavalry Brigade vice Captain H.J. CLARKE A.S.C transferred to ENGLAND.	
" 12th, " 13th, " 14th	Nothing unusual to report	
" 15th	Transport Inspection at INVAL of the 30th Lancers by O.C. A.S.C.	
" 16th, " 17th, " 18th, " 19th, " 20th, " 21st	Nothing unusual to report	
" 22nd	Inspection by O.C. A.S.C. of Head Quarters Transport	
" 23rd	Inspection of Machine Gun Squadron AMBALA Cavalry Brigade at LILETTE at 10 A.M. by O.C. A.S.C.	

1247 W 3299 200,000 (E) 8/14 J.B.C. & A. Forms/C. 2118/11.

Instructions regarding War Diaries and Intelligence Summaries are contained in F. S. Regs., Part II. and the Staff Manual respectively. Title pages will be prepared in manuscript.

WAR DIARY
or
INTELLIGENCE SUMMARY
(Erase heading not required.)

Army Form C. 2118.

Hour, Date, Place		Summary of Events and Information	Remarks and references to Appendices
OISEMONT	March	24th Weather cold & snowing towards evening	
	"	25th Heavy fall of snow during night, but thaw set in during day	
	"	26th } 27th } Nothing unusual to report	
	"	28th Inspection of the MHOW, MEERUT, & SECUNDERABAD Cavalry Field Ambulances by G.O.C. 2nd I.C.D.	
	"	29th } 30th } 31st } Nothing unusual to report.	

(1-4-16)

[illegible] Capt & Adj
A.S.C. 2nd I.C.D.

1247 W 3299 200,000 (E) 8/14 J.B.C. & A. Forms/C. 2118/11.

SERIAL NO. 123.

Confidential

War Diary

of

O.C. Army Service Corps, 2nd Indian Cavalry Division

FROM 1st April 1916 TO 30th April 1916.

18/5

Instructions regarding War Diaries and Intelligence Summaries are contained in F. S. Regs., Part II. and the Staff Manual respectively. Title pages will be prepared in manuscript.

WAR DIARY
or
INTELLIGENCE SUMMARY
(Erase heading not required.)

Army Form C. 2118.

Hour, Date, Place	Summary of Events and Information	Remarks and references to Appendices
OISEMONT April 1st	The Divisional Ambulance Workshop A.S.C. for the Motor Ambulance Cars of the Division is abolished, and the whole of the personnel and vehicles, with the exception of one 30-cwt lorry, one motor car, and three drivers, have been transferred to the permanent establishment of the Divisional Supply Column. The surplus transport and personnel will be evacuated under instructions which will be issued by the Director of Transport. In future the O.C. Divisional Supply Column will be held responsible for the maintenance and upkeep of the Motor Ambulance Cars of the Field Ambulances allotted to the Division. Authority G.R.O. No 1484 dated 30th March 1916	
" 2nd	2nd Lieut. E. BURT 2nd Indian Cavalry Supply Column proceeded today to take over Command of the 7th Divisional Field Ambulance Workshop Unit. vide Q.M.G's No. A.S.C. 9718 dated 29-3-16.	
" 3rd	X and V Batteries R.H.A rejoined the Division today from the X Corps also the Gun Section of the Ammunition Column.	
" 4th	Nothing unusual to report	
" 5th	A British Watering Party left Railhead today to relieve the regimental details of the Watering Party at present attached to the 36th Division.	
" 6th	Temp'y Lieut. R.H. BECK A.S.C. having reported his arrival is posted to the 2nd I.C.D. Supply Column vide Q.M.G's No A.S.C. 9718 dated 29-3-16	

Instructions regarding War Diaries and Intelligence Summaries are contained in F. S. Regs., Part II. and the Staff Manual respectively. Title pages will be prepared in manuscript.

WAR DIARY
or
INTELLIGENCE SUMMARY
(Erase heading not required.)

Army Form C. 2118.

Hour, Date, Place	Summary of Events and Information	Remarks and references to Appendices
OISEMONT April 7th	Inspection of all Remounts by G.O.C. Division received during the last five months.	
" 8th	One British and one Indian Working Party left Railhead today to join the 48th Division and 1st Corps respectively in relief of similar parties who are being returned to the Division	
" 9th	The CANADIAN Cavalry Brigade which has been attached to this Division left today for the 3rd Cavalry Division Area where they will be attached to G.H.Q. Troops.	
" 10th	Nothing unusual to report	
" 11th	The MEERUT Cavalry Brigade proceeded today to ST RIQUIER for Brigade Training in that Area.	
" 12th, 13th, 14th	Nothing unusual to report	
" 15th	Nine G.S. Limbered Wagons have been drawn from the Horse Transport Depot at ABBERVILLE (complete with [illegible]) for the Division at the scale of one per Regiment for the carriage of [illegible] ammunition	
" 16th, 17th, 18th, 19th	Nothing unusual to report.	
" 20th	The SECUNDERABAD Cavalry Brigade proceeded today to ST. RIQUIER for Brigade Training in relief of the MEERUT Brigade who returned today to their original billeting area, with the exception of V. Battery R.H.A to remain at ST RIQUIER for further training	

1247 W 3299 200,000 (E) 8/14 J.B.C.&A. Forms/C. 2118/11.

Instructions regarding War Diaries and Intelligence Summaries are contained in F. S. Regs., Part II. and the Staff Manual respectively. Title pages will be prepared in manuscript.

WAR DIARY
or
INTELLIGENCE SUMMARY

(Erase heading not required.)

Army Form C. 2118.

Hour, Date, Place	Summary of Events and Information	Remarks and references to Appendices
OISEMONT April 21st	Captain G. H. BOROUGH A.S.C. O.C. Auxiliary Horse Transport Company was evacuated sick to the Base today.	
" 22nd	O.C. 2nd Indian Cavalry Supply Column reports that Lieutenant C. MACRAE A.S.C. died during the night of the 21st–22nd.	
" 23rd, " 24th	Nothing unusual to report	
" 25th	Temporary 2nd Lieut D. C. HOLMES A.S.C. reported his arrival today to the O.C. 2nd Indian Cavalry Supply Column vice Lieutenant C. MACRAE A.S.C. Deceased. vide Q.M.G. No A.S.C/10103 dated G.H.Q. 23-4-16	
" 26th	Proposal to slaughter meat for Indians at unit HQ not approved, but arranged to issue meat on day of arrival at railhead making only 60 hours between slaughter & consumption	
27	Horse [illegible] [illegible] ration [illegible]	
28	[illegible] position of Supply Column as refitting unit for motor vehicles of Field Ambulances [illegible] on consultation with ADMS	
29	Inspection of A.H.T. Coy with ADVS in view of adverse reports from Brigades	
30	Saw 4 [illegible] [illegible] horses of 13th Hussars, and arranged for [illegible] of 3. [illegible] would be preferable if [illegible] to [illegible]	
~~1 [illegible] approved proposal [illegible]~~		

[illegible] Major
OC ASC 2nd I.C.Dn

1247 W 3299 200,000 (E) 8/14 J.B.C. & A. Forms/C. 2118/11.

SERIAL NO 123

Confidential

War Diary

of

O.C. A.S. Corps, 2nd Indian Cavalry Division

FROM 1st May 1916 TO 31st May 1916.

Instructions regarding War Diaries and Intelligence Summaries are contained in F. S. Regs., Part II. and the Staff Manual respectively. Title pages will be prepared in manuscript.

WAR DIARY
or
INTELLIGENCE SUMMARY
(Erase heading not required.)

Army Form C. 2118.

Hour, Date, Place		Summary of Events and Information	Remarks and references to Appendices
[illegible]			
May	1	Approved suggestion to reduce [illegible] ration by half & substitute fresh vegetables	
	2	Rum issue stopped	
	3	ADVS' report on 4 Div H T Coy satisfactory. Cases of negligence regarding wagons & components dealt with as matters of discipline	
	4	Various samples of oats taken at random & sent to DDST not as complaint but for information. Apparently Charles Richardson's oats are the best, and the oats packed in 128.16 [Ontario] sacks without name are the worst	
	[illegible]	Issued orders regarding supplies for Divisional Training	
	6	46th Reserve Park left to join 8th Corps. Issued letter directing units to indent(?) direct on DADOS for replacements of Horse Transport vehicles & not through B.T.O., which delays matters	
	7th	Nothing unusual to report	

1247 W 3299 200,000 (E) 8/14 J.B.C. & A. Forms/C. 2118/11.

Army Form C. 2118.

Instructions regarding War Diaries and Intelligence Summaries are contained in F. S. Regs., Part II. and the Staff Manual respectively. Title pages will be prepared in manuscript.

WAR DIARY
or
INTELLIGENCE SUMMARY

(Erase heading not required.)

Hour, Date, Place	Summary of Events and Information	Remarks and references to Appendices
ST. RIQUIER May 8th	8th Division moved this morning to billeting area near ST. RIQUIER for Divisional Training. Brigades & Divisional Troops moved independently. Distance from OISEMONT about 20 miles. Head Quarters at ST. RIQUIER. Division moved at full strength with the exception of a few details left with surplus kits in old billets & the Ammunition Column which remains in RAMBURELLES. Railhead is also still at GAMACHES.	
" 9th	9th Nothing unusual to report	
" 10th	10th Whole Division out on training. O.C. A.S.C proceeded to the Training Area & inspected the A Echelon Transport of the SECUNDERABAD Cavalry Brigade which was accompanying the Brigade. He also inspected the B Echelon of part of the AMBALA Brigade which had remained in billets.	
" 11th	11th O.C. A.S.C proceeded to Railhead on inspection	
" 12th	12th Divisional Field Day. O.C. A.S.C accompanied the Q. Staff	
" 13th	O.C. A.S.C inspected the A+B Echelon Transport in their standings of the 18th Lancers & 3rd Skinner's Horse, also the B Echelon Transport of the 20th Deccan Horse.	
OISEMONT " 14th	Division left ST. RIQUIER this morning & returned to old Billeting area. Head Quarters again in OISEMONT. Nothing special to report regarding the march. Brigades & Divisional Troops moved independently.	

Instructions regarding War Diaries and Intelligence Summaries are contained in F. S. Regs., Part II. and the Staff Manual respectively. Title pages will be prepared in manuscript.

WAR DIARY
or
INTELLIGENCE SUMMARY
(Erase heading not required.)

Army Form C. 2118.

Hour, Date, Place	Summary of Events and Information	Remarks and references to Appendices
OISEMONT May 15th	15th Nothing unusual to report	
" 16th	16th O.C. A.S.C attended inspection of the A & B Echelon Transport of the AMBALA Cavalry Brigade by the G.O.C. Division at ANDAINVILLE at 11AM.	
" 17th	17th Nothing unusual to report.	
" 18th	18th O.C. A.S.C proceeded to Railhead on Inspection.	
" 19th	19th Inspection of the A & B. Echelon Transport of the SECUNDERABAD Cavalry Brigade by O.C. A.S.C. The Reserve Park joined the 2nd I.C. Division today & is being billeted at BOUILLANCOURT.	
" 20th	20th Nothing unusual to report	
" 21st	21st O.C. A.S.C proceeded to BOUILLANCOURT to inspect the arrangements made as regards the billeting of the Reserve Park & as regards the ground chosen for the ~~...~~ picketing of all animals.	
" 22nd	22nd Inspection of the A & B Echelon Transport of the MEERUT Cavalry Brigade by the O.C. A.S.C. at 10AM on the MAISNIERES – TOURS road.	
" 23rd	23rd Inspection of the SECUNDERABAD & MEERUT Field Ambulances by O.C. A.S.C near AUMATRE at 9-45AM. and of the MHOW. Cav. Field Ambulance at BIENCOURT at 11-45AM.	
" 24th	24th Inspection of Auxiliary Horse Transport Company at 10AM.	

1247 W 3299 200,000 (E) 8/14 J.B.C. & A. Forms/C. 2118/11.

Instructions regarding War Diaries and Intelligence Summaries are contained in F. S. Regs., Part II. and the Staff Manual respectively. Title pages will be prepared in manuscript.

WAR DIARY
or
INTELLIGENCE SUMMARY
(Erase heading not required.)

Army Form C. 2118.

Hour, Date, Place	Summary of Events and Information	Remarks and references to Appendices
OISEMONT May 25th	25th O.C. A.S.C inspected the lines of the Supply Reserve Park at BOUILLENCOURT.	
" 26th	26th Inspection of Auxiliary Horse Transport Company by O.C.A.S.C at 10AM, also Inspection at AUMATRE of SEC'BAD & MEERUT Field Ambulance Transport Animals in their Lines at 12pm.	
" 27th	27th Captain G.H. BOROUGH A.S.C. having reported his arrival on discharge from Hospital, assumed Command of the Auxiliary Horse Transport Company from this date.	
28th 29th 30th	28th 29th 30th Nothing unusual to report	
" 31st	31st 2nd Lieut. L. HANSON-HOTTE A.S.C having reported his arrival from the M.T. School of Instruction ST. OMER is posted to the 2nd I.C.D. Supply Column vide D.D S&T 4th Army No 114/81 dated 29th May 1916.	

C.A. Steel Capt. for Lt Col
OC ASC 2nd Ind Cav Dn
1.6.16.

1247 W 3299 200,000 (E) 8/14 J.B.C. & A. Forms/C. 2118/11.

SERIAL NO. 123.

Confidential

War Diary

of

O.C., A.S.C., 2nd Indian Cavalry Division

FROM 1st June 1916 TO 30th June 1916

Instructions regarding War Diaries and Intelligence Summaries are contained in F. S. Regs., Part II. and the Staff Manual respectively. Title pages will be prepared in manuscript.

WAR DIARY
or
INTELLIGENCE SUMMARY
(Erase heading not required.)

Army Form C. 2118.

Hour, Date, Place	Summary of Events and Information	Remarks and references to Appendices
OISEMONT June 1st	1st A Working Party consisting of 800 men of all ranks found by the MEERUT Cavalry Brigade proceeded today to BRIQUEMESNIL to be attached for duty with the 18th Division XIII Corps. Party proceeded by road being returned on arrival by Lorries up to T for the 3rd inst. Sufficient spare mounted men accompanied the party to bring back the led horses on the 2nd inst, rations for the 2nd being issued to them by lorries before leaving BRIQUEMESNIL. Rations for Digging Party for the 4th inst. onwards being sent up by lorries to 18th Division Railhead. O.C. A.S.C proceeded to 18th Division today to make all arrangements regarding the etc.	
2nd	2nd SECBAD Cavalry Brigade proceeded today for training into the Belgian Training area. Rations will be sent [illegible] by Supply Column from Divisional Railhead. Also Coal, wood [illegible] being sent by Lorry from OISEMONT. T/Captain G. L. EVANS A.S.C. [illegible] J.C. Ammunition Park proceeded today to report for duty to O.C. 1st Base M.T. Depot ROUEN. T/Captain E. G. FELLY A.S.C. [illegible] Supply Column [illegible] posted to the [illegible] Ammunition Park. Inspection of Div. Head Quarters [illegible] Transport by O.C A.S.C.	vide D.D. S&T [illegible] No 114/88 dated [illegible]

1247 W 3299 200,000 (E) 8/14 J.B.C. & A. Forms/C. 2118/11.

Army Form C. 2118.

Instructions regarding War Diaries and Intelligence Summaries are contained in F. S. Regs., Part II. and the Staff Manual respectively. Title pages will be prepared in manuscript.

WAR DIARY
or
INTELLIGENCE SUMMARY
(Erase heading not required.)

Hour, Date, Place	Summary of Events and Information	Remarks and references to Appendices
OISEMONT June 3rd	3rd } Nothing unusual to report	
" 4th	4th }	
SENARPONT " 5th	5th Divisional Head Quarters changed billets from OISEMONT to SENARPONT today. O.C. A.S.C proceeded to Head Quarters of the 4th Army during the day	
" " 6th	6th } Nothing unusual to report	
" " 7th	7th }	
" " 8th	Inspection by the D.D. S&T IV ARMY of the 2nd I.C.D. SUPPLY Column, Ammunition Park, Reserve Supply Park & Auxiliary Horse Transport Company. All units inspected in their own lines. SECUNDERABAD Cavalry Brigade returned to their old billeting area today.	
" " 9th	9th Nothing unusual to report	
" " 10th	10th MEERUT and AMBALA Cavalry Brigades proceeded today from their permanent billets to ST. RIQUIER for training. O.C. A.S.C inspected Transport of both Brigades on the line of march. Rations will be supplied for these Brigades as usual from Railhead by Lorries.	
" " 11th }	11th Nothing unusual to report.	
" " 12th }		

1247 W 3299 200,000 (E) 8/14 J.B.C. & A. Forms/C. 2118/11.

Army Form C. 2118.

Instructions regarding War Diaries and Intelligence Summaries are contained in F. S. Regs., Part II. and the Staff Manual respectively. Title pages will be prepared in manuscript.

WAR DIARY
or
INTELLIGENCE SUMMARY
(Erase heading not required.)

Hour, Date, Place	Summary of Events and Information	Remarks and references to Appendices
SENARPONT June 12th	12th Nothing unusual to report.	
13th	13th O.C. A.S.C & S.S.O. proceeded to St. RIQUIER to see the method adopted by the MEERUT. Brigade for loading up Iron Rations on to Pack Animals.	
14th	14th The following transfers have been ordered within the Division vide O.C. A.S.C's Telegram No S.T. 750 dated 14th inst. Captain HUNT A.S.C. is transferred as B.T.O to AMBALA Brigade vice Captain WOODHOUSE S&T Corps transferred to MEERUT Brigade in same capacity. 2nd Lieut PEMBERTON. A.S.C. is transferred as Requisitioning Officer to SEC'BAD. Brigade vice Lieut. DUNNING transferred as R.O. from SEC'BAD to MEERUT. Brigade vide O.C. A.S.C telegram No S.T. 793 dated 14th inst. MEERUT Cavalry Brigade returned from training area to permanent billets today also the 30th Lancers of the AMBALA Brigade.	
15th	15th AMBALA Cavalry Brigade returned from ST RIQUIER to permanent billets today less 30th Lancers who returned yesterday	
16th	16th The following transfer between Brigades has been ordered. The 18th Lancers MEERUT. Cavalry Brigade transfer to the AMBALA Brigade in place of 30th Lancers transferred to MEERUT Cavy Bde.	
17th	17th Nothing unusual to report.	
18th	18th Under orders from the G.M.G the SEC'BAD and AMBALA Cavalry Brigades & Divl Troops handed over today 62 Limbered G.S. Wagons to the MEERUT Cavy Bde	

Instructions regarding War Diaries and Intelligence Summaries are contained in F. S. Regs., Part II. and the Staff Manual respectively. Title pages will be prepared in manuscript.

WAR DIARY
or
INTELLIGENCE SUMMARY
(Erase heading not required.)

Army Form C. 2118.

Hour, Date, Place	Summary of Events and Information	Remarks and references to Appendices
SENARPONT June 18th	18th (Continued) MEERUT Cavalry Brigade in exchange for 31 G.S. Wagons. Each Brigade taking over 15 complete & Divisional H.Q. one complete. These Wagons will be eventually handed over to Base Horse Transport Depot ABBEVILLE in exchange for 62 Limbers of which 31 will be complete limbered.	
" 19th	19th First portion of MEERUT Cavalry Brigade entrained today at PONT REMY taking 3 days Train Rations for Men & Animals. O.C. A.S.C proceeded to PONT REMY to see about Supply & Transport arrangements. Also went to BASE Horse Transport Depot ABBEVILLE to arrange for the issue of Limbered G.S. Wagons to SEC'BAD & AMBALA Brigades to replace those handed over to MEERUT Brigade as mentioned above also for the handing in of the 31 G.S. Wagons which became surplus. CANADIAN Cavalry Brigade joined the Division on 18th inst. being attached in replacement of MEERUT Cavalry Brigade now struck off the strength of the Division.	
" 20th	Meerut Brigade continued entraining at PONT. REMY today. Sixty Two G.S. Limbers were issued to SEC'BAD & AMBALA Brigades & Divl. Troops from Horse Transport Depot today at ABBEVILLE. O.C. A.S.C superintended distribution. The 31 G.S. Wagons surplus were handed in in exchange	
" 21st	The last of MEERUT Brigade entrained today.	

Instructions regarding War Diaries and Intelligence Summaries are contained in F. S. Regs., Part II. and the Staff Manual respectively. Title pages will be prepared in manuscript.

WAR DIARY
or
INTELLIGENCE SUMMARY
(Erase heading not required.)

Army Form C. 2118.

Hour, Date, Place	Summary of Events and Information	Remarks and references to Appendices
PONT REMY June 22nd	22nd Division marched this morning & billeted in ST. RIQUIER training area. H.Q. at PONT. REMY. Before leaving all surplus stores were dumped at OISEMONT. Also all Units & A. Echelon issued with one extra day Iron Rations which was carried in Units Cook Wagons. A second days Iron Ration was also [illegible] along in Lorries. These two days Emergency Rations are in addition to the daily issue by Supply Column. Railhead still at ~~LONGPRE~~ GAMACHES	
23rd	23rd Nothing unusual to report	
24th	24th Whole Division out on training, ~~[illegible]~~ during afternoon & evening.	
25th	25th Orders received for the 2nd days Emergency Ration at present in Brigade charge to be issued to all units, which will be carried in improvised pack [illegible] under unit arrangements.	
26th	26th The Auxiliary Horse Transport Company having been converted into a water Company left today to join the III Corps IV ARMY & are struck off the strength of the Division. Rationed up to & for the 27th. The Division march on the nights June 26th/27th and 27th/28th to a bivouac between DAOURS and QUERRIEU. Brigades & A. Echelon Transport march straight through to new area but B. Echelon [illegible] do the distance in two marches.	
BUSSY-Les-DAOURS 27th	27th Division H.Q. left PONT REMY for new area at BUSSY-Les-DAOURS. & A & B Echelon Transport marched via FLIXECOURT – HANGEST – PICQUIGNY – AMIENS to BUSSY.	

1247 W 3299 200,000 (E) 8/14 J.B.C. & A. Forms/C. 2118/11.

Instructions regarding War Diaries and Intelligence Summaries are contained in F. S. Regs., Part II. and the Staff Manual respectively. Title pages will be prepared in manuscript.

WAR DIARY
or
INTELLIGENCE SUMMARY
(Erase heading not required.)

Army Form C. 2118.

Hour, Date, Place	Summary of Events and Information	Remarks and references to Appendices
BUSSY-LES-DAOURS June 28th	28th. Brigades arrived during the night & this morning. Supply Column drew for today from FRECHENCOURT Railhead. Whole Division now in camp around here & Divisional H.Q. & Brigade Head Quarters all in BUSSY. A Divisional DUMP consisting of 8 lbs of Oats per Horse has been formed here to be issued before Division moves up to its position of readiness. Orders were received to issue to fighting troops & A. Echelon today. These extra oats will only be utilised if the usual daily issue of forage cannot be made. The British and Indian Working Parties which have been attached to the IV Army rejoined the Division today. Issue of Rum having been authorised was issued to all troops this evening. Weather bad, heavy rain last night & all the morning. Roads very bad & very cut up mostly owing to Motor traffic & mud.	[signature] Lieut Col OC ASC 2nd Ind Cav Div
June 29th	29th. Weather fine but dull. Strong wind blowing which is drying up the roads fast.	
30th	30th. Weather fine. Orders issued for the Division & A Echelon Transport to move to a position of assembly between BUIRE and RIBEMONT tomorrow morning.	

1247 W 3299 200,000 (E) 8/14 J.B.C. & A. Forms/C. 2118/11.

SERIAL NO 123.

Confidential

War Diary

of

O.C. Army Service Corps, 2nd Indian Cavalry Division.

FROM 1st July 1916 TO 31st July 1916.

ORIGINAL.

Instructions regarding War Diaries and Intelligence Summaries are contained in F. S. Regs., Part II. and the Staff Manual respectively. Title pages will be prepared in manuscript.

WAR DIARY
or
INTELLIGENCE SUMMARY
(Erase heading not required.)

Vol I

of O.C. A.S.C. 2nd D. C. Div.

Army Form C. 2118.

Hour, Date, Place	Summary of Events and Information	Remarks and references to Appendices
BUSSY-LES-DAOURS July 1st	1st Division & A ECHELON Transport moved at 3-30am to a position of assembly between BUIRE and RIBEMONT. B. Echelon Transport of Brigades & Divisional Troops remain in present areas, also the transmitted Reinforcements, all under the command of the O.C. A.S.C. At 4-30pm Division returned back into original billeting area at BUSSY. Rations delivered from Supply Column on arrival back of Division to original Brigade & D.T. Dumps.	
" 2nd	2nd Nothing unusual to report	
" 3rd	3rd Division under orders to move 3 hours after receipt of orders.	
" 4th " 5th " 6th	4th 5th } Nothing unusual to report 6th	
" 7th	7th Inspection by G.O.C. Division of Canadian Field Ambulance & Ammunition Column. Inspection attended by O.C. A.S.C.	
" 8th	8th A course of lectures has now been started on Transport Generally and is being attended by the R.T.O.s & Transport N.C.O's of Canadian Cavalry Brigade.	
" 9th	9th Nothing unusual to report	
" 10th	10th Ditto	
" 11th	11th Orders issued for Division less B Echelon to move forward & billet in area ALBERT	
" 12th	12th Orders regarding move of Division cancelled, but to be ready to move at two hours notice	

Instructions regarding War Diaries and Intelligence Summaries are contained in F. S. Regs., Part II. and the Staff Manual respectively. Title pages will be prepared in manuscript.

WAR DIARY
or
INTELLIGENCE SUMMARY
(Erase heading not required.)

Army Form C. 2118.

Hour, Date, Place	Summary of Events and Information	Remarks and references to Appendices
BUSSY-LES-DAOURS July 13th	13th Orders received during the night for the Division's A Echelon to move today to a bivouac in the area MEAULTE — DERNANCOURT. B. Echelon Transport of Brigades and Divisional Troops remain in present area, also the Dismounted Reinforcements, all under the command of the O.C. A.S.C. Rations for 14th issued to Brigades in new area at 5pm.	
" 14th	14th Captain HEXT STC Corps transferred temporarily to Reserve Park 2nd ICD for work in connection with improvisation of a Horse Train ~~from~~ their unit	
15th	Horse train scheme has not so far materialised but Capt Hext still retained with Reserve Park.	
16th	Supply Column camp shelled in night. Shells said to be from French anti-air-craft guns in AMIENS	
17th	Ammunition Park left for MERICOURT. CAPT HEXT promoted temporary major from 17-5-16 Authority W.O. Letter No 100/India/1316 MSC Train dd 17.5.16	
18th	Nothing unusual to report.	

1247 W 3299 200,000 (E) 8/14 J.B.C. & A. Forms/C. 2118/11.

Instructions regarding War Diaries and Intelligence Summaries are contained in F. S. Regs., Part II. and the Staff Manual respectively. Title pages will be prepared in manuscript.

WAR DIARY
or
INTELLIGENCE SUMMARY
(Erase heading not required.)

Army Form C. 2118.

Hour, Date, Place	Summary of Events and Information	Remarks and references to Appendices
DERNANCOURT July 19th	O.C. A.S.C left BUSSY in command of B Echelon Transport of the Division & proceeded to Head Quarters of the Division at DERNANCOURT, moving via DAOURS – HEILLY & BUIRE. On arrival B Echelon rejoined their respective Brigades.	
" 20th	Whole Division now in bivouac in & around DERNANCOURT.	
" 21st	~~Captain~~ Major C.W. Hext rejoined H.Q of O.C. A.S.C 2nd I.C.D from Supply Reserve Park.	
" 22nd	Nothing unusual to report	
" 23rd	O.C A.S.C inspected the lines of Supply Reserve Park at MORLANCOURT & later visited the Supply Dump of AMBALA Cavalry Brigade. Orders received at 1-30 am from the Division to return ~~B.D~~ to BUSSY-LES-DAOURS. A & B Echelon Transport [illegible] of the Division moved under orders of O.C. A.S.C. Brigades returned into bivouac in the same area as before.	
" 24th	~~[illegible]~~ Nothing unusual to report.	

1247 W 3299 200,000 (E) 8/14 J.B.C. & A. Forms/C. 2118/11.

Instructions regarding War Diaries and Intelligence Summaries are contained in F. S. Regs., Part II. and the Staff Manual respectively. Title pages will be prepared in manuscript.

WAR DIARY
or
INTELLIGENCE SUMMARY
(Erase heading not required.)

Army Form C. 2118

Hour, Date, Place	Summary of Events and Information	Remarks and references to Appendices
BUSSY-LES-DAOURS		
July 25th	Inspection by the G.O.C. Division of A & B Echelon Transport of all Brigades. Inspection attended by O.C. A.S.C.	
" 26th	26th The following parties left today for work under XV Corps – 4 Officers & 100 men of Canadian Cav. Bde, 4 Officers & 100 men found from 8th Hussars & 7th Dragoon Guards. These two parties are for salvage & burial work in XV Corps Area. In addition to the above all Officers & N.C.O's & 600 men of the Dismounted Regiment left by Bus for work on entrenchments in XV Corps Area. All these parties are rationed up to & for 27th inst. The latter party will	
" 27th	27th continue to be rationed daily by 2nd I.C.D. Supply Column. Inspection of the Canadian Cavalry Field Ambulance by O.C. A.S.C.	
28th	28th O.C. A.S.C & S.S.O proceeded to BECOURT with reference to the rationing of the Dismounted Regiment as from [illegible] duty with the 15th Corps	
29th 30th	29th 30th Nothing unusual to report	
31st	31st O.C. A.S.C inspected the 2nd I.C. Ammunition Park at MERICOURT at 10.30 AM & 2nd I.C. Supply Column near BUSSY at 3pm	

[illegible] Lt Col
O.C. A.S.C.
2nd Ind. Cav. Div.

1247 W 3299 200,000 (E) 8/14 J.B.C. & A. Forms/C. 2118/11.

SERIAL NO. 123.

Confidential

War Diary

of

O.C., A.S.C., 2nd Indian Cavalry Division.

FROM 1st August 1916 TO 31st August 1916

Army Form C. 2118.

Vol. II

Divisional A. S. C., 2nd Ind. Cav. Div.

WAR DIARY
or
INTELLIGENCE SUMMARY

(Erase heading not required.)

Instructions regarding War Diaries and Intelligence Summaries are contained in F. S. Regs., Part II. and the Staff Manual respectively. Title pages will be prepared in manuscript.

Hour, Date, Place		Summary of Events and Information	Remarks and references to Appendices
August BUSSY-LES-DAOURS	1st	1st Inspection at MERICOURT of 2nd I.C. Ammunition Park also Canadian by the G.O.C. 2nd ICD at 10-30 AM. Inspection of Canadian & 2nd I.C. Supply Column at 2-30 pm near BUSSY by G.O.C. Division. Both inspections attended by O.C. A.S.C.	
"	2nd	2nd Nothing unusual to report	
"	3rd	3rd O.C. A.S.C proceeded to 4th Cav. H.Q to see D.D.S&T.	
"	4th	4th Inspection at 10 AM of Pack Section MHOW. F[illegible] Ambulance by O.C. A.S.C & A.D.M.S. to see the new system of carrying collapsible stretchers on Pack Animals	
"	5th	5th Nothing unusual to report	
"	6th	6th O.C. A.S.C proceeded to near TRICOURT to visit the Dismounted Detachment at present attached to 15th Corps with reference to the delivery of the [illegible] by the Supply Column	
"	7th	7th Nothing unusual to report	
LONGPRE	8th	8th 2nd I.C. Division left BUSSY for the BLANGY area where they go into bivouac. B Echelon Transport of Divn H.Q. & Divn Troops, & SECUNDERABAD & Canadian Cavy Brigades marched at 5 AM under O.C. A.S.C. to LONGPRE where they bivouacked for the night.	
RIEUX	9th	9th B Echelon under O.C. A.S.C marched at 10-20 AM & arrived in new billeting area at 7-20 pm. Head Quarters of Division in and around the village of RIEUX near BLANGY.	

Instructions regarding War Diaries and Intelligence Summaries are contained in F. S. Regs., Part II. and the Staff Manual respectively. Title pages will be prepared in manuscript.

WAR DIARY
or
INTELLIGENCE SUMMARY
(Erase heading not required.)

Army Form C. 2118.

Hour, Date, Place	Summary of Events and Information	Remarks and references to Appendices
RIEUX. August 10th	10th Division (less AMBALA Cavalry Brigade & Digging Parties) bivouac round RIEUX & SENARPONT. The AMBALA Cavy Brigade remained at BUSSY also digging & working parties attached to 14th Corps remain for the present. The above are rationed by a detachment of the Supply Column which remains at BUSSY & draws rations etc from FRECHENCOURT. Railhead for the Division at GAMACHES from 9th inst.	
" 11	Major HEXT Asst to [illegible], Capt RENDALL Supt, Lieut WHITAKER 2nd I C Supply Column (Cav S.T. Coy) all left for England on 10 days leave preparatory to proceeding to MESOPOTAMIA. Had done what I could to prevent the division losing so many S&T Officers at once, but it appeared inevitable.	
12	Question of putting certain lorries at [illegible] to save petrol being taken up but [illegible] owing to forthcoming move of division & different units.	

1247 W 3299 200,000 (E) 8/14 J.B.C. & A. Forms/C. 2118/11.

Army Form C. 2118.

Instructions regarding War Diaries and Intelligence Summaries are contained in F. S. Regs., Part II. and the Staff Manual respectively. Title pages will be prepared in manuscript.

WAR DIARY or INTELLIGENCE SUMMARY

(Erase heading not required.)

Hour, Date, Place	Summary of Events and Information	Remarks and references to Appendices
RIEUX Aug 12th	Weather changeable. Question of H.Q for S.O.D.T has arisen – SENARPONT too far for Div HQ, but Div HQ too far from bulk of Div Troops	
Aug 13th	Scheme for saving petrol now being worked out.	
14th	Took Supply Officers to Selected dumps for Hay oats & coal in connection with above scheme. In Capt. Bird's absence with Ambulance Bde and with Lt Whitaker in [illegible] the 2 Canadian Column Supply Officers are acting as Column Supply Officers for the division	
15	above scheme started. No particular hitch. Hope precautions taken against blocking traffic will work out satisfactorily. Calculate petrol consumption reduced 50%.	
16	~~[illegible]~~ Seed & Ambulance Bde on exchanging duties, former proceeding to BUSSY to furnish working parties, latter coming here. Move will take some days & involves considerable movements of Supply column.	
17.	Lt Wood. 2nd Lieut BRITTS & Lt FARRELL arrived yesterday. Latter to Supply column. BRITTS to RO [illegible]. Lt WOOD at present to act as asst [illegible]	

1247 W 3299 200,000 (E) 8/14 J.B.C. & A. Forms/C. 2118/11.

Instructions regarding War Diaries and Intelligence Summaries are contained in F. S. Regs., Part II. and the Staff Manual respectively. Title pages will be prepared in manuscript.

WAR DIARY
or
INTELLIGENCE SUMMARY
(Erase heading not required.)

Army Form C. 2118.

Hour, Date, Place	Summary of Events and Information	Remarks and references to Appendices
RIEUX Augst 18th	~~[struck out]~~ I inspected the transport of the following units:- Divl H.Q.rs, Divl H.Q.rs A.S.C, A.D.M.S H.Q.rs, Signal Squadron & Canadian Cav Field Amb. Also the hay, oats & coal dump of the Can Cavy Bde, Sec Cav Bde & Amm Col, 2nd I.R.H.A Bde H.Q, Can Cav Field Amb & the Mhow Cav F.A at BOUTTENCOURT	
Augst 19th	Nothing unusual to report. Horse standings getting sloppy	
Augst 20th	The Ambala Cav Bde came into SENARPONT. H.Q.rs of S.O.D.T transferred to BOUTTENCOURT. Improvement in weather	
Augst 21st	Major General McAndrew commanding the Division inspected the horses & transport of the following units:- Divl H.Q.rs, Signal Squadron, Amm Col, Mhow F.A & Can F.A. He spoke well of the transport but said the animals ears should be a bit cleaner	
Augst 22nd	Nothing unusual to report. 2nd I.C.D Reserve Park harness competition judged by ~~[struck out]~~ me	
Augst 23rd	Nothing unusual to report.	
Augst 24th	Extension of the scheme for saving petrol by utilising wagons of the 2nd I.C.D Reserve Park, 50 wagons being used from this unit. The O.C. A.S.C inspected the filling up of supplies at R.H. also the dump at BOUTTENCOURT	
Augst 25th	R.H.A units ordered to front area, involving changes in S&T arrangements	
Augst 26th	~~[struck out]~~ visited Fourth Army H.Q.rs & Sec'bad Bde with A.A.Q.M.G & S.S.O to arrange S&T details for (a) Return of Sec'bad Bde (b) Parties remaining in front area.	
Augst 27th	Nothing unusual to report.	

Instructions regarding War Diaries and Intelligence Summaries are contained in F. S. Regs., Part II. and the Staff Manual respectively. Title pages will be prepared in manuscript.

WAR DIARY
or
INTELLIGENCE SUMMARY
(Erase heading not required.)

Army Form C. 2118.

Hour, Date, Place	Summary of Events and Information	Remarks and references to Appendices
RIEUX		
Aug[st] 28th	Nothing unusual to report	
29th	Very heavy rain. Standings getting very bad ~~[illegible]~~ I met the OC ASC 1st Ind Cav Division at ABBEVILLE to discuss various points	
30th	The Sec'bad Cavalry Brigade arrived at NESLE-NORMANDEUSE from BUSSY and have been ordered to participate in petrol saving Scheme from 1st Sept.	
31st	Nothing unusual to report. Great scarcity of cars for A.S.C duties at present; two are in dock	

[illegible] Lt Col
OC ASC
2nd Ind Cav Div

1247 W 3299 200,000 (E) 8/14 J.B.C. & A. Forms/C. 2118/11.

SERIAL NO. 123.

Confidential

War Diary

of

Headquarters, A.S.C., 2nd Indian Cavalry Division

FROM 1st September 1916 TO 30th September 1916.

Instructions regarding War Diaries and Intelligence Summaries are contained in F. S. Regs., Part II. and the Staff Manual respectively. Title pages will be prepared in manuscript.

WAR DIARY
or
INTELLIGENCE SUMMARY
(Erase heading not required.)

Army Form C. 2118.

Garr. A.S.C. 2nd Ind. Cav. Div. Vol. III

Hour, Date, Place		Summary of Events and Information	Remarks and references to Appendices
1st September RIEUX			
Sept	1st	By direction of the Major General commanding the Division I gave a lecture on Pack Loading at SENARPONT, which was attended by officers & N.C.O's of the Canadian Cav Bde, Amballa Cav Bde, Sec'bad Cav Bde & Field Ambulances.	
	2nd	Improvement in weather, nothing unusual to report	
	3rd	Shifted the position of hay, oats & coal dump a few hundred yards on account of condition of roads	
	4th	Divisional Horse Show held at NESLE-NORMANDEUSE. Several transport classes, General turn out of transport competing considered good.	
	5th	Orders received at 6 pm to be ready to move at 4 am next day. Reserve Park at once reloaded their Supplies	
	6th	"B" Echelon moved up from their different areas to BUSSY arriving at 10 am on 7-9-16. Condr BOSWORTH, S.T.C proceeded on leave to ENGLAND prior to going to Base MARSEILLES under orders for INDIA.	

1247 W 3299 200,000 (E) 8/14 J.B.C. & A. Forms/C. 2118/11.

Instructions regarding War Diaries and Intelligence Summaries are contained in F. S. Regs., Part II. and the Staff Manual respectively. Title pages will be prepared in manuscript.

WAR DIARY
or
INTELLIGENCE SUMMARY
(Erase heading not required.)

Army Form C. 2118.

Hour, Date, Place	Summary of Events and Information	Remarks and references to Appendices
BUSSY Sept 7th	The whole of the Division arrived at BUSSY area	
8th	Sergt MACLEOD STC reported for duty in my office.	
	Sub Condr FROST S.T.C and Sub Condr GREGORY S.T.C joined from Base MARSEILLES, the former relieved Sub Condr MARTIN S.T.C the latter relieved Sergt MACLEOD S.T.C with Supply HdQrs Amballa Cav Bde.	
9th	"B" Echelon rejoined their own Brigades. I visited the A.D.S.T at QUERRIEU in the afternoon in connection with formation of new Limber Train.	
10th	I visited A.D.S.T and O.C. Xth Reserve Park in connection with Limber Train which is to be formed from limbers detached from that unit	
11th	Sub Condr DUKES S.T.C arrived from Base MARSEILLES & relieved Sub Condr WARD S.T.C in Amballa Cav Bde.	
	Sub Condr MARTIN S.T.C left for Base MARSEILLES.	
12th	LIEUT E.M WOOD A.S.C representing "B" Echelon proceeded to FRICOURT and MAMETZ to see site chosen for "B" Echelon camping ground and also Supply Dump at MAMETZ.	
	CAPT F BROWNE Cav A.S.C appointed to command Limber Train.	
	Limber Train seen into its bivouac by me in the afternoon	
	Sub Condr WARD S.T.C left for Base MARSEILLES.	

Instructions regarding War Diaries and Intelligence Summaries are contained in F. S. Regs., Part II. and the Staff Manual respectively. Title pages will be prepared in manuscript.

WAR DIARY
or
INTELLIGENCE SUMMARY
(Erase heading not required.)

Army Form C. 2118.

Hour, Date, Place	Summary of Events and Information	Remarks and references to Appendices
BUSSY Sept 13th	I attended a conference at Divl H^d Q^rs at 10-30 A.M Major General commanding the Division also called a meeting of all the officers of the Div^n & gave a brief summary of the work the Cavalry would be expected to do in the present operations.	
FRICOURT Sept 14th	The Division moved to bivouacs at DERNANCOURT. I accompanied the Div^l H^d Q^rs which were established at FRICOURT. "B" Echelon remained at BUSSY	
15th	The Division moved to a position of readiness about MAMETZ. In readiness for the Div^n to move forward till 6 pm. when orders were received that it should stand fast till 9 AM the following day	
16th	In readiness till the evening when the Div^n received orders to return to their bivouacs in the BUSSY area the following day	
BUSSY 17th	The Division returned to BUSSY, "B" Echelon joining Brigades & D. T.	
18th	Change for the worse in the weather. Much occupied with report demanded from Cavalry Corps regarding failure of certain rations to reach 'B' Echelon	

Instructions regarding War Diaries and Intelligence Summaries are contained in F. S. Regs., Part II. and the Staff Manual respectively. Title pages will be prepared in manuscript.

WAR DIARY
or
INTELLIGENCE SUMMARY
(Erase heading not required.)

Army Form C. 2118.

Hour, Date, Place	Summary of Events and Information	Remarks and references to Appendices
BUSSY Sept 19th	Saw A.D.S.T regarding use of horse transport at railhead He decided to do nothing at present owing to congestion of other traffic at railhead.	
20th	Visited the Supply Column bivouac from which supplies were being drawn by horse transport of the different Brigades, & D Troops. Very bad weather, horse standings getting in a very bad state. Inspected Lumber Train in bivouac. Accompanied the A.A.&QMG round Canadian Cav Bde in connection with shortage of supplies.	
21st	Visited the Supply Column bivouac in the morning in connection with shortage of supplies. Visited the Major General Commanding the Division at 5 pm. in connection with shortage of supplies. LT HALL relieved of duties as Column Supply officer & becomes B.S.O Can Cav Bde. Capt THOMAS becomes Column Supply officer Capt SMILLIE becomes Brigade Supply officer Can Cav Bde	
22nd	Visited the Supply Column & also the B.T.O Sec'bad Cav Bde Inspected the Aux H.T Coy in bivouac	

1247 W 3299 200,000 (E) 8/14 J.B.C. & A. Forms/C. 2118/11.

Instructions regarding War Diaries and Intelligence Summaries are contained in F. S. Regs., Part II. and the Staff Manual respectively. Title pages will be prepared in manuscript.

WAR DIARY
or
INTELLIGENCE SUMMARY
(Erase heading not required.)

Army Form C. 2118.

Hour, Date, Place	Summary of Events and Information	Remarks and references to Appendices
BUSSY Sept 23rd	Improvement in weather. Held instructional parade of pack animals of the Secunderabad Cav Bde.	
24th	Held further inspection of the Aux H T Coy in their bivouac. Presented ribbon of the Military Medal to one of their Company. Visited the ADS.T in connection with WE of Aux H T Coy. Received orders in the evening that the Zero hour would be 12.35 pm on 25-9-16 & that we were to be prepared to move at 1½ hours notice from that hour.	
25th	Stood by in readiness for a move until the evening, when orders were received that the Division would move WESTWARDS the following day. Orders received that the Lumber Train after unloading its supplies at railhead CORBIE would rejoin the Xth Reserve Park.	
DREUIL 26th	The Division moved Westwards. B Echelon under my command left BUSSY at 10-30 A.M. arrived at DREUIL at about 7 p.m. Wagons parked on field adjoining road	

1247 W 3299 200,000 (E) 8/14 J.B.C. & A. Forms/C. 2118/11.

Instructions regarding War Diaries and Intelligence Summaries are contained in F. S. Regs., Part II. and the Staff Manual respectively. Title pages will be prepared in manuscript.

WAR DIARY
or
INTELLIGENCE SUMMARY
(Erase heading not required.)

Army Form C. 2118.

Hour, Date, Place	Summary of Events and Information	Remarks and references to Appendices
DREUIL Sept 27th	Threatened to rain, so moved wagons on to road; road narrow & therefore some difficulty in ensuring traffic not being blocked.	
CAVILLON 28th	Orders received for units of B Echelon to rejoin their brigades. Moved A.S.C. H^d Q^rs to CAVILLON. Informed that a farmer intended to claim for 40 bundles unthrashed straw. Instituted immediate search through lines & found no trace of any unthrashed straw.	
29th	Conference at Canadian Cavalry Bde H^d Q^rs regarding relation of Canadian Cavalry Supply Column and 2^d Indian Cavalry Supply Column.	
30th	Interview with O.C. 2^d Ind Cav Supply Column on subject of yesterday's conference, also with S.S.O & O.C. Canadian Cavalry Bde Supply Column on same subject.	

[signature] Lt Col.
OC A.S.C. 2nd Indian Cavalry Division

1247 W 3299 200,000 (E) 8/14 J.B.C. & A. Forms/C. 2118/11.

SERIAL NO. 123.

Confidential

War Diary

of

A.S.C. Hd. Qrs., 5th Cavalry Division, (late 2nd Ind. Cavy. Divn).

FROM 1st October 1916 TO ~~31st October~~ 30th November 1916.

Instructions regarding War Diaries and Intelligence Summaries are contained in F. S. Regs., Part II. and the Staff Manual respectively. Title Pages will be prepared in manuscript.

WAR DIARY
or
INTELLIGENCE SUMMARY
(Erase heading not required.)

Hqrs. A. S. Co.

Vol IV

Army Form C. 2118

Place	Date	Hour	Summary of Events and Information	Remarks and references to Appendices
CAVILLON	1-10-16		Nothing unusual to report.	
	2.10.16		Change for the worse in the weather	
	3-10-16		nothing unusual to report	
	4-10-16		The Divisional Commander inspected the MHOW Ind. Cav. F. A, Can. Cav F. A & the S.A.A Section Amm Col at FOUDRINOY at 4 p.m. The MHOW I. C. F. A pronounced by the Divisional Commander to be faultless. The Can Cav F. A needed attention in certain respects. An officer of the S.A.A Amm Col had reported to the A.A.&Q.M.G earlier in the day that he was not getting any locally purchased fodder, I investigated the case & obtained the acknowledgement of the officer that the report was without foundation.	
	5.10-16		I gave a lecture on Pack Loading & Transport knots to the AMBALLA Cav Bde at MOLIENS-VIDAME, to officers & other transport ranks who were unable to attend previous lecture.	
	6.10.16		Had a parade of pack animals of AMBALLA Bde, including those loaded with entrenching tools. Sent report on parade to AMBALLA Bde H^d Q^rs. The parade included instruction in transport loading knots. Orders received that MAJOR A.S. NOAKE S&TC, Capt A.C. BIRD S&TC & Capt G.G. WEITZMANN IARO were to proceed to ENGLAND & report in writing to WAR OFFICE on arrival. Capt G.O. HUNT A.S.C reported for duty from B.H.T DEPOT HAVRE. L^T A.A. GREGORY A.S.C reported for duty with 2nd Ind Cav Supply Column	

Instructions regarding War Diaries and Intelligence Summaries are contained in F. S. Regs., Part II. and the Staff Manual respectively. Title Pages will be prepared in manuscript.

WAR DIARY
or
INTELLIGENCE SUMMARY
(Erase heading not required.)

Army Form C. 2118

Place	Date	Hour	Summary of Events and Information	Remarks and references to Appendices
CAVILLON	7-10-16		Issued orders for Capt A.C BIRD S&T.C & Capt G.G WEITZMANN I.A.R to proceed to ENGLAND via BOULOGNE tomorrow. Orders for Major A.S NOAKE S&T.C to proceed to ENGLAND temporarily held in abeyance. Lt GREGORY to BUSSY to relieve Capt BIRD. Lt PEMBERTON to officiate as BSO Sec'bad Bde, vice Capt WEITZMANN in addition to requisitioning duties. Orders for Lt COL M. SYNGE to proceed to ENGLAND received.	
	8-10-16		Major R.R.B JACKSON arrived to relieve Lt COL M SYNGE. The relief held in abeyance by orders from Q.M.G. Started handing over as provisional measure, meanwhile handing over in same way to Capt HUNT.	
	9-10-16		The Divisional Commander inspected the animals & transport of the following:– Divisional HdQrs, including Police, A.S.C HdQrs and Signal Squadron. He expressed satisfaction at the general turnout of the transport & animals of the A.S.C. HdQrs including the riding horses.	
	10-10-16		2nd Lt H.W. COLDRIDGE A.S.C arrived & posted as R.O of Sec'bad Bde. Lt Col SHAW arrived as O.C A.S.C Can Cav Bde in spite of the G.O.C's recent recommendation that this appointment should be abolished.	
	11-10-16		Question of relief of Major NOAKE & me still pending. Major JACKSON made a tour of Bdes & D.T units to acquaint himself with the A.S.C officers.	

WAR DIARY
or
INTELLIGENCE SUMMARY
(Erase heading not required.)

Place	Date	Hour	Summary of Events and Information	Remarks and references to Appendices
CAVILLON	12.10.16		Continued handing over	
	13.10.16		Took Major JACKSON round the different units in the forward area.	
	14.10.16		Completed handing over.	
			[illegible] Lt Col. O.C. A.S.C. 2nd Ind. Cav. Divn.	
	15.10.16		Lt Col M SYNGE S,TC and Major A.S. NOAKE, S,TC left for ENGLAND on 7 days leave.	
			Instructed SEC'BAD Cav Bde that there would be an inspection of the transport of the Bde at 2.30 pm on Wednesday 18th by ADS,T Cavalry Corps	
	16-10-16		Directed Lt Col J.A. SHAW C.A.S.C to reconnoitre the new area with a view of ascertaining it capabilities as regards the winter billets, supplies etc	
			Visited the DDS,T IVth Army at QUERRIEU	
	17.10.16		nothing unusual to report.	
	18.10.16		The ADS,T Cav Corps came & inspected the transport of the SEC'BAD Cav Bde at CROUY at 2-30 pm. The Indian transport was good, the British not so good. The animals of the DECCAN HORSE were especially good & reflected great credit on the Transport Officer	

Instructions regarding War Diaries and Intelligence Summaries are contained in F. S. Regs., Part II. and the Staff Manual respectively. Title Pages will be prepared in manuscript.

WAR DIARY
or
INTELLIGENCE SUMMARY
(Erase heading not required.)

Army Form C. 2118

Place	Date	Hour	Summary of Events and Information	Remarks and references to Appendices
CAVILLON	19-10-16		Owing to the appointment of Major R.V. HUNT A.S.C as S.S.O of the Division & the early departure to INDIA of Capt B.M.C. TYLER. S&T.C. IAR & L^T E.A. NESBITT S&T.C. IAR the following moves have been made: Capt F. BROWNE from Adj to O.C. C.A.S.C to B.T.O AMBALLA Cav Bde vice Major R.V. HUNT A.S.C to S.S.O. L^T H.W. COLDRIDGE. A.S.C to understudy L^T E.A. NESBITT S&T.C IAR as a temporary measure. L^T H. PEMBERTON A.S.C to temporarily carry on the duties of B.S.O SEC'BAD Cav Bde as well as R.O. Very wet & cold weather all day, an issue of rum to all ranks was sanctioned.	
	20-10-16		L^T COL J.A. SHAW. C.A.S.C the officer detailed to report on the reconnaisance of the new area returned & reported that the FRENCH had been buying up supplies I went to Cav Corps H^D Q^RS & reported the matter to the A.D.S&T. Heavy frost at night.	
	21-10-16		L^T COL J.A. SHAW. C.A.S.C again went on reconnaisance duty in the new area Fairly severe frost at night.	
	22-10-16		Nothing unusual to report.	
	23-10-16		L^T COL. J.A. SHAW. C.A.S.C returned from reconnaisance duty in the new area & reported having bought 27 tons of Hay & 1 ton of straw, he also arranged for, but did not pay for 30 tons hay. Some of the purchases were made outside the new area, but this was owing to the area having been altered after the departure of L^T COL. J.A. SHAW & it was impossible to notify him. The S.S.O visited the Digging parties in the front area.	

1875 Wt. W593/826 1,000,000 4/15 J.B.C. & A. A.D.S.S./Forms/C. 2118.

Instructions regarding War Diaries and Intelligence Summaries are contained in F. S. Regs., Part II. and the Staff Manual respectively. Title Pages will be prepared in manuscript.

WAR DIARY
or
INTELLIGENCE SUMMARY
(Erase heading not required.)

Army Form C. 2118

Place	Date	Hour	Summary of Events and Information	Remarks and references to Appendices
CAVILLON	24-10-16		Very wet weather.	
			Went round all Brigades to make arrangements regarding Conveyance of Reserve Rations in case of a move WESTWARDS	
	25-10-16		Weather continues wet, standings getting very sloppy	
			Directed my adjutant to visit the new area & arrange about the billeting of the A.S.C H^o Q^rs Staff.	
	26-10-16		Owing to inclement weather an issue of rum to all ranks was sanctioned.	
			The S.S.O visited the D.D S&T IVth Army at QUERRIEU, also saw L^T GOLD A.S.C, S.O Detachments, brought back L^T GREGORY from FRECHENCOURT posted him to No 71 Coy 2nd I.C Supply Column.	
	27-10-16		I visited the new area & arranged purchases	
	28-10-16		Bad weather continues a further issue of rum to all ranks was sanctioned.	
			Detailed L^T Col J.A SHAW C.A.S.C to inspect the Can Cav Bde F.A. he reported that it was satisfactory.	
			A further issue of rum to all ranks was sanctioned owing to bad weather.	
	29-10-16		Horse rugs had to be brought in from DARGNIES, detailed 9 lorries from 2nd I.C Amm Park & 7 from 2nd I.C Supply Column for the duty, horse rugs were delivered at 5 pm. Small arms ammunition dumped under orders of the G.O.C, same put under Cover.	
			Weather still very bad, a further ~~of~~ issue of rum to all ranks was sanctioned.	

1875 Wt. W593/826 1,000,000 4/15 J.B.C. & A. A.D.S.S./Forms/C. 2118.

Instructions regarding War Diaries and Intelligence Summaries are contained in F. S. Regs., Part II. and the Staff Manual respectively. Title Pages will be prepared in manuscript.

WAR DIARY
or
INTELLIGENCE SUMMARY
(Erase heading not required.)

Army Form C. 2118

Place	Date	Hour	Summary of Events and Information	Remarks and references to Appendices
CAVILLON	30-10-16		Still very wet weather & heavy gale. Lt Col J.A. SHAW. C.A.S.C left to report to A.D.S.&T Cav Corps for duty under authority Cav Corps Q S.T.W 200 of 29.10.16.	
	31.10-16		Improvement in weather.	
			Orders received from A.A.&Q.M.G this morning that the Division would move WESTWARDS tomorrow.	
			All arrangements made for the conveyance of horserugs & tents of the Division	

A. A. Jackson Lt Col.
O.C. A.S.C. 2nd Indian Cavalry Division

1875 Wt. W593/826 1,000,000 4/15 J.B.C. & A. A.D.S.S./Forms/C. 2118.

Instructions regarding War Diaries and Intelligence Summaries are contained in F. S. Regs., Part II. and the Staff Manual respectively. Title Pages will be prepared in manuscript.

WAR DIARY
or
INTELLIGENCE SUMMARY
(Erase heading not required.)

Army Form C. 2118

H.Q.s 5th Cav. Divn.
A.S.C.
Vol. V

Place	Date	Hour	Summary of Events and Information	Remarks and references to Appendices
DARGNIES	1-11-16		The Division moved WESTWARDS. Divl. H.Q.rs at DARGNIES.	
			appointed 2nd/Lt M.H.G BRITTS as Divisional Purchasing Officer in accordance with instructions received from A.D.S.T Cav Corps.	
	2-11-16		Railhead altered to WOINCOURT.	
			General condition of the A.S.C of Divl. H.Q.rs was indifferent owing to being scattered all about, amalgamated the whole of the A.S.C under me and started a proper mess for them.	
	3-11-16		Commenced making standings for the animals.	
	4-11-16		Nothing unusual to report	
	5-11-16		Visited the A.D.S.T Cav Corps in connection with the purchasing of hay & straw in the Divisional area.	
	6-11-16		The G.O.C held an inspection of the S.A.A Section of the 2nd Ind. Cav. Divn & Can Cav Bde Ammunition Column at BEAUCHAMPS.	
			Very bad weather.	
	7-11-16		The G.O.C inspected the A & B Echelons of the transport of the Can Cav Bde at 3 pm. I was in attendance. The condition of the animals & wagons was very good & compared most favourably with the transport of infantry divisions I have recently inspected. Opened the Canteen.	
			The Aux H.T. Coy returned by route march from the SOMME marching via QUERRIEU - AMIENS - PICQUIGNY - SOUES - ARRAINES - OISEMONT - TRANSLOY - GAMACHES to ~~(?)~~ billets in OUST-MAREST. Very bad weather & heavy gales.	
			Arranged for the hire of a petrol chaff cutting machine for cutting oat straw into chaff & so saving 2 lbs hay per horse per day.	

Instructions regarding War Diaries and Intelligence Summaries are contained in F. S. Regs., Part II. and the Staff Manual respectively. Title Pages will be prepared in manuscript.

WAR DIARY
or
INTELLIGENCE SUMMARY
(Erase heading not required.)

Army Form C. 2118

Place	Date	Hour	Summary of Events and Information	Remarks and references to Appendices
DARGNIES	8-11-16		Condition of Aux H.T Coy wagons in an awfully bad state, the horses were good considering the hard time they had had on the SOMME. The wagons require thorough overhauling.	
	9-11-16		Selected Refilling Points for the Divisional Troops & the three Brigades as follows:-	
			D.T's at DARGNIES.	
			Amballa Cav Bde 100 yds from ruined church N.W of the GAMACHES-BEAUCHAMPS road about ½ mile from GAMACHES.	
			Secbad Cav Bde Clump of trees on AIGNEVILLE-FEQUIRES road.	
			Can Cav Bde About 300 yds from BETHENCOURT on the BETHENCOURT-ALLENAY road	
	10-11-16		Information received that Capt G.H. BOROUGH A.S.C O.C. Aux H.T. Coy died on 7-11-16 at No 24 General Hospital ETAPLES. Cause of death Cerebral Meningitis. L^T G.E.C EAGAR & S.S.M. J BEAN of the Aux H.T. Coy were temporarily isolated. Appointed L^T T.E.A. HALL. CASC to command Aux H.T Coy as a temporary measure.	
	11-11-16		On recommendation of the A.D.M.S the Aux H.T Coy was isolated.	
			The working parties rejoined the Division.	
	12-11-16		Information received that the cause of Capt G.H. BOROUGH'S death was diabetes so that the restrictions on the Aux H.T Coy were removed & L^T G.E.C. EAGAR and S.S.M. J. BEAN rejoined for duty.	

1875 Wt. W593/826 1,000,000 4/15 J.B.C. & A. A.D.S.S./Forms/C. 2118.

Instructions regarding War Diaries and Intelligence Summaries are contained in F. S. Regs., Part II. and the Staff Manual respectively. Title Pages will be prepared in manuscript.

WAR DIARY
or
INTELLIGENCE SUMMARY
(Erase heading not required.)

Army Form C. 2118

Place	Date	Hour	Summary of Events and Information	Remarks and references to Appendices
DARGNIES	14-11-16		Accompanied the A.A. Q.M.G to the inspection by the G.O.C of the transport of the 8th Hussars, transport very good.	
			no supplies arrived from BASE for this Division on enquiring I ascertained from R.C.O ABBEVILLE that IVth Army had wired Base "no pack required for 14th at Railhead" apparently this was due through mistake of Signals which should have read 5A, i.e. the pack for the working party at the front. The 13 pounder Section of Cav Amm Park rejoined its unit at 7 pm	
	15-11-16		Accompanied the A.A. Q.M.G to the inspection of the transport of the 7th D.G's, great improvement in turnout of transport	
	16-11-16		Went round the R.H.A Bdes, found horses suffering tremendously ordered linseed & chaff to be provided at once. Still a day behind with men's rations.	
			Very cold & frost during night.	
	17-11-16		A double pack arrived today which made up the deficiency of men's rations. The lorries which supplied the detached parties of the division returned under Lt R.H. BECK. 2nd Lt C.M. GOLD rejoined at the same time.	
	18-11-16		Snow fell last night, cold rain during the day. Got all animals under cover. Frost again.	
	19-11-16		The 13 pdr Section of the 2nd Ind Cav Amm Park arrived at MERS at 2.30 pm complete with ammunition	
	20-11-16		Inspected the Aux H.T. Coy in conjunction with the A.D.S.&T Cav Corps	

1875 Wt. W593/826 1,000,000 4/15 J.B.C. & A. A.D.S.S./Forms/C. 2118.

Instructions regarding War Diaries and Intelligence Summaries are contained in F. S. Regs., Part II. and the Staff Manual respectively. Title Pages will be prepared in manuscript.

WAR DIARY
or
INTELLIGENCE SUMMARY
(Erase heading not required.)

Army Form C. 2118

Place	Date	Hour	Summary of Events and Information	Remarks and references to Appendices
DARGNIES	21-11-16		Visited the A.D.S.&T. Cav Corps in connection with the transport of the Can Cav Bde Machine Gun Squadron	
	22.11.16		Held a meeting of all R.O's & French Interpreters to discuss purchases and requisitioning matters in the different districts.	
	23.11.16		Nothing unusual to report.	
	24.11.16		Nothing unusual to report.	
	25.11.16		Very wet weather.	
			It was decided to change the titles of the 1st & 2nd Ind. Cav Divns as follows:-	
			Old Title: 1st Ind Cav Div — New Title: 4th Cav Divn	
			Old Title: 2nd Ind Cav Div — New Title: 5th Cav Divn	
			The inspection of the Aux H T Coy by the G.O.C the division was cancelled owing to the inclemency of the weather.	
	26.11.16		Weather continues bad.	
			Nothing unusual to report.	
	27.11.16		Had a meeting of all R.O's to discuss matters regarding purchasing of hay & straw impressed upon them the necessity of getting in as much as possible of both.	
			Two days supplies delivered to Can Cav Bde & half D.Ts in order to enable horse transport to draw from Railhead to day.	

Instructions regarding War Diaries and Intelligence Summaries are contained in F. S. Regs., Part II. and the Staff Manual respectively. Title Pages will be prepared in manuscript.

WAR DIARY
or
INTELLIGENCE SUMMARY
(Erase heading not required.)

Army Form C. 2118

Place	Date	Hour	Summary of Events and Information	Remarks and references to Appendices
DARGNIES	28-11-16		30 Wagons of the 4th Cav Div Reserve Park joined to day & were attached to the Aux H. T. Coy. Drew supplies by horse transport from Railhead for the Can Cav Bde & half D.Ts	
	29-11-16		The G.O.C Division inspected the transport of the MHOW I.C.F.A & SEC'BAD F.A in marching order, the transport was good; the MHOW I.C.F.A. being better than the SEC'BAD F.A.	
	30-11-16		The G.O.C Division inspected the transport of the Can. Cav Bde F.A and the Can Machine Gun Squadron, there was an improvement on the last inspection but they were not up to the standard of the two units inspected yesterday	

H H Jackson Lt Col
OC A.S.C 5th Cav. Divn

1875 Wt. W593/826 1,000,000 4/15 J.B.C. & A. A.D.S.S./Forms/C. 2118.

SERIAL NO. 123.

Confidential

War Diary

of

Headquarters, A.S.C., 5th Cavalry Division

FROM 1st December 1916 TO 31st December 1916.

Instructions regarding War Diaries and Intelligence Summaries are contained in F. S. Regs., Part II. and the Staff Manual respectively. Title Pages will be prepared in manuscript.

WAR DIARY
or
INTELLIGENCE SUMMARY
(Erase heading not required.)

HQrs A. S. C.
5th Cav Divn
Vol VI

Army Form C. 2118

Place	Date	Hour	Summary of Events and Information	Remarks and references to Appendices
DARGNIES	1-12-16		Weather fine but inclined to be foggy. Worked out scheme so that the rest of the Division viz Amballa Cav Bde, Sec'bad Cav Bde & the other half of D.Ts should be supplied by horse transport. The Scheme to come into effect on Monday next. Major R.E. SANDERS A.S.C reported for duty to act as S.S.O vice Major R.V. HUNT A.S.C transferred to take over Command of the VIth Reserve Park.	
	2-12-16		Had a meeting of all B.S.Os & B.T.Os to discuss arrangements for the new scheme to carry supplies for the whole Division by horse transport. Dull weather frosty.	
	3-12-16		Visited the A.D.S.&T Cav Corps in connection with the question of forage for the Division. An issue of rum to all ranks was approved. Evacuated 1 G.S. Wagon turn out complete to Base H.T. Depot ABBEVILLE →	A.D.S.&T Cav Corps T/634 D 29-11-16
			Dull weather frosty.	
	4-12-16		Supplies for the whole division were delivered by horse transport from Railhead.	
	5-12-16		Dull & showery weather. Nothing important to report.	
	6-12-16		Weather fine. Nothing unusual to report.	
	7-12-16		Brig General The Rt Hon J.E.B. SEELY C.B. DSO inspected the billets of the Divl HdQrs at DARGNIES & of the Aux H.T. Coy & Detachment of the IVth Cav Div Reserve Park attached to the Aux H.T. Coy at WOINCOURT, he expressed himself as satisfied on the whole, but that some of the approaches to the Horse Standings were in a very muddy state & that same should be taken in hand. The necessary orders were issued for this to be done.	

1875 Wt. W593/826 1,000,000 4/15 J.B.C. & A. A.D.S.S./Forms/C. 2118.

Instructions regarding War Diaries and Intelligence Summaries are contained in F. S. Regs., Part II. and the Staff Manual respectively. Title Pages will be prepared in manuscript.

WAR DIARY
or
INTELLIGENCE SUMMARY
(Erase heading not required.)

Army Form C. 2118

Place	Date	Hour	Summary of Events and Information	Remarks and references to Appendices
DARGNIES	8.12.16		Wet weather. Nothing unusual to report.	
	9.12.16		Weather continues wet. Nothing important to report.	
	10.12.16		Major R.V. HUNT A.S.C left to day to take over command of the VI Reserve Park. Very wet weather all day.	
	11.12.16		Nothing important to report. Improvement in weather.	
	12.12.16		The G.O.C. Division inspected the billets of the 5th C.D. Supply Column & 5th C.D. Amm Park at MERS & expressed himself as satisfied. The Canadian & Sec'bad Pioneer battalions went up in the front area today. The Canadian to the XV Corps & Sec'bad to the XIV Corps. With a view to relieving some of the Aux H.T. Coy wagons of daily duty the following units detailed wagons to help in transporting supplies:- 5th Cav Div R.H.A. Bde Amm Column — 6 wagons R.C.H.A. Bde Amm Column — 5 wagons Can Field Amb — 3 wagons.	
	13.12.16		The Amballa Pioneer battalion & the relieved party of Sec'bad Pioneer battalion rejoined their units to day.	
	14.12.16		Supplies were delivered by lorries direct to units, to enable the Aux H.T. Coy to prepare for the G.O.C's inspection on Saturday.	
	15.12.16		Lorries again delivered supplies direct to units. Weather dull & foggy	
	16.12.16		The G.O.C Division inspected the Aux H.T. Coy & Detachment of IV C.D Reserve Park in marching order in Column of Route & expressed himself as satisfied.	

Instructions regarding War Diaries and Intelligence Summaries are contained in F. S. Regs., Part II. and the Staff Manual respectively. Title Pages will be prepared in manuscript.

WAR DIARY
or
INTELLIGENCE SUMMARY
(Erase heading not required.)

Army Form C. 2118

Place	Date	Hour	Summary of Events and Information	Remarks and references to Appendices
DARGNIES	17-12-16		Horse transport again delivered supplies as per former arrangements. Fine weather, slight frost. 2/Lt M.H.G. BRITTS A.S.C. proceeded to ENGLAND to report at War office, authority Cav Corps "Q" No S.T.W 475 of 17.12.16.	
	18-12-16		Nothing unusual to report.	
	19-12-16		Dull ~~foggy~~ frosty weather. Nothing important to report.	
	20-12-16		Fine sunny weather. Nothing unusual to report	
	21-12-16		Wet dull weather. The G.O.C Division inspected the 5th Cav Div Supply Column and the 5th Cav Div Ammn Park at MERS	
	22-12-16		Weather mild. Nothing unusual to report.	
	23-12-16		Cold, wet weather. Rain all day. Nothing important to report.	
	24-12-16		Weather wet & windy. Nothing unusual to report.	
	25-12-16		Auxiliary Horse Transport Co. were relieved from loading & delivering rations today, rations being loaded & delivered by Supply Column, assisted by some Ammn Park lorries. Weather mild.	
	26/27 12/16		Nothing unusual to report. Weather still mild.	
	28-12-16		Delay at railhead too great owing to loading in detail. Arranged to load forage only in detail, and rations in bulk by Brigades, these being dumped at Brigade dumps, and drawn at 2 pm daily by Horse Transport. Weather fine and mild.	
	29/30/31 12/16		Nothing unusual to report. Weather mild. Wet on 29th, but fine on 30th & 31st.	

R. M. Jackson Lt. Col.
O.C. A.S.C. 5th Cavalry Division.

1375 Wt. W593/826 1,000,000 4/15 J.B.C. & A. A.D.S.S./Forms/C. 2118.

BEF

2 IND CAV DIV TROOPS

(71 Coy ASC) 1 SECTION
(83 " ") NO 2 "

DIV SUPPLY COL

1914 SEPT to 1915 MAR

1916 JULY to 1916 ~~DEC~~ ~~SEPT~~ OCT SEPT.

TO 5 CAV DIVN 74 DIVN SUPPLY COLUMN Box 1163.

1184

DIV SUPPLY COLUMN

War Diary
of
O C 71 M.T. Coy
Secunderabad Cavalry Bgd Supply Column
(Changed to 2nd Indian Cavalry Division Supply Column on 31st December/14)

25th Septr 1914.
L[illegible]nded at LE HAVRE at 11.0 a.m.
Strength of Coy 6 officers, 208 N C O's & men, 40 lorries 30 cwts, 4 cars, 7 motor bicycles.
Camped in open space in Docks.

26th Unloaded lorries, cars & bicycles. Weather fine. 2 men admitted into hospital.

27th Left LE HAVRE 10.15 a.m.

arrived	BOLBEC	1.0 P.m.	28½ Kilos.
"	YVETOT	3.5 P.m.	21½ "
"	ROUEN	6.30 P.m.	36 "

much delayed by columns in front
Roads excellent, weather fine.
Country people pressed flowers, fruit, cakes

cigarettes etc on the troops.
One lorry ran out big end 2 miles out of
ROUEN & was towed in.
Camped for night under shed of quay.
Days run 86 Kilos.

28th. Left ROUEN 8·30 a.m.
arrived LOUVIERS 10·45 a m
" EVREUX 1·30 P.m
" NONANCOURT 4·0 P.m

Roads good, weather fine.
Left repair lorry, spare part lorry & one
broken down lorry at Rouen, to join
convoy as soon as possible.
days run 90 Kilos.

29th. Repair lorry & spare part lorry with
broken down lorry which has been repaired
joined column at NONANCOURT at
8·30 a.m.
Column left NONANCOURT at 10·30
am. arrived DREUX " 12·15
" ~~HOUDAN~~
FAVEROLLES 1·45
RAMBOUILLET 3·10
VERSAILLES at 6·25 P.m

3

[illegible] parked in the Avenue de Paris.
[illegible] were good + weather fine.
Days run 98.5 Kilos.

30th Septh.
Column remained in avenue de Paris.
Obtained 1000 galons of petrol from
WILLENEUVE ST GEORGE,
Obtained 105 blankets for men in PARIS
after great difficulty.

1st Octh
Column left VERSAILLES at 9.30 a.m.
arrived WILLENEUVE ST GEORGE 11.30
" CORBEIL 12.45
" LA FERTE ALAIS 2.10
" ETAMPES 4.55
" MONNERVILLE 6.20

Roads good on the whole, but bad between CORBEILLE + LA FERTÉ ALAIS.
Pavé in villages very bad, especially in ETAMPES.
Weather perfect.
Days run 96.5. Kilos

2nd Octh Left MONNERVILLE 9.30 a.m.

reached ANGERVILLE 9.55 a.m.
" ARTENAY 12.15 p.m.
" point on main road 5
miles out of ORLEANS
on ARTENAY road 1.30 p.m.

camped on right hand side of road. Road is wide & there is a nice strip of grass at the side for fires, stores to be stacked etc. Water rather scarce but can be obtained from village of Chevilly about one mile away. Borrowed water cart from mayor of town, & put in for one from Ordnance. Days run 50 Kilos.

3rd October.

6 lorries paraded at 6.30 & 15 at 7.0 a.m to carry stores from Orleans railway goods siding to Cercottes camp for Indian contingent. Men left in camp were employed on erecting small marquee, fatigues, cleaning lorries drills etc.

Weather still fine.

4th October.

Last night was warmer than it has been lately but fine rain fell early in the morning

5

15 lorries were required at the station at 8.0 a.m for the purpose of carrying more stores from the station to Cercottes.

5th October. ~~Weather still~~

Weather still remains fine though cold. Workshops busy making wooden frames on lorry bodies to carry tarpaulines, also overhauling engines. Nearly all the 24 men in the workshop branch are excellent workers. Strength of company 213 including officers. Transport & supply men had a route march, foot drill & aiming drill.

6th Octr.

Still no rain. 10 lorries required for transport duty in the afternoon. Work & drills as yesterday.

7th Octr

No orders to move yet. Weather fine. Strength of Company 211. Men feel the cold a bit. Remainder of blankets received from ordnance ~~received~~ today. Each man now has one blanket. Workshops busy on superstructures.

8th Octr.

Very cold last night with a sharp white frost. Another man admitted to hospital.

85

suffering from the cold. still no rain & no orders to move. the native troops, some of them at any rate, have been here several days now.

9th Octr.

Weather fine, lorries employed on conveying supplies from Orleans goods station to Cercottes camp.

10th Octr.

Weather fine, lorries employed same as yesterday.

11th Octr & 12th Octr

Weather still fine. Pouches cartridge, & some boots obtained from the ordnance at La Chapelle.

Strength of company 210 officers & men. Workshops still busy on con[s]pies of lorries.

13th Octr

Warmer last night. Rain at 7 a.m. this morning for ½ an hour. High wind all day. 10 lorries required for duty from station to Cercottes camp.

14th Octr.

High wind & rain last night.

10 more lorries required for duty to Cercottes camp.

15th Octr.

Complete change in the weather much rain though temperature not so low. Non skids on lorries prove indespensible in the various camps.

16th Octr.

Still rather wet. All available lorries employed between Cercottes camp & the railway goods siding at Orleans.

17th Octr

Weather finer. Strength of company reduced to 208 N.C.O's & men.

18th Octr.

Employed non skids with much effect in Les Groues camp. Helped out lorries belonging to 87, 70, & 72 Companies besides my own.

19th Octr

No sign of spare parts for lorries yet. Have put in three separate indents for them. Workshop staff working very well & so far all lorries are being kept in very fair running order. Have ordered a number of new tyres for the worst wheels. Other companies have better lorries than ours nearly all of which are old, but I could not wish for a better lot of men on the whole. Some of the supply men have given a little trouble, but they have been suitably dealt with. Gen. Landon saw all officers comm'g companies this evening with regard to the spare part question.

20th Oct.

Still damp & overcast. All available lorries out on duty to various camps.

21st Oct.

Weather warmer. All lorries out again.

22nd Much work for lorries of 71 & 72 Coys as all other companies left Orleans. Weather warm.

23rd. Sent Lt Truman off early this morning to Rouen to try & obtain some spare parts. He returned about 8 P.M., having covered about 260 miles. He was able to bring a considerable amount of stuff

including springs, lamps, a magneto etc. 9
Lorries working very hard night & day.
Four common lorries & 12 men joined company today from England to carr supplies for Jodhpur Lancers attached to Indian Cavalry Brigade supply column.

24th Octh.

Seven drivers joined company to replace casualties, a very rough looking lot. Received orders to leave for Abbeville tomorrow. Weather is now absolutely perfect & no difficulty is experienced in getting into & out of camps.

25th Octh

Loaded up at 7.a.m. a supply siding with two days supplies for Indian Cavalry Brigade. at last moment had orders to leave behind four lorries & 12 men for Jodhpur Lancers. By mistake one extra man was left behind. Strength of company 210 men & 40 lorries.

Column left Aircottes at 12.0 mid day 14 Km
Reached Artemay 1.15 P.m. distance 13.5
" Allonnes 3.30 P.m. 33.0

Column was somewhat delayed by 7 2 Coy

99

who had taken the wrong road last night.

26th Octr.

Column left allonnes 8.0 a.m. weather threatening. Roads so far have been level & good. Distance of trip 98 Kils.

Column reached CHARTRES at 9. a.m
NONANCOURT at 12. a.m.
EVREUX at 2.30 P.m.
LOUVIERS at 4.0 P.m

Thornycroft lorry No 1263 broke spring but arrived an hour after remainder of column.

office Leyland was delayed by magneto trouble.

27th Octr

Leyland lorry was repaired. Thornycroft lorry left behind to follow on an hour later after new spring had been fitted.

Convoy left LOUVIERS at 9.0 a.m.
arrived at ROUEN at 12.5 P.m.
" " NEUCHATELLE at 4.30 P.m

Court Martial on two wheelers & one loader was promulgated by the road side just before reaching ~~ORLE~~. ROUEN. The three prisoners were then taken to the prison in ROUEN & left there. Roads mostly good but very bumpy round ROUEN.

and a bad hill up out of the town. otherwise the country was mostly flat. Lorries parked in the town square at NEUFCHATEL for the night. Distance 97.5 Kilos.

28th Octr

Much rain last night.

Column left NEUFCHATEL at 8.25 am
reached BLANGY at 12.5 p.m
" ABBEVILLE " 4.15 p.m.

Total distance Kilos.

The road today was very hilly & the convoy was much delayed in consequence. There is a steep hill out of NEUFCHATEL and there are several hills round BLANGY. Two lorries were delayed at the start by water in their petrol tanks. State of the roads was uniformly good. The column on entering ABBEVILLE was turned back & ordered to halt by the road side about two miles out of the town to wait instructions.

29th Octr

Very cold last night; some rain storms in the evening. The spirits of the men are excellent & now that we have got rid of the few bad characters I anticipate very little trouble. Spent day outside ABBEVILLE. Drew 4500 francs from bank to pay men also obtained 127 pairs of gloves for men on authority of ordnance officer.

30th Octr

Received orders at 8·30 to move on to AIRE at once. Weather wet & cold.

Column left ABBEVILLE at 9·15 a.m.
Reached HESDAN at 12·30 P.m
" FRUGES at 1·45 P.m
" AIRE at 4·30 P.m.

Roads very hilly & much rain. Distance 78 Kil.

Reported arrival of column to Head Qrs Indian army corps at ~~Merville~~ MERVILLE as ordered. Was told to await further orders at AIRE.

31st Octr

Went to St VENANT at 9 a.m. to draw rations. Met staff officer of 9th Indian Cavalry Brigade. Recd instructions to move supply column to St VENANT. Did so, column arrived there at 4·0 P.m. Issued some provisions to part of a few units that evening. Was

told to unload one days rations on ground 13
as Brigade would stay at ST VENANT
for two days.
1st November.
Received orders to take one days supplies
to VIEILLE CHAPELLE as the whole
Brigade is moving there this evening
Loaded lorries up again sending one
section to VIEILLE CHAPELLE & the
other section with head qrs to ~~Choques~~
CHOQUES which is rail head. Dumped
one days supplies at ~~Vielle~~ VIELLE
CHAPELLE. Remainder of column
reached camping ground ½ mile out of
CHOQUES at 3.30 P.m. Column parked
at side of broad main road. Water to be
obtained in village ¼ mile away
2nd November. Weather very fine.
No 2 section started at 5.30 a.m &
reached VIEILLE CHAPELLE at
7. a.m. distance about 15 kilos.
Much transport on the road. No 1
section loaded up at CHOQUES
station at 8.15 a.m. with following 74

14

days supplies. Weather still fine roads cut up by guns & transport off main roads.

3rd Novb.

No 1 section left camp at 7.30 a.m. & arrived at ~~Vieille Ch~~ VIEILLE CHAPELLE at 8.45 a.m. Unloaded by 9.45 a.m and returned to camp. No 2 section loaded up at station at 8.0 a.m & returned to camp at 11.0 a.m. Weather fine. Roads into Head Qrs narrow & very wet at the sides. Country round here appears nice and flat for the lorries.

4th November

Very misty all day & colder. Heavy rain at night. BETUNE was shelled by the Germans this afternoon. Only one woman was killed. This place is about ¾ mile from here. Convoy ran to station & Head Qrs at VIEILLE CHAPELLE as before. Judpur Lancers have now arrived.

Brigade consists at present of the following units, though casualties alter the numbers of men each day. The horses or very few of them are being used at present so that their numbers remain much the same 15

	British	Indians	animals
Head Quarters	53	23	81
7th Dragoon Gds	538	14	623
20 Decan Horse	27	583	590
30 Poona Horse	17	573	603
Judpur Lancers	10	490	620
N. Battery R.A.	178	24	245
Ammunition Column R.A.	23	111	175
Signal Troop R.E.	14	22	34
Field Troop R.E.	8	92	93
S+T. (Indian) Head Qrs	6	40	43
Postal	2	3	—
Ambulance R.A.	37	159	82
71 Coy ASC, Supply Col	224	—	—
72 Coy A.S.C. Am. Col.	86	—	—
	1223	2134	3189

5th November.

Much rain last night, fine today + quite warm, Supply column running smoothly. Some lorries used to bring in hay, other to carry wounded to trains at railhead + others to convey corpses to station. These men apparently died in Hospital. An aeroplane dropped a bomb with ¼ mile of our [illegible] camp today. I think they destroyed a cottage!

6th November.

Weather fine, misty in the early morning
No 1 section loaded at station at 9.0 a m
finished loading at 2.15 p.m.
No 2 section left camp at 7.0 a m, reached
VIEILLE CHAPELLE at 8.0 a.m with
rations for Cavalry Bgd. Returned to camp 12.5 pm.

7th Novr

Some rain in the night. Work carried
out same as yesterday.

8th Novr

Fine & slightly warmer. Nothing of note to
record.

9th Novr

Very heavy gun fire heard today. Brigade
was ordered to be prepared to move at a
moments notice. Order was afterwards
cancelled. 2 German prisoners were
conveyed from ~~Vieille Ch~~ VIEILLE
CHAPELLE to CHOQUES station
in our lorries today.

10th November

Cold early this morning. Bombardment
of BETHUNE continues at intervals

in a spasmodic manner. 17
Colonel Vaughn has taken over the duties of S & T officer for the Cavalry Brigade from Capt Harrison.

Nov. 11th

Four more lorries were received from H.Q. Qrs. at St OMER today for the purpose of carrying hay for the Brigade. Eight men joined with the lorries, 2 of which are Milnes Daimlers and 2 are Halleys. Our lorries now consist of the following:—

Thornycroft	7
Commer	7
Albion	6
Daimler	5
Milnes Daimler (Mercedes)	5
Halford	4
Leyland	3
Austin	3
Straker Squire	3
Halley	3
Maudsley	1
Wolseley	1
	48

17 lorries in No 1 section carry 1 day's food
17 " " No 2 " " 1 " "
2 workshop lorries
2 store lorries.
2 1st aid lorries with skidding etc.
1 office lorry, also carrying ammunition, petrol etc.
1 lorry for rations, water, wood etc for Coy.
1 Post lorry
1 ordnance store lorry.

a tremendous wind blowing today, increasing in violence towards the evening.
Supplies are coming up pretty well by the train now & articles are not so short as they have been up to the present. Plenty of rum & cigarettes have been sent up, but the jam is often short & the bacon nearly always bad. It does not in many instances appear to have been properly cooked.

Novr 12th

Wind has gone down today, though it was violent in the night & accompanied by heavy showers of rain. The roads to the head qrs of the different units of the brigade are narrow & very greasy. It is necessary to keep lorries well on the crown of the road.

Novr 13th

Wet and cold. Hay has now arrived by train for the brigade. Sent 8 lorry loads up to Head Qrs at VIEILLE CHAPELLE.

Novr 14th

Moved the column ½ a mile down the road nearer CHOQUES in the position occupied by 69 Coy. The men are now able to sleep in some empty houses. They have fresh straw on the wooden floors and are quite comfortable.

Novr 15th.

Very cold & wet. Snow fell for a short time this morning.

Novr 16th.

Still very wet but slightly warmer. The section which has loaded up at the station on the previous day now has to make a second journey to Head Quarters with hay, which comes up by train, no hay being obtainable locally now.

Novr 17th

Moved supplies of Head Quarters from VIEILLE CHAPELLE to QUAI DE RIVAGE just outside BAETHUNE. All head quarters of the different units are now moved to position near BETHUNE. Shells are frequently falling in this town now.

Novr 18th

Units of the Brigade are rather scattered. N Battery RHA is about 3 miles beyond ESSARS the remainder of the brigade are on the CHOCQUE

and St VENANT side of BETHUNE.
Radiators are now emptied every night.
Novr 19th
Frost last night. Water in the lorry tubs was covered with ice. Railway truck with supplies for British troops broke down on train & did not arrive this morning. This truck came in later on in the day. Snowed at night.
Novr 20th
Very hard frost last night & some snow. Water in lorry tubs frozen solid. Two Daimler cylinder heads cracked in spite of all water having been drained out of cylinders in the evening & engines run to convert remainder of water into steam.
Nov 21st
Still freezing hard. No more lorries damaged by frost. Daimler engines kept running all night to prevent them freezing up. These engines have a flange round the inside of the cylinder head which retains a certain amount of water after rest of water jacket has been drained. This is now to be syphoned out if possible. ∞

Novr 22nd

Still freezing hard. Fur lined coats boots, flannel belts etc have been ordered for the troops & I hope that they arrive soon. An issue of 6 lbs of wood per man is now made every day. Tonight the idea of putting the side lamps under the bonnet to keep the radiator warm is to be tried.

Novr 23rd

Still very cold. The use of lamps under the bonnets of the lorries seems to be successful in preventing the radiators from freezing up combined with the necessary precaution of emptying the radiators to start with. One of the Daimler cars was unfortunately run into by a lorry of 69 Coy yesterday & put completely out of action. This will be sent off to Paris to be repaired as soon as possible, but I don't suppose we shall see it again. The full amount of hay is now being sent up each day by train. Carrying the supplies, this hay, wood for the troops burn wood to the trenches for the engineers ordnance stores etc, keeps the section quite busy enough.

24th November.

Thaw this morning. It was quite impossible for the motor cyclists to ride their machines on the roads owing to the snow being washed off the coating of ice which lay underneath. after mid day the roads became better. 3 men were admitted to hospital yesterday, suffering from colds & bronchitis. The strength of the company is now 220 men.

25th November.

Still much warmer & fine.

Daimler Motor Car No M 1696 arrived for this company from Brigade Head quarters. in place of Daimler No 857 sent to Paris damaged. A new Sunbeam car was sent for my use, but this was kept by the G.O.C. the Brigade who sent on his worst car to me instead. It may possibly be of some use when the workshop branch have thoroughly overhauled it, It appears though fairly new to have been very much knocked about

23

Two Daimler lorries, & 1 G.o.c. chassis are in the shops, the two former with cracked cylinder heads, & the latter with a broken driving cap to the near hand whe[el].

26th Novb.

The supply train arrived very late today. The supply train is now divided into two portions ours was the second half & we were not loaded up until after dark. Have asked the R.T officer to arrange for our part to come in first so that we may load up & get away before the other columns arrive. He promised to do so.

27th Novb.

Sent Halley 3 ton lorry to Rouen today to be retired.

Weather still very mild.

Supplies coming up better on trains & supply train came in earlier today.

28th Novb.

One half of supply train came in early in the morning, the other half in the afternoon. Col Vaughan, B. G. S. supply

94

officer came down to superintend the loading this afternoon, but every thing was finished

29th Novr.

Still warm. Supply train came in early today. N Battery R.H.A. have moved to a spot between HINGES and BETHUNE for a rest.

30th Novr.

Supply train came in very late today. Loading was not completed until after dark. I went to St Omer to try & get permission to have one of the new workshops which have arrived at Rouen, in place of one of my own workshops which are not well enough fitted up. Moore was in so I left a note for Major Wilder.

1st Decr.

Fine weather continues. Supplies come up now in more accurate quantities, although many articles are still marked as being of a greater weight than is actually the case. The rations are now as follows & the articles come up in bags, boxes etc as marked against them.

English rations.

1 lb preserved meat in cases of 48 or 60 rations.
1 lb biscuit in 100 lb bags or 50 lb boxes, 5 to lb, 11 to lb
or biscuits to lb.
4 oz bacon in 65 lbs to 70 lbs boxes.
$\frac{5}{8}$ oz tea in average of 50 lb boxes.
3 oz sugar in 80 lb bags.
4 oz jam in 1 lb tins, 40 to the box.
$\frac{1}{2}$ oz salt in 80 lb bags.
$\frac{1}{36}$ oz pepper in 1 lb tins, 40 in a box
$\frac{1}{10}$ oz mustard in $\frac{1}{4}$ lb tins, 60 in a box.
3 oz cheese, in 9 lb dutch or 60 lb cheddars.

Native ration.

ata $1\frac{1}{2}$ lbs in 80 lb bags.
Dhall 4 oz in average 80 lb bags.
ghi 3 oz in 60 lb box containing 2 tins of 30 lbs each.
goor 3 oz in 60 lb box " " 2 " " 30 lb " .
mixed fruits 2 oz in boxes of 50 lbs.
tea $\frac{1}{3}$ oz in average 50 lb boxes.
salt $\frac{1}{2}$ oz in 80 lb bags.
ginger $\frac{1}{3}$ oz chillies $\frac{1}{6}$ oz turmeric $\frac{1}{6}$ oz garlic $\frac{1}{6}$ oz. well all mixed up at first in bags of about 20 lbs, now they come up separately. a 20 lb bag is sufficient for 160 men.

The following extras come up by the train 36

are taken to Head Qrs where they are distributed. 26
Jam 4 oz per native per week, (usually Wednesdays)
Rum twice a week, for all troops on Wednesdays & Saturdays. British 1/64 gallon, native 2 oz. = about 43 gallons per issue.
Maconachie rations 1½ lbs each. Meat & vegetable once a week in lieu of preserved meat for British only (usually on Fridays.)
1 tin of Maconachie = 4 rations of bacon.
Matches 1 box per man, twice a week on Wednesdays & Saturdays.
Tobacco & cigarettes once a week on Saturdays, 2 oz of tobacco, 4 packets of english or 3 packets of french cigarettes per man. 1250 packets of french cigarettes in a case.
Candles about 3 times a week in 60 lb boxes are taken to head qrs where they are distributed.

No leakage of supplies is possible once the food & forage has been taken off the train. The driver of every lorry carrying supplies to the various units signs for what he has received from the train. He in turn gets a receipt from the Q. M. of the regt concerned for what he hands over. This receipt is handed to Bgd supply officer, who keeps it

100

hands the column supply officer a duplicate signed by himself.

2nd Decb

The C.I.M.T. made an inspection of colm in today & made enquiries as to running of lorries etc. Still warm, & a strong drying wind.

3rd Decb

7 lorries were ordered by the G.O.C. the Bgd for 5.30 P.m. this evening to convey the 7th D. Guards from the trenches back to their head qrs. The native troops have to walk. This is just as well, for it is difficult always to find the necessary number of lorries for this sort of duty when so many are required for supplies.

4th Decb.

I hear the Brigade is shortly to be moved. Strength of company today 217 all ranks. Coal is now issued in lieu of part of the wood. 3 lbs of coal or coke = 6 lbs of wood. The issue per man at present is 1½ lbs coal, 1 lb ~~charcoal~~ coke & 1 lb of wood.

5th Decb

Very strong wind & wet today.

The local prices paid for various articles whic

are purchased when they do not come up by the train, are as follows 38

meat per
bread per
potatoes per
wood per

6th Deck
Still very wet & high wind. The head quarters of the Brigade are moving to BUSNES tomorrow. This place is about 10 Kilometers from here and is nearer AIRE. The Brigade are not to be used in the trenches any more for the present.

7th Deck
The train was late owing to a breakdown on the line at ABBEVILLE and did not arrive until late in the afternoon, but 4.30 P.M. One hundred fur lined coats have arrived for car & lorry drivers. These are excellent garments. Have put in for leather jackets for the workshop branch, as they are more suitable for them to work in than overcoats.

8th Deck
A beautiful day, but I am afraid nothing but a good frost can now make the roads good. 104

as they are so soaked with rain.
The roads to BUSNES are not very good. The short cut road is narrow, & the long way round by LILLERS is very rough. The lorries go by the short was under charge of an officer, & when anything is met the convoy is halted until it has passed by. One bridge does not seem to be very strong but this is being watched.
Strength of Company now 215 including officers.

9th Decr.
Weather warm but heavy mist & much rain. The darkest day we have had so far.
Lt Macdonell went on leave to England today for a week.

10th Decr.
Little rain today but gloomy & overcast.
An addition of 3 officers + 40 men arrived today for the Jodhpur Lancers.
The supply train now comes up about 8 a.m every morning.

11th Decr.
Still warm. Motor Car No M 1 676 was sent to G.H.Q. St OMER today. This leaves us with only three cars.

12th Decb.
Weather mild & wet.
A French interpreter has arrived for the company. He messes with the sgts. I don't think he will be much use, as so many officers & some n c o's speak french.
13th Decb
All leave for officers & N. C.O's is stopped for the present; this may mean an advance.
Weather still keeps mild.
14th Decb.
A fine day & no rain.
More fur coats have arrived for the men, They are now well provided with two sets of underclothes, one good & one bad pair of boots, a fur coat & waterproof. The men are now sleeping mostly in two empty houses, though some still prefer their lorries.
15th Decb.
Mild & damp again.
Received orders to be ready to move off at half an hour's notice. Brigade [illegible]

expected to be about to make an advance. 31
16th Decb.
Orders to move were cancelled at 10.30 a m this morning,
Lt Macdowell returned from leave this evening.
Am promoted Major.
Weather finer but colder.
Lorries running well, only two still under repair, the L. G. O. waiting a new driving plate on rear hind wheel & an austin waiting a new wheel in gear box.
17th Decb
Weather same as yesterday.
Nothing special to Report. Hear we are definitely to be turned into a cavalry division soon.
18th Decb.
Weather wet, roads bad in direction of BUSNES.
19th Decb
Weather wet. all lorries ordered to proceed to BUSNES instead of being distributed to [illegible]

different units as usual. a change of refilling points was contemplated owing to the military situation. Lorries were kept waiting until 3.0 P.M & were then sent to usual refilling points.

20th Decr

a beautiful day, no rain & a fine drying wind. Roads slippery in the morning but drying up in places in the afternoon. at [illegible].45 P.M. received sudden orders to move column at once to a position on main CHOCQUES - LILLERS road, that is west of CHOCQUES. Move was completed by 4.30 P.M. Column drawn up on side of road 3 Kilometers West of CHOCQUES facing towards LILLERS, about 50 men were accomodated in a barn, the rest sleeping on their lorries. The six officers slept in a small loft & the senior NCOs in a farm kitchen. Supplies were delivered today, same as usual, but rations for men in trenches were taken up to GORE.

21st Decr

very wet & windy again today. Took supp[illegible]

to head qrs of units as usual & also sent out a proportion of rations for men in trenches out to GORE. Severe fighting taking place & ration lorries for Jodhpur Lancers & Deccan Horse had to wait from 12.30 P.m till 6.0 P.m before they could deliver the rations.

22nd Decr

Received sudden orders to move column to BERGUETTE at 2.30 P.m. Column moved off at 2.55 P.m. & reached BERGUETTE a distance of about 15 Kilometers via LILLIERS at 4.0 P.m. Billets were obtained for officers & some of the N.C.Os & the men were accomodated in a large barn with plenty of fresh straw. The lorries completely fill the village street, only allowing room for passage of one vehicle past them at a time. Some supplies had to be sent out in the evening to N. Battery & H supply column. Fine day.

23rd Decr

Very cold today & heavy snow storm about mid day but snow did not lie. Papers were sent to LILLIERS but were collected & distributed to units. Supplies also went to LILLIERS, but supply train was afterwards shunted to BERGUETTE

34

& supplies collected by column at 12 0 mid day, afterwards being taken round to the units.

H.Q. Qrs of Bgd	are at	ISBERGUES.
7th D Guards	" "	MOLINGHAM
Supplies		MAZINGHAM
Deccan Horse		" "
Poona Horse		WITHERNESSE.
Judhpore Lancers		LIETTRES

24th Decr.

Supplies were drawn from the railway train at 7.15 a m & distributed to the troops. N Battery & H ammunition column are still out near BETHUNE. The distance from BERGOETTE to their head Qrs & back is about 60 miles. G.H.Q now require a return of all cars drivers, etc in the Brigade. Roads round here are narrow & few are wide enough to permit of two lorries passing one another. Goats & papers for Bgd are still obtained from LILLIERS & the rest of the supplies from here. Freezing hard today.

25th Decr.

True Christmas weather. Fine, bright & frosty. The roads are in much better condition. The supplies have been sent to LILLIERS again.

All the men were issued with the King & Queen's Xmas cards & also with one of Princess Mary's presents of tobacco, pipe & cigarettes. Non smokers had some sweetmeats. All presents were enclosed in little metal boxes. Both cards & presents were much appreciated both by officers & men. All work as far as possible stopped after one p.m. 35

26th Decbr.

Still frosty. Supplies again were sent to LILLIERS. Capt Macdonell has gone in to ST OMER for orders & will ask if supplies cannot be sent to BERGUETTE station.

27th Decbr

Frost all gone. Muggy & warm, supplies now coming to AIRE station but meat and papers being still sent to LILLIERS.

28th Decbr

Wet and cold. High wind. Hear the 2nd and 3rd Brigades of the 2nd Indian Cavalry Division start arriving on 31st inst.

29th Decbr

Reported to Col. Ford A.D.S. G.H.Q. He informed me officially of pending arrival of 2nd Cav Division.

118

30th Decr

Reported at H.Q.rs of Indian Cavalry Corps at ST ANDRE FERME at 10.0 a.m. & 12.0 mid day. Expect rest of my supply column this evening.

General Rimmington is commanding the Indian Cavalry Corps, consisting of the 1st & 2nd Divisions.

General Cookson is commanding the 2nd Div.

Col A.S. Cobbe is A.Q.M.G. 2nd Div.

" E.G. Vaughan is A.D.S.&T. 2nd Div.

Col R.E. Vaughan is A.Q.M.G Indian Cavalry Corps.

31st Decr

Column did not arrive last night, although it was looked for by me in a car & by motor cyclists. It arrived at 10.30 a.m. this morning, under command of Lt Pinder A.S.C. 117 lorries, 2 cars & about 570 men. Other officers besides Lt Pinder are

2nd Lt R Kirke transport

" " F.G. Pratt transport

2nd " C.O. Marshall workshops

" " J. Clarke.

Capt Brown Indian S&T

Lt Bloomfield " S&T.

Column was parked N.W. of AIRE.
Major Fox Bgd supply officer for MOW Bgd.
Major Chamier " " " " MEERUT " .
Capt Rendall, Div troops supply officer.

1st Jany 1915.
Different units of the Division have started to arrive & have received their rations. No time to day to square up supply column.

2nd Jany
Troops continue to arrive. Have sent transport officers round to visit the different head quarters of the units in the brigades & Divisional troops.

3rd Jany
Have managed to transfer several lorries from section B of column to Section A. Took supplies to different H.Q. qrs of Bgds for distribution to troops. Very busy but all going well & troops being fed, which is the chief thing.

4th Jany
Transferred 50 lorries & one workshop from "B" section to "A" section. The new

company which is No 83 is called B section, the old No 71 Coy is A section. Weather very wet & windy.

5th Jany

Mhow Bgde & Divisional H^d Q^rs are at MAMETZ, MEERUT Brigade H^d Q^rs are at ESTREÈ BLANCH & the SECUNDERABAD H^d Q^rs are at ISBURQUES.

6th Jany.

A section now has 79 lorries & B section 82. Seven workshops in company. Still very wet and windy. Supplies are now delivered regularly, but fresh units keep on turning up & asking for rations.

7th Jany

I have arranged with A D of S & T 2nd Ind Cav Division (Col E.G. Vaughan) that units are to send in their numbers to him weekly & that the supply officers get the numbers from him once a week only. We shall then work on those numbers for the following week.

8th Jany

Still very wet & windy, though warm

I have arranged that all papers, presents for troops etc now go to AIRE instead of LILLIERS.

9th Janry.

Very stormy, floods out all round the neighbouring country. Went in to St Omer today. Saw Major Gibb, & reported on some of the officers. Recommended Capt Macdonell to command a supply column. Issued definite instructions to Capt Brown & Lt Bloomfield Indian S+T Corps as to their duties.

10th Janry.

Ran round the units in the car & saw that all was well. Got a lorry out of the ditch at DELETTE. Received 28 pairs of gloves from Messrs Leyland Motors Ltd for distribution to the troops. Day fine & dry.

11th Janry

Fine in morning but wet again in the afternoon. Took lorries into BETHUNE with food for troops of Mhow Brigade who are going into the trenches.

12th Janry. Cold but dry. Everything now

running smoothly. Have a bad cold & am unable to do much. 40

20th Jany

Returned from leave this evening. Fi[nd] everything going on all right. Capt Macdonell in bed with fever & cold. 2nd Lt Gaymer & 2nd Lt Marshall laid up with scarlet fever. 2nd Lt Wein on leave. Oats are being drawn from various reserve parks instead of from the train, as they were [f]ound to be sprouting with the damp.

21st Jany

Warm but overcast & very wet still under foot. Went round to see that all was going on well with the different Brigades supply depots. G.O.C. wants marmalade instead of plum jam & hind quarter instead of forequarter of beef, & dry sugar instead of wet sugar.

22nd Jany.

Dull and warm again. Very busy changing men & lorries between the two sections. No [c]omplaints about supplies at Bgd. Hd. Qrs.

23rd Jany

Froze hard last night. Roads in excellent condition. Went into St Omer to see Major

Gibb & Capt Davidson. Reported on various officers.

24th Janry.

Capt Macdonell was admitted into hospital at St OMER with a bad throat. Now that he is gone & one officer from A section on leave, this section is reduced to 4 officers. Lt Clark is also in bed with a sore throat so there is plenty of work for the few who are left. During my absence on leave last week 4 workshops were sent away. Bitter complaints have been received by the us from the officers who took over our two old workshops. Weather fairly cold.

25th Janry.

Very cold & looks like snow. No complaints from troops about rations.

26th Janry

4 old 30 cwt lorries arrived for A section. This section now has 71 lorries & B section 75. Still cold but no snow has fallen. Lt Truman went on leave today for a week & 2nd Lt Weir returned off leave. 5% of the men are now allowed on leave at a time.

27th Janry. Capt Macdonell returned from

42

hospital. New Vauxhall Car No 1398 arrived in place of the Lancia which Lt Truman took back to England with him.

28th Janry.

Very cold last night. Roads in splendid condition.

29th Janry.

Still cold & a hard frost during last night. Everything going well. 10 lbs of hay per horse are being sent up on the train but far more hay is shown on the ticket on the truck than actually comes up. Strength of column, Nos 71 and 83 Coys = 565 all told.

30th Janry.

Received orders at 2.30 a.m. to be ready to move at two hours notice. However, nothing happened all day. Very fine day, a bright sun & gentle thaw. Froze again in the evening.

31st Janry.

Men of both sections getting on well with their drill. All leave stopped for the present. Very wet today. Snow & sleet in the afternoon

1st Febry.
The French authorities have temporarily closed all road to motor traffic except the AIRE-MAZINGHAM & AIRE – MAMETZ road. also the MAZINGHAM – ESTREÉ BLANCHE road for half loaded vehicles.
2nd Febry
Weather continues mild but cloudy & damp.
3rd Febry
a beautiful day. Roads still closed.
4th Febry. Weather still very fine. War has now lasted six months. Received orders today to send Capt Macdonell back to England. also Staff Sgts Watts & Moore, two Sgts & 2 corporals.
5th Febry.
Capt Macdonell & the six N C O's left for England today to join other formations. The roads have now been opened again by the French authorities. Have asked for another officer. Weather today perfect, warm, dry & very sunny. Major General Remmington inspected the B

section at AIRE at 4.30 P.m & was very pleased with the men & condition of the camp.

6th Feby

Weather slightly colder, roads getting in good condition.

7th Febr

Capt Pinder went on leave to day for a week. Lt J.D Truman has taken over temporary command of B section in his absence.

8th Feby

2nd Lt M.B.S. Whiteside arrived today from Advanced M.T. Depot Rouen in the place of Capt Macdonell. He is posted to A section. Weather splendid now. I attended a conference in the office of Gen. Hobbs, at 2.P.M. to discuss measures for regulating the road traffic in AIRE. ~~It would seem that~~ perhaps not.

9th Feby.

Have been ordered to return several 3 ton lorries & take 30 cwt in their place. Shall also ask for some 30 cwt in place of a number of

are ten lorries which we have. Heavy rain today & tearing wind.
Food continues to be first rate & all the men seem quite satisfied. Men are getting on well with their drill.

10th Febry

Slight frost this morning, but it was soon dispelled by the sun. Road picquets & controlls started in AIRE today.

11th Febry.

Received orders today that all schools were to be evacuated & not to be used as billets. Have found a mess for the sgts in an empty house & a room for the officers in a large house in the village. Weather rather unsettled.

12th Febry

Moved out of the school today & had the whole place thoroughly cleaned out. It is a pity we have had to move, as the school is not going to be used for any other purpose.

13th Febry

Very wet last night & this morning, fine but very windy in the afternoon. The hay has been coming up irregularly by the train for the lorry

week, being short or even entirely deficient one
day, & a double issue coming up the next.

14th Feby.

Received intimation that 18 three ton lorries
had to be returned to G.H.Q. & received two extra
30 cwt Napier lorries for extra postal
work. Cap Pinder returned from leave
and Lt Bloomfield went on leave.

15th Feby

very wet day. I fetched the 18 lorries from
St Omer, consisting of 1 Daimlers, 1 Halley
4 Commers, 1 Hallford, 11 L.G.O's.

16th Feby.

Sent one 3 ton Wolesley to Paris for repairs
& the remaining 3 lorries consisting of
1 Halley, 1 Leyland, 1 Maudesley, 1 Commer
2 Straker Squires, 12 Daimlers to St Omer.

17th Feby

I was obliged to go to bed with slight
ptomaine poisoning.

18th Feby

Better & was able to rise. 8 N.C.O's ordered
to be sent back to England for duty with
Kitchener's new army, am endeavouring

to retain CQSM Huskar as he is the only 47
regular N.C.O in the company. Strength
of Company by new establishment should
be 569 all ranks. Lorries 148, which
we have. We are about 18 men short.

Feby 19th

General James was to have gone round
the various units to see the supplies delivered
but had to put off his visit till Tuesday
next. Only half rations of bacon & jam came
up in the train for the whole division. These
articles have been rather short for the last
few days.

Feby 20th

The two cylinder albion gave out today. The
driving shaft in the gear box having become
bent through the gears jamming. It is to go
back to Rouen. This is the last of the two
cylinder lorries.

Feby 21st

Beautiful day. The roads in most places
very good. The wind here seems to dry
the roads up at a great pace. Paraded
all the men from 83 coy who were transferred
to 71 coy & got 1 franc per man out of

them for their Xmas dinner which they had promised to refund to Capt Pinder. The best way to get the money from men who are disinclined to pay, is obviously to have them all on parade & then ask those who don't wish to pay to fall out". No one will move. New Hallford in place of Albion was taken over today from Corps troops supply column.

22nd Febry

All leave is stopped for men & officers from the end of this month. Weather fine.

23rd Febry

Nothing of importance happened today.

24th Febry

Heavy snow showers all day off and on. Snow soon melted. Lieut G. Vaughan went on leave this evening till the end of the month

25th Febry

Snow fell to a considerable extent during the night, but later in the day the sun melted most of it. Roads etc in a very bad condition. 49

Feby 26th

Lieut Clarke returned from a week's leave last night. Is laid up with chill & fever which officer of R.A.M.C pronounced to be non infectious.

Weather frosty & dense mist ~~mist~~ making driving dangerous. Lieut Vaughan went on leave for three days.

Men of both A and B sections are getting on very well with their drill and the specially enlisted officers are doing very creditably.

Feby 27th

Snow in morning fine in afternoon. Roads drying up quickly with strong N.E. wind.

Two cases of gonorrhoea having occurred in "A" section, the village of ISBORGUES is now placed out of bounds for all N.C.Os & men.

Strength of column is now 553.

Feby 28th

Rain in morning fine in afternoon

very strong wind. Lieut Vaughan returned from leave this evening all leave being now for the present stopped.

Daimler car Government No M 855 stripped 3rd speed gears & will have to be replaced as repairs ~~have~~ cannot be carried out in our own workshops.

March 1st.

Cold & wet. Roads getting in a bad condition again round ISBURGUES. Main pavé roads appear to be giving way in places between AIRE and BETHUNE owing to the heavy motor traffic. Daimler car No M 855 sent off to Paris today by rail, driver accompanying car.

March 2nd

all batteries & gun sections of ammunition columns sent to join VIII Division temporarily at MERVILLE – LA GORGUE. Sent Lieut Clarke at 6.0 P.M. with 6 lorries loaded with hay & 6 with rations for above units to VIII Divisional supply

column at CAUDESCURE.
Weather fine. One 30 cwt Wolseley lorry broke torque rod & differential casing so will have to be returned to base. New lorry demanded from AD of S+T 2nd cavalry corps.

March 3rd

2nd Lt M B Whiteside took six lorries loaded with hay over to CAUDESCURE for batteries & ammunition column attached to VIII Division temporarily. Six hay lorries were returned to this supply column leaving 12 lorries attached to VIII Divn supply column to carry for attached batteries etc.
New L G O lorry arrived in place of damaged Wolseley lorry sent to ROUEN.
New Daimler car Government No 9013 arrived in place of damaged Daimler car No 855 sent to Paris.
Weather dull, wet and cold.

C A Lawley-Bovey Major
A.S.C

4-3-15

SERIAL NO 56.

Confidential

War Diary

of

2nd Indian Divisional Supply Column.

FROM 1st July 1916 TO 31st July 1916.

Vol. I.

Instructions regarding War Diaries and Intelligence Summaries are contained in F. S. Regs., Part II. and the Staff Manual respectively. Title Pages will be prepared in manuscript.

WAR DIARY or ~~INTELLIGENCE SUMMARY~~

2nd L. I. C. Divl. Supply Col.

Army Form C. 2118

(Erase heading not required.)

134

Place	Date	Hour	Summary of Events and Information	Remarks and references to Appendices
			left at mid day, Meerut lorries under Lieut. Pratt at 12.30 P.m & H.Q. Qrs + workshops at 1.0 P.m. A section arrived at 1.30 P.m, workshops at 7.30 P.m. Roads good, distance 70 Kilometers. I chose dumping places for Brigades & Divn Troops with O.C. A.S.C. Rations were dumped at 5.30 P.m. Weather wet in morning, fine in afternoon.	
AMIENS-BUSSY road.	28 6/16		Rations were delivered to dumps at 9.0 a.m. Rations were drawn from FRÉCHENCOURT station at 10.0 a.m. Weather dull	
" "	29 6/16		Rations were drawn from FRECHENCOURT railhead at 12.0 mid day by B section. A section delivered to units at 10.30 a.m. Weather wet & standing for lorries at side of road bad.	
" "	30 6/16		Rations drawn from railhead at 11.0 a.m, delivery at 10.30 a.m. Lieut. Pratt 2nd Lt Holmes, 101 M.T. drivers, 24 workshop personnel, 30 loaders + issuers, 36 lorries, 2 workshops, 2 stores, 1 motor car, 2 motor cycles left today at 12.0 mid day for HESDIN, via Abbeville. Weather fine.	
" "	1 7/16		Weather fine. Sent 8 lorries from A section to CANAPLES to fetch wood (30.000 lbs) for fuel for Division. Train arrived late this morning. Canadians loaded first at 10.30 a.m. Loading completed & lorries returned to camp	

1875 Wt. W593/826 1,000,000 4/15 J.B.C. & A. A.D.S.S./Forms/C. 2118.

Army Form C. 2118

(135)

WAR DIARY
or
~~INTELLIGENCE SUMMARY~~
(Erase heading not required.)

Instructions regarding War Diaries and Intelligence Summaries are contained in F. S. Regs., Part II. and the Staff Manual respectively. Title Pages will be prepared in manuscript.

Place	Date	Hour	Summary of Events and Information	Remarks and references to Appendices
			at 3.45 P.M.	
AMIENS–Bussy road	2/7/16		Weather dull & rather cold. Recd instructions re secret location of billet in ALBERT in case of an advance. Sent 4 lorries from B section ALLONVILLE for coal & wood for division. Roads bad & full of holes.	
" "	3/7/16		Very heavy thunderstorm in afternoon. Rain continued for two hours, but as ground was hard, most of it ran off & lorries are still able to stand on ground off the road. Train still continues to come up late.	
" "	4/7/16		Court of enquiry held on accident to a child at Gamaches by a motor lorry. Court found that driver of lorry was in no way to blame. Divn order published today giving me command of Canadian supply column thus ensuring my 3/- a day command pay.	
" "	5/7/16		Sent 2 lorries to ST RIQUIER for R.E. pontoons. 2 lorries to AMIENS for live sheep. 6 lorries to railhead for coal, 8 lorries to DOULLENS for wood. Sent copies of Divn & IV Army orders to Canadians for information & guidance. Weather finer but very cool & cloudy.	
" "	6/7/16		Canadians commenced loading at railhead at 8.30 a.m, 1st British Cav Divn having left this railhead. We commenced loading at 9.15 a.m. Recd instructions to put an 18" white square on near side of all lorries	

1875 Wt. W593/826 1,000,000 4/15 J.B.C. & A. A.D.S.S./Forms/C. 2118.

Instructions regarding War Diaries and Intelligence Summaries are contained in F. S. Regs., Part II. and the Staff Manual respectively. Title Pages will be prepared in manuscript.

WAR DIARY
or
~~INTELLIGENCE SUMMARY~~
(Erase heading not required.)

Army Form C. 2118

(136

Place	Date	Hour	Summary of Events and Information	Remarks and references to Appendices
			and also on tail boards with an 8" black horse shoe in centre. This appears to be Fourth army sign for car supply Col.	
AMIENS–BUSSY road.	7 7/16		Rain at intervals during the day. sent three lorries to SAMACHES to fetch 8 tons of potatoes for SSO Divn. Also went there myself to settle two claims, one for Am Park & one for railway staff.	
" "	8 7/16		very heavy rain during last night. Loaded at station this morning at 4.30 a.m. Canadian Brigade were an hour late.	
" "	9 7/16		Twenty one loaders arrived from the Base to replace labourers at special 3/- a day rate of pay. weather fine.	
" "	10 7/16		Lt Col Mark Synge held a conference at supply column head Qrs with O.C.s different B echelon units, assigning to each their place on the ground adjoining our lines. We moved our bivouacs into a more concentrated area.	
" "	11 7/16		Lorries were sent to railhead for 10 tons of wood, also 10 tons of coal & 30,000 lbs of wood were fetched from near DOULLENS for use of Division. Roads round camp had to be cleared by 6. a.m for passage of troops.	
" "	12 7/16		Weather still very fine. Took lorry with rations for field squadron up to	

1875 Wt. W593/826 1,000,000 4/15 J.B.C. & A. A.D.S.S./Forms/C. 2118.

Army Form C. 2118

(137)

Instructions regarding War Diaries and Intelligence Summaries are contained in F. S. Regs., Part II. and the Staff Manual respectively. Title Pages will be prepared in manuscript.

WAR DIARY
or
~~INTELLIGENCE SUMMARY~~
(Erase heading not required.)

Place	Date	Hour	Summary of Events and Information	Remarks and references to Appendices
			MÉAULTE near ALBERT: Found the Fourth army route map has the arrows pointing the wrong way on many roads. Reconnoitred the roads around DERNINGCOURT	
AMIENS–BUSSY road	13/7/16		5 lorries were sent up to new Divisional area round MÉAULTE and DERNINCOURT at 9 a.m. under command of Capt Vaughan with rations for Field squadron & 4 lbs of grain per horse. Took remainder of A section myself at 2.0 P.m having sent off Canadians at 1.30 P.m. Arrived at rendezvous at 4.30 P.m. Div: Troops, Ambala Bgd & Canadian Bgd rations were delivered at once, lorries returning to camp by 7.30 P.m. Distance travelled 44 miles, roads flat, fairly wide, surface rough, especially round DERNINGCOURT. Sec'bad bgd rations were delivered ¾ mile up a very bad side road blocked with mule carts & horses. 3 lorry ~~loads~~ loads of hay were afterwards taken on to a spot on the BRAY CARNOY road ½ mile from BRAY. Lorries returned to camp at 10.30 P.m.	
" "	14/7/16		Weather fine though overcast. Received four different orders re delivery of rations today. Finally rendezvoused on MOURLANCOURT – MÉAULT road at 7.30 P.m. After waiting several hours all units rations were delivered & lorries returned to camp at 1.0 a.m on 15th inst. Capt Stafford & I reconnoitred road round	

1875 Wt. W593/826 1,000,000 4/15 J.B.C. & A. A.D.S.S./Forms/C. 2118.

Instructions regarding War Diaries and Intelligence Summaries are contained in F. S. Regs., Part II. and the Staff Manual respectively. Title Pages will be prepared in manuscript.

WAR DIARY
or
~~INTELLIGENCE SUMMARY~~
(Erase heading not required.)

Army Form C. 2118

(138)

Place	Date	Hour	Summary of Events and Information	Remarks and references to Appendices
			FRICOURT – CARNOY – BRAY for Sec'bad Bgd Dump. Rations were finally dumped at same place as yesterday. Lorries returned to camp at 3.30 a m on 15th inst. Roads round FRICOURT surprisingly good. Shell holes have already been filled up.	
AMIENS – BUSSY road	15 7/16		Fine day. Lorries delivered to usual billets around MEAULT. Rendezvous at 5.0 P.M, rations delivered at 7.0 P.M. Last lorries returned to camp at 9.30 P.M.	
" "	16 7/16		Four new M.T. drivers arrived up from Base. Rations were delivered same as yesterday. German aeroplanes passed over this camp about 11.0 P.M & dropped bombs on AMIENS. All lights were extinguished in camp immediately. several french shells fired from the batteries round AMIENS fell in & around the camps of the 2nd Ind Cav Supply Col & the Canadian Cav Bgd Supply Col.	
" "	17 7/16		Capt Stafford, Lt Stafford & I were sent by the DA & Q.M G. of the Division this morning to reconnitre the MAMETZ road as far as MAMETZ wood. It was found the lorries could only proceed as far as FRICOURT, the road through MAMETZ being impassable. The road running by the wood was under shell fire. Rations dumped at 5.0 P.M today. Weather wet & roads greasy. Sec'bad section returned to camp at 10.30 P.M. One I.G.O.C broke a back axle. A fresh axle was taken out to replace the broken one, & lorry arrived in camp at 3.30 a.m. on 18th.	

1875 Wt. W593/826 1,000,000 4/15 J.B.C. & A. A.D.S.S./Forms/C. 2118.

Instructions regarding War Diaries and Intelligence Summaries are contained in F. S. Regs., Part II. and the Staff Manual respectively. Title Pages will be prepared in manuscript.

WAR DIARY
or
~~INTELLIGENCE SUMMARY~~
(Erase heading not required.)

Army Form C. 2118

(139

Place	Date	Hour	Summary of Events and Information	Remarks and references to Appendices
BUSSY AMIENS road.	18 7/16		very wet in night. Roads very bad. Loaded at station very late today. Loading completed at 5.0 P.m. Delivery at 5.0 P.m last lorries returned to camp at 9.15 P.m	
" "	19 7/16		Finer today, camp drying up. Very heavy bombardment heard this morning. Delivered rations at 4.45 P.m. Roads very congested with transport & troops. 3rd British Cavalry Division delayed lorries passing through CORBIE for 45 minutes. Time of delivery had been fixed for 3.30 P.m. Lorries returned from station at 4.30. P.m.	
" "	20 7/16		Fine day. Terrific bombardment heard during the night & at 9.0 a.m this morning for half an hour. Roads nice & dry again. B echelon of Division joined up with A echelon round MEAULT yesterday.	
" "	21 7/16		Weather beautifully fine. Rations delivered same time & place as yesterday. Dismounted reinforcements & all animals are being sent after today to MERICOURT so that the lorries will not in future be overcrowded with additional men. 48 men were taken up to Divn Troops today from railhead on the lorries. 20 Tons of coal from railhead.	
" "	22 7/16		Dull & cool today. Fetched 12 tons of wood from rail head. Recd 6 bell tents from ordnance. Delivery same as yesterday. Loading finished at 3.0 P.m. lorries returned to camp at 4.30 P.m.	
" "	23 7/16		Weather still overcast. Ground in camp very hard now & lorries can run anywhere. Received wire from D.A.Q.M.G. at 2.30 a.m saying ~~were~~ we were to load	

Instructions regarding War Diaries and Intelligence Summaries are contained in F. S. Regs., Part II. and the Staff Manual respectively. Title Pages will be prepared in manuscript.

WAR DIARY
or
~~INTELLIGENCE SUMMARY~~
(Erase heading not required.)

Army Form C. 2118

V40

Place	Date	Hour	Summary of Events and Information	Remarks and references to Appendices
			at 4.30 a.m. On arrival at railhead R.S.O said we were not required to load before the usual time, namely 8.0 a.m. There were two divisions to load before us. Strength of column 444 all ranks, Canadian Bgd supply Column attached 202 all ranks.	
BOSSY – AMIENS Road	24/7/16		Weather cool & cloudy. Rations delivered to Bgds & Divl Troops at 5.0 P.m. in old area round BOSSY. Loading commenced at railhead this morning at 8.0 a.m. last lorries returned to camp at 1.30 P.m.	
" "	25/7/16		Loading & delivery the same as yesterday. Weather cloudy & dull, no rain.	
" "	26/7/16		Canadian Bgd delivered at 9.0 a.m this morning, & afterwards 12 lorries were sent to an unknown destination with troops for digging trenches. Remainder of delivering lorries dumped supplies at 12.0 mid day. Large number of guns & horse transport passed camp making lorries rather late in starting for delivery. Loading commenced at 9.45 a.m this morning.	
" "	27/7/16		Rations for Field Squadron & Sec'bad Field Ambulance delivered at MÉAULT at 8.0 a.m. Rations for digging party (2 lorries) delivered on the FRICOURT – ALBERT Road at 4.0 P.m. Remainder of rations delivered at 5.0 P.m. Rations drawn from	

Army Form C. 2118

141

Instructions regarding War Diaries and Intelligence Summaries are contained in F. S. Regs., Part II. and the Staff Manual respectively. Title Pages will be prepared in manuscript.

WAR DIARY
or
~~INTELLIGENCE SUMMARY~~
(Erase heading not required.)

Place	Date	Hour	Summary of Events and Information	Remarks and references to Appendices
			railhead at 9.30 a.m. Weather still dull & overcast.	
BUSSY–AMIENS road	28/7/16		Weather very fine. 2 days mails were delivered to Field Squadron at MEAULT as no mails were delivered to them yesterday owing to rations being delivered at 8.0 a.m. Delivery to Div & dismounted party same time as usual	
" "	29/7/16		Weather very hot. Took A section on foot parade from 10.0 a.m. to 11.15 a.m. Men & officers know their drill very well. Delivered dismounted party's rations at 7.0 P.M.	
" "	30/7/16		Still very hot. 10 M.T. Drivers arrived from Base to replace casualties. These men do not appear to be up to the usual good standard of M.T. drivers. Rations for digging party delivered just south of MAMETZ. Other rations delivered as usual.	
	31/7/16		Field Cashier has been attached to supply column. He has brought 1 horse, 1 batman & one staff sgt. The money box has been put in charge of the guard. Strength of column including 2 RE's, 2 RAMC, 1 MO, 1 interpreter = 254. Train arrived at station at 2.0 P.M. today. Last lorries returned to camp at 2.0 P.M. Weather continues very fine.	

C.A. Crawley Boevey Major
O.C. 2nd Cav Supply Col.

1/8/16

1875 Wt. W593/826 1,000,000 4/15 J.B.C. & A. A.D.S.S./Forms/C. 2118.

SERIAL NO. 56.

Confidential

War Diary

of

2nd Indian Cavalry Division Supply Column.

FROM 1st August 1916 TO 31st August 1916

Army Form C. 2118

Vol II

2nd Ind Supply Column 142

WAR DIARY
or
~~INTELLIGENCE~~ SUMMARY
(Erase heading not required.)

Instructions regarding War Diaries and Intelligence Summaries are contained in F. S. Regs., Part II. and the Staff Manual respectively. Title Pages will be prepared in manuscript.

Place	Date	Hour	Summary of Events and Information	Remarks and references to Appendices
BOSSY—ALLONVILLE road.	1 8/16		Weather very hot. Supply train came in late. Lorries did not finish loading until 4.0 P.m. Maj Gen Macandrew G.O.C. 2nd I.C. Div inspected the supply column at 2.30 P.m. today. He expressed himself as very pleased with everything he saw & ordered me to convey his appreciation to the troops.	
" "	2 8/16		Very hot again today. Supply train was once more late & loading was not finished until 7.0 P.m. Last lorries arrived in camp at 8.30 P.m. Took O.C. A.S.C. to FRICOURT & BEAMAULT to see digging parties & arrange about post for all detachments in this area.	
" "	3 8/16		Weather still very warm. Rations train was again very late. Lorries did not return from railhead till 9.30 P.m. Visited digging parties near FRICOURT & arranged about delivery of letters.	
" "	4 8/16		Cooler today. Attended conference in office of O.C. A.S.C. 2nd I.C.D. at 5.0 P.m re combining duties of Canadian Bgd supply officers with the duties of Divn supply ed supply officers. Various minor alterations in present system were agreed to.	
	5 8/16		Much colder today & cloudy. B section had 1 hour's foot drill this morning at 8.0 a.m.	

1875 Wt. W593/826 1,000,000 4/15 J.B.C. & A. A.D.S.S./Forms/C. 2118.

Instructions regarding War Diaries and Intelligence Summaries are contained in F. S. Regs., Part II. and the Staff Manual respectively. Title Pages will be prepared in manuscript.

WAR DIARY
or
~~INTELLIGENCE SUMMARY~~
(Erase heading not required.)

Army Form C. 2118

(143

Place	Date	Hour	Summary of Events and Information	Remarks and references to Appendices
BUSSY-ALLONVILLE road	6/8/16		warmer again today. Supply train came in at 2.0 P.m ~~today~~. Rec'd orders to load in bulk at rail head + to be clear in two hours instead of three. This means that rations have to be unloaded again in camp + redistributed, causing an extra handling.	
" "	7/8/16		Weather very fine. Held foot drill of A section from 8.0 a.m to 9.30. Practised marching on markers + on a square. Rec'd orders that column is moving back to GAMACHES rail head ~~tomorrow~~	
" "	8/8/16		A ~~section~~ company less AMBALA section + lorries for digging + dismounted parties left camp at 6.0 a.m. for LONGPRE via AMIENS + PICQUIGNY. Rations were delivered at 3.0 P.m to Sec'Bad Bgd + 6.0 p.m to Div Troops. Last lorries arrived at camp at WATTLEBLERY above BLANGY at 8.5 P.m. Total distance covered during day 36 miles. Delivering section of Canadian Cav Bgd left camp at 5.50 a.m. + proceeded by same route to FONTAINE, delivered rations at 10 P.m + arrived at camp at WATTLEBLERY at 1.0 a.m on morning of 9/8/16. B sect of column + other section of Canadian supply column loaded at railhead at FRECHENCOURT at 2.30 P.m left at 4.30 P.m. + arrived at WATTLEBLERY via MOLLIENS-VIDAME at 11.15 P.m. Canadian workshops + spare lorries left camp at 8.30 a.m + arrived at WATTLEBLERY at 5.0 P.m. 2nd S.C.S.Col workshops + pool lorries left an hour after Canadians + arrived at WATTLEBLERY an hour ~~after them~~. Column is on Route national No 28 with head at—	

1875 Wt. W593/826 1,000,000 4/15 J.B.C. & A. A.D.S.S./Forms/C. 2118.

Army Form C. 2118

(144)

Instructions regarding War Diaries and Intelligence Summaries are contained in F. S. Regs., Part II. and the Staff Manual respectively. Title Pages will be prepared in manuscript.

WAR DIARY
or
~~INTELLIGENCE SUMMARY~~
(Erase heading not required.)

Place	Date	Hour	Summary of Events and Information	Remarks and references to Appendices
			cross roads on top of hill, & facing towards BLANGY. Lieut Beck is left in charge of detachment camped on BUSSY-ALLONVILLE road, assisted by Lt Owen & Lt Whittaker. Strength of detachment 165 N.C.O's & men, 3 officers, 41 lorries 1 workshop, 1 store lorry.	
WATTERBLERY	9/8/16		A section loaded at GAMACHES at 6.30 a.m., Canadian Cav Supply Col at 7.15 a.m. Rations were delivered at 6.0 P.m. - Sec'bad Bgd at NESLE NORMANDEUSE, GUIMERVILLE, BOURDEL, Canadians round RAMBURELLES. Longest run for lorries was to SENARPONT about 10 miles altogether. Very steep hill up to WATTERBLERY from BLANGY. Weather fine roads good. Lorries run to station by road south of river BRESLE & return along road north of the river. Paid out men this morning & sent money up to detachment at BUSSY.	
BOULLANCOURT	10/8/16		Lorries loaded at station same time as yesterday. Moved into BOULLIANCOURT this afternoon with Canadian Cav Bgd Supply Column. 2nd S. C. Am Park. moved out at 2.30 P.m. Billets for men & officers fairly good. Fair standing for lorries. Distance from WATTLEBLERY to BOUILLANCOURT one mile, distance to rail head 3 miles. Weather Fine	
" "	11/8/16		Weather still fine, slightly cooler. Went to ARBEVILLE in afternoon to get hay which was short on train. Lt WHITTAKER left for England today.	

1875 Wt. W593/826 1,000,000 4/15 J.B.C. & A. A.D.S.S./Forms/C. 2118.

Instructions regarding War Diaries and Intelligence Summaries are contained in F. S. Regs., Part II. and the Staff Manual respectively. Title Pages will be prepared in manuscript.

WAR DIARY
or
~~INTELLIGENCE SUMMARY~~
(Erase heading not required.)

Army Form C. 2118

(145)

Place	Date	Hour	Summary of Events and Information	Remarks and references to Appendices
BOUILLANCOURT	12/8/16		Weather still very fine. Saw R.S.O. & arranged about earlier loading at station. Recd instructions that Field Cashier would use one of column cars every Monday for drawing money from Abbeville.	
" "	13/8/16		Some rain in the night & early morning. 3 ton Berna for ~~Divisional~~ H.Q. Qrs returned to column from Divn today.	
" "	14/8/16		Some rain in the afternoon. Issued special circular memo to O.C.'s coys & H.Q. Qrs also Canadian Bgde Supply Column re precautions to be taken against fire.	
" "	15/8/16		Lorries of A section for H.Q. Qrs of Divn & Canadian Cav Bgde lorries after loading at station took on hay, oats & coal to a dump on left hand side of BOUTTENCOURT – SENARPONT road, 200x beyond cross roads on BLANGY – ABBEVILLE road. Lorries with British & native rations will deliver at same time tomorrow. B section lorries which loaded yesterday delivered at ~~usual time~~ 3.9 p.m. in the afternoon. The units above specified have therefore 1 days men's rations & 2 days horses rations in hand. Sec'bad Bgde less Battery leave tomorrow to relieve AMBALA Bgde at BOSSY.	

1875 Wt. W593/826 1,000,000 4/15 J.B.C. & A. A.D.S.S./Forms/C. 2118.

Army Form C. 2118

146

Instructions regarding War Diaries and Intelligence Summaries are contained in F. S. Regs., Part II. and the Staff Manual respectively. Title Pages will be prepared in manuscript.

WAR DIARY
or
~~INTELLIGENCE SUMMARY~~
(Erase heading not required.)

Place	Date	Hour	Summary of Events and Information	Remarks and references to Appendices
BOUILLANCOURT	16 8/16		Weather cloudy. A section delivered rations to Divn Troops at 10.0 a.m. Canadian Cav Bgd rations ~~at~~ same as yesterday drew at 6.0 a.m. delivered to dump at 8.30 a.m. Sec'bad brigade rations were drawn at 7.0 a.m. & the section under Lieut ~~Stafford~~ Harper then proceeded to camp near BUSSY, via MOLLIENS-VIDAME and AMIENS arriving at 2.0 P.m. Lieut Stafford delivered rations for Brigade for consumption today at RIANCOURT at 5.0 P.m.	
" "	17 8/16		Lt M. Farrell a.s.c joined the column today in the place of Lieut Whittaker. arrival reported by wire in usual manner. Was member of a court of enquiry on a fire which occured in the Motor machine guns lines in this village on the 10th inst. amount claimed £104, amount suggested as suitable compensation 500 francs. Lieut Stafford took Sec'bad section of ration lorries to BUSSY, leaving BOUILLANCOURT at 11.0 a.m. this morning. Heavy rain in the afternoon.	
" "	18 8/16		Rained at intervals throughout the day. Lieut Stafford returned at 6.0 P.m. with his section of lorries from BUSSY.	
" "	19 8/16		Re issued orders & instructions in case of fire. sent round correspondence re joy riding, saving of petrol etc for all officers to sign. Thunderstorm in morning Lorries leave for station now at 6.30 a.m., loading commences at 11.0 a.m.	

Instructions regarding War Diaries and Intelligence Summaries are contained in F. S. Regs., Part II. and the Staff Manual respectively. Title Pages will be prepared in manuscript.

WAR DIARY
or
~~INTELLIGENCE~~ SUMMARY
(Erase heading not required.)

Army Form C. 2118

147

Place	Date	Hour	Summary of Events and Information	Remarks and references to Appendices
BOUILLANCOURT	20 8/16		visited section at BOSSY & found all correct, ordered 4 canadian lorries attached to this section to return to BOUILLANCOURT. weather fine roads rather greasy from recent rain. canadian R.C.H.A. went to BRUTELLE yesterday for 2 days.	
"	21 8/16		saw rations delivered at BRUTELLE near CAYEUX today at 4.0 P.m. various units of canadian Cav Bg^e are going to this place every 2 days. The canadian supply column are delivering the rations.	
"	22 8/16		Have made arrangements to store oats, preserved meat & biscuits of Reserve Park in BOUILLANCOURT, total weight approx. 90 tons. O C Reserve Park came over today & arranged to dump his supplies at 11.30 a m tomorrow. weather continues fine. Strength of column, including detachment at BOSSY, MO, 2 RE drivers, 2 RAMC men + 1 interpreter = 457.	
"	23 8/16		weather fine. Reserve Park wagons commenced unloading oats preserved meat biscuits & petrol at 11.30 a.m. in an empty house & barn in this village. Unloading was completed by 3.30 P.m. Lt Fairclough R.A.M.C went on 5 days leave ~~yesterday~~ today.	
"	24 8/16		one lorry sent to BLANGY station to take yeomanry officers from thence (at 7.0 a.m) to SENARPONT. Reserve Park commenced drawing hay & oats from the station on their waggons this morning, 50 waggons & 8 lorries were used. The latter for mens rations	

Instructions regarding War Diaries and Intelligence Summaries are contained in F. S. Regs., Part II. and the Staff Manual respectively. Title Pages will be prepared in manuscript.

WAR DIARY
or
~~INTELLIGENCE SUMMARY~~
(Erase heading not required.)

Army Form C. 2118

(148)

Place	Date	Hour	Summary of Events and Information	Remarks and references to Appendices
			the former for animal rations. Weather fine. I visited the detachment at BUSSY this afternoon to see Lt Beck re charge against Sgt Seawright, & 2nd Lt Owen re his application for artillery commission.	
BODILLANCOURT	25/8/16		Some rain in morning. Recd notification that RCHA Bde are going up to the forward area, rations to be delivered tomorrow at AILLY. Inoculation return sent in today shows a percentage of 93·30 inoculated. 9th Hodsons Horse are going up to BRUTELLE tomorrow for 2 days. Their rations to be loaded on lorries tomorrow thus releasing 4 Reserve Park waggons from duty at station. RCHA Brigade move releases 4 more waggons.	
" "	26/8/16		All smoke helmets & goggles in the section of the column at BODILLANCOURT were inspected by an expert from the Division ~~upon~~ at my request. B section held foot drill parade & practised fixing & unfixing bayonets. Much rain in the evening.	
" "	27/8/16		Much rain at intervals throughout the day. Recd secret memo re Divn being formed into infantry bde, number of lorries & amount of personnel required to be supplied by me.	
" "	28/8/16		Lt Farrell left at 8.30 am this morning with 12 lorries for detachment's camp at BUSSY. 5 lorries are to bring back Canadian dismounted men from XV Corps digging party at ERICOURT.	

1875 Wt. W593/826 1,000,000 4/15 J.B.C. & A. A.D.S.S./Forms/C. 2118.

Instructions regarding War Diaries and Intelligence Summaries are contained in F. S. Regs., Part II. and the Staff Manual respectively. Title Pages will be prepared in manuscript.

WAR DIARY
or
~~INTELLIGENCE~~ SUMMARY
(Erase heading not required.)

Army Form C. 2118

(149

Place	Date	Hour	Summary of Events and Information	Remarks and references to Appendices
			+ 7 lorries are required to assist Secunderabad Bgd to bring back surplus stores, kits etc from their area near BUSSY to present Divisional area near SENARPONT. Route for lorries via OISEMENT, AIRAINES, PICQUIGNY, AMIENS. Visited 9th Hodgson's Horse, 8th Hussars, Fort Garry horse & machine gun sections at BRUTELLE. Fine day.	
BOUILLANCOURT ~~BRAS~~	29 8/16		Much rain during last night, roads round this village getting very soft in places.	
" "	30 8/16		Capt Stafford reported to me this morning that Lieut Farrell had returned without the Coy motor bicycle last night. I saw Lt Farrell who said he had had the bicycle stolen in AMIENS, I rendered copies of statements by Lt Farrell & Lt Beck together with my forwarding minute to O C A.S.C. Bought 35 francs worth of paper bags in ABBEVILLE. Rained hard all day many roads round here under water in places. Capt HANSON left this day for 48 am sub Park. 2nd Lt P.L. Blunt A.S.C reported for duty this morning. Loading at station is now at 6.0 a.m. 12 lorries were used today	
"	31 8/16		Lieut Thiersch proceeded to Bussy this morning in the side car to fetch over the workshop & store lorry to BOUILLANCOURT. All lorries returned safely from BUSSY: 9 have been left behind temporarily for feeding the digging parties. Capt Bird is in charge with 10 supply men. Weather fine, roads dryer. Reissued orders to Canadian supply column re roads to be used by their lorries in the vicinity of BOUILLANCOURT.	

C A Crawley-Boevey Major
31/8/16 O C 2nd I.D. Cav Supply Col.

1875 Wt. W593/826 1,000,000 4/15 J.B.C. & A. A.D.S.S./Forms/C. 2118.

SERIAL NO. 56

Confidential

War Diary

of

2nd Indian Cavalry Supply Column

FROM 1st September 1916 TO 30th September 1916.

Instructions regarding War Diaries and Intelligence Summaries are contained in F. S. Regs., Part II. and the Staff Manual respectively. Title Pages will be prepared in manuscript.

WAR DIARY
or
INTELLIGENCE SUMMARY
(Erase heading not required.)

Army Form C. 2118

2nd Cav Supply Column. Vol. III

150

Place	Date	Hour	Summary of Events and Information	Remarks and references to Appendices
BOUILLANCOURT.	1 9/16		Finer today, roads fairly dry. Rained a little in the evening. standing for lorries in this village will be bad in the winter as the sides of most of the roads are very soft. Lt Thiersch went over to see D.D. S&T re lost motor cycle. Lt Farrells application for commission in the infantry returned for want of certificate, vide para 242 Kings Regs. Lieut Fairclough returned from leave to England today.	
" "	2 9/12		Received information that P.M. Fourth army is in possession of missing motor cycle. Weather fine. Several lorries required by Div H.Q. Qm today & also for tomorrow, 16 lorries required at rail head today. 1 lorry sent to replace an L.G.O.C attached to 3rd Corps troops supply Col. which has differential trouble.	
" "	3 9/12		weather fine. Motor cycle was brought back from P.M. Fourth army by M S M Marsh this afternoon. Cancellation of old divisional sign, black horse shoe on white ground. The lorry from N Bat. attached 3rd Corps Troops returned today. Strength of column 456 including attached.	
" "	4 9/12		very wet early in the morning. Pte Owen H. who had been missing two days has been discovered in the hospital at LE TREPORT. Lieut Pratt reports the section at HESDIN is being broken up. Lorry 30 cwt for carry entrenching tools is now ready for taking over at 4th army Troops supply col.	

1875 Wt. W593/826 1,000,000 4/15 J.B.C. & A. A.D.S.S./Forms/C. 2118.

Instructions regarding War Diaries and Intelligence Summaries are contained in F. S. Regs., Part II. and the Staff Manual respectively. Title Pages will be prepared in manuscript.

WAR DIARY
or
~~INTELLIGENCE SUMMARY~~
(Erase heading not required.)

Army Form C. 2118

(151)

Place	Date	Hour	Summary of Events and Information	Remarks and references to Appendices
BOUILLANCOURT	5/9/16		Received orders at 8.30 P.m. that Divn is under orders to move at 4.0 a.m tomorrow morning. Handed over all oats, petrol & reserve rations to reserve park at 10.30 P.m. sent out lorries to pick up all rations delivered for today to units for consumption on the 7th. sent out 4 lorries to BRUTELLE to pick up hay from 9th Hodsons Horse & 8th Hussars.	
" "	6/9/16		B section left camp at 1.30 P.m. & delivered rations to Divn in the neighbourhood of MOLLIENS VIDAME at 4.30 P.m. Canadian Cav Bgd supply column delivered rations to their Bgd at same hour near SOUES. The two columns afterwards proceeded to old camping ground on BOSSY – ALLONVILLE road, which was reached at 7.30 P.m. 6 lorries from No 2 I.C.S.C & 2 lorries from C.C.B.S.C were sent back to late Bgd supply H.d qrs in BLANGY area to bring on surplus oats for Divn. weather fine.	
BOSSY – ALLONVILLE road.	7/9/16		A section left camp at 7.0 a.m. & arrived at this camp at 11.15 a.m. Delivered rations to units in close billets round BOSSY at 1.0 P.m. H.d qrs of column left camp at 11.0 a.m. towing 1 lorry + 1 car & arrived in camp at 7.0 P.m. workshops took up old position. Canadian Cav Bgd supply column all left camp at BOUILLANCOURT at 5.30 a.m + reached this camp at 10.30 a.m. weather very fine & camping ground nearly dry again	

Instructions regarding War Diaries and Intelligence Summaries are contained in F. S. Regs., Part II. and the Staff Manual respectively. Title Pages will be prepared in manuscript.

WAR DIARY
or
~~INTELLIGENCE SUMMARY~~
(Erase heading not required.)

Army Form C. 2118

152

Place	Date	Hour	Summary of Events and Information	Remarks and references to Appendices
			after recent heavy rains. Saw D.A.Q.M.G. of Divn re getting stones to fill in holes in road on NE side of BOSSY which is very bad.	
BOSSY – ALLONVILLE Road.	8 9/16		11 lorries rejoined column from No 625 company. Names of Captains Vaughan and Stafford were sent up to Fourth army today, recommended for independent commands. Loaded A section at CORBIE rail head this morning. Time of loading supposed to be 7.0 a.m. actually commenced at 11.30 a.m. Two lorry loads of rations had to be drawn from reserve dump on barges as rations on train were short.	
" "	9 9/16		One lorry load of rations has to be drawn from FRECHENCOURT every day for a detachment of the 1st Indian Cav Divn until its arrival in this area. Rations have also to be drawn at CORBIE for a detachment of the 3rd British Cav. Divn with the digging parties. 40 tons of coal was drawn at railhead today + dumped in supply column camp. With digging parties away + "B" echelon loaded separately, there are no spare lorries in the ~~column~~. weather very fine.	
" "	10 9/16		N Battery + Canadian R.H.A rejoined the Division this evening. 10 tons of coal were fetched from the station this morning. Two Canadian + 2 "A" section lorries had to be unloaded for the purpose of fetching it. Obtained O.C. A.S.C's	

1875 Wt. W593/826 1,000,000 4/15 J.B.C. & A. A.D.S.S./Forms/C. 2118.

Instructions regarding War Diaries and Intelligence Summaries are contained in F. S. Regs., Part II. and the Staff Manual respectively. Title pages will be prepared in manuscript.

WAR DIARY
or
~~INTELLIGENCE SUMMARY.~~
(Erase heading not required.)

Army Form C. 2118.

153

Place	Date	Hour	Summary of Events and Information	Remarks and references to Appendices
ALLONVILLE -BUSSY ROAD	10 9/16	continued	sanction to my detailing all Canadian Cav Bgd lorries & cars as may be found necessary. 2 lorries were sent to ALBERT rail head to take kits of details of 1st 2nd C. Divn to FRICOURT. 2 lorries (1 A sect + 1 Canadian) were sent from BUSSY to FRICOURT with officers & kits in relief of other officers with digging parties who will return in lorries to BUSSY. Weather very fine.	
" "	11 9/16		Weather still very fine. Loaded in bulk at the railhead for the first time. Received orders to repaint divisional sign on all Lorries.	
" "	12 9/16		Recd orders from Divn at 12.15 am to send 16 lorries to 3rd Can Divn Reinforcements attached to Sec'bad Bgd near BUSSY church at 7.0 a m to take 330 men out to FRICOURT. Lorries were sent off at 5.0 a m under 2/Lt Owen after the rations had been dumped. They returned to camp at 2.0 P m. One days hay for division, two days oats & the greater part of two days rations were drawn from barges at CORBIE commencing at 3.0 P m today & were taken to spot in centre of MAMETZ village where they were dumped. Last lorries returned to camp at 1.35 a.m. All available lorries of A & B sections were used, B section dumping their rations at units on the way to the barges at CORBIE. Weather fine. Distance from camp to MAMETZ approx 22 miles.	

Instructions regarding War Diaries and Intelligence Summaries are contained in F. S. Regs., Part II. and the Staff Manual respectively. Title pages will be prepared in manuscript.

WAR DIARY
or
INTELLIGENCE SUMMARY.
(Erase heading not required.)

Army Form C. 2118.

(154

Place	Date	Hour	Summary of Events and Information	Remarks and references to Appendices
ALLONVILLE -BUSSY road.	13/9/16		Misty in the morning with slight rain. Received orders at 5.0 P.M. to move column at once to a point on the ALBERT - MILLENCOURT road ¼ mile S W of ALBERT. Distance approx 13 miles. all column less workshops arrived by 10.30 P.M. Parked on road for the night. Lieut Smith was left behind with 5 lorries in case they should be wanted by Divn staff or O.C A.S.C for any purpose. Rain fell from 10.15 P.M to 10.45 P.M.	
ALBERT MILLENCOURT road.	14/9/16		Recd orders for single line of traffic only along this road in direction of ALBERT at 9.30 a.m from A.P.M of 3rd Corps. at 5 30 P.M. recd an order from IV army through A.A.Q.M.G. of Divn that all lorries are to be parked off the road. Lorries were moved accordingly. Head of column was shelled during the afternoon, several shells fell near the lorries, one in the road beside a lorry but no damage was done. Canadian Cav Bgd supply Col workshops were moved from top of the hill to the valley as they were considered to be within view of a german observation baloon. Train arrived at rail head at 11.15 P.M. Rail head ALBERT.	
	15/9/16		Weather fine. Train again arrived at 11.0 P.M. B echelon ~~lorries~~ british rations & animal rations will in future be fetched direct from FRECHINCOURT rail head by horse transport, thus releasing 4 lorries for each echelon. Division	

Instructions regarding War Diaries and Intelligence Summaries are contained in F. S. Regs., Part II. and the Staff Manual respectively. Title pages will be prepared in manuscript.

WAR DIARY
or
~~INTELLIGENCE SUMMARY.~~
(Erase heading not required.)

Army Form C. 2118.

(155

Place	Date	Hour	Summary of Events and Information	Remarks and references to Appendices
			are bivouacked round MAMETZ. Only rations for digging party & B echelon were delivered today.	
ALBERT–MILLENCOURT road.	16 9/16		From 5.45 P.m. to 8.15 P.m the column was shelled at the rate of two shells per minute. The workshops were hastily removed to a less exposed position & shortly afterwards six shells fell where they had been standing. The only damage sustained was a company notice board smashed & some splinters of shell through the tents. The canadian supply column men retired into some dugouts, but there was no room for the remainder of the men. Rations arrived at railhead at 11.0 P.m.	
" "	17 9/16 & 18 9/16		Recd orders to deliver one days rations to units by Brigades in old area round BUSSY. "A" section delivered at 5.0 P.m. This section then returned to ALBERT, loaded again at railhead at 1.15 a m on morning of 18th took rations straight to old column camp on BUSSY–ALLONVILLE road, dumped them there at 6.0 a m, returned to camp near ALBERT, picked up extra days rations which had been dumped there & returned to BUSSY camp at 11.30 a m. "B" section on 17th collected remains of MAMETZ dump & brought it to camp near ALBERT. at 9.0 P.m left camp with one days rations for D divn which it dumped at 11.15 P.m proceeding thence to BUSSY camp. at	

WAR DIARY
or
~~INTELLIGENCE SUMMARY.~~
(Erase heading not required.)

Instructions regarding War Diaries and Intelligence Summaries are contained in F. S. Regs., Part II. and the Staff Manual respectively. Title pages will be prepared in manuscript.

Army Form C. 2118.

(156

Place	Date	Hour	Summary of Events and Information	Remarks and references to Appendices
			10.45 a m on morning of 18th this section loaded at CORBIE railhead. Ten lorries were afterwards sent to old camp near ALBERT to fetch remainder of oats, bran & coal which had been left there. Rain commenced to fall at about midnight 17th–18th & continued until evening of 18th at 6.30 P.m. Everyone very tired but all officers & men worked very willingly & well.	
BUSSY–ALLONVILLE road	19 9/16		Very wet all day. Great difficulty experienced in manoeuvering the lorries in camp during the process of sorting out the rations. Rations delivered at 5.0 P.m. Men were paid out this evening, 13235 francs for 440 men. Train arrived at 4.0 P.m. There was a special rum issue this evening.	
" "	20 9/16		Units drew from supply column dump today commencing at 3.0 P.m at intervals of ¾ an hour by horse transport. Another wet day.	
" "	21 9/16		20 tons of coal & 15 tons of wood arrived at railhead this morning & were fetched up to camp by 17 lorries of "B" sect & 8 lorries of Canadians. One lorry of "B" sect took 1 officer & 19 natives from BUSSY to digging party. Capt Thomas of Canadian Bgd is taking the place of Lieut Hall as column supply officer from tomorrow morning. Weather finer today, a drying wind has made the camp much easier for the lorries.	

Army Form C. 2[illegible]8.

(157)

Instructions regarding War Diaries and Intelligence Summaries are contained in F. S. Regs., Part II. and the Staff Manual respectively. Title pages will be prepared in manuscript.

WAR DIARY
or
INTELLIGENCE SUMMARY.
(*Erase heading not required.*)

Place	Date	Hour	Summary of Events and Information	Remarks and references to Appendices
BUSSY – ALLONVILLE Road.	22 9/16		Fine day, bright sun. Camp nearly dried up. Train arrived at 9.0 a m today. Four lorries have been ordered to report at H^d Q^rs of Ambala and Sec'bad brigades at 7.30 a m tomorrow morning to fetch kits of men from rear billets. Aeroplanes passed over the camp at 3.30 a m & bombarded AMIENS. Four unexploded shells from the Amiens anti-aircraft guns fell in our camp.	
" "	23 9/16		Weather still continues fine. Loading commenced at station at 8.30 a m & was completed by 10.0 a.m. 20 tons of coal & 10 tons of wood were also fetched from railhead by "B" section lorries, the section which was not loading.	
" "	24 9/16		Weather very fine, roads good. A church of England service was held for the column at 2.0 P.m. Drawing & delivery of rations was the same as yesterday.	
" "	25 9/16		Rations were delivered to units by lorry today at 5.30 P.m. German aeroplanes passed over the camp about 9.45 P.m. & bombed AMIENS. Several french shells which did not explode fell in the neighbourhood of the camp as usual.	
CAMPS EN AMIENOIS	26 9/16		Recd orders after midnight 25–26th that Divn was moving to old billets near GAMACHES. at 11.30 a m. the orders were amended for the Divn to stay in the CAVILLON, – MOLLIENS VIDAME district. Supply column moved to CAMPS EN AMIENOIS, arriving there at	

Instructions regarding War Diaries and Intelligence Summaries are contained in F. S. Regs., Part II. and the Staff Manual respectively. Title pages will be prepared in manuscript.

WAR DIARY
or
~~INTELLIGENCE SUMMARY.~~
(Erase heading not required.)

Form C. 2118.

(158)

Place	Date	Hour	Summary of Events and Information	Remarks and references to Appendices
			7.0 P.M. distance 35 kilometres. Billets & standing for lorries good. delivering section (A) delivered rations at 7.0 P.M. all correct. Weather fine.	
CAMPS EN AMIENOIS	27 9/16		Rations were drawn from HANGEST railhead at 7.0 a.m. In order to avoid the MOLLIENS-VIDAME SOUES road along which all the cavalry Divn are encamped, the lorries were sent round by AIRAINES, SOUES distance 26 kilometres. Rations were delivered at 5.0 P.M. Cpl. Milvaine reports the loss of his company motor cycle in AMIENS yesterday. Have informed A.P.M. AMIENS, AD of S+T Cav Corps, & OC O.S.C 2nd I C.D.	
" "	28 9/16		Rations were drawn at railhead at 6.0 am today. Lorries proceeded via MOLLIENS-VIDAME & SOUES direct today. Delivery of rations at 4.0 P.M. today. No trace of motor cycle as yet. a little rain in the afternoon. The column is settled down very comfortably in this village, which is most suitable for lorries.	
" "	29 9/16		Time of drawing & delivering rations the same as yesterday. Rained during morning and till 4.0 P.M. in afternoon.	
" "	30 9/16		Rations for Sec'bad Bgd delivered in CROUY-ST PIERRE A GOUY area today at same time as before. Weather fine. Strength of column 441 all ranks, 2 M T men & 4 supply men deficient.	

C A Crawley-Boevey Major
OC No2 Ind Cav Supply Col.

T.2134. Wt. W708-776. 500000. 4/15. Sir J. C. & S.

SERIAL NO. 56.

Confidential War Diary of

Supply Column 5th Cavalry Divn. (late 2nd Ind. Cavy. Divn.)

FROM 1st October 1916 TO ~~30th November~~ ~~31st October~~ ~~31st Oct~~ 30th November 1916.

Instructions regarding War Diaries and Intelligence Summaries are contained in F. S. Regs., Part II. and the Staff Manual respectively. Title pages will be prepared in manuscript.

WAR DIARY
or
~~INTELLIGENCE SUMMARY.~~
(*Erase heading not required.*)

2nd Supply Col. Army Form C. 2118.

Vol. IV

(159)

Place	Date	Hour	Summary of Events and Information	Remarks and references to Appendices
CAMP EN AMIENOIS	1/10/16		Steam disinfector should have arrived at 9.0 a.m. At 12.15 a.m. found that the Canadians had appropriated it. Commenced on our blankets & underclothing at 1.0 P.M. Finished "B" sect & workshops only. Shall have to do A section on another occasion. Drawing & delivery of rations as usual. Weather fine.	
" "	2/10/16		Very wet today. Road to station slippery, & being narrow in places is difficult for lorries to avoid getting ditched when passing traffic. A case of measles was reported in the town & the house has been placed out of bounds. Circular memo recd today warning troops against drinking syrups & water in cafés. Lieut Fairclough left the unit this day by order of A.D.M.S.	
" "	3/10/16		Wet in morning, fine rest of day. 12970 francs were drawn for pay of company tomorrow. Nothing special to report.	
" "	4/10/16		Rain off & on all day. The camp at BUSSY where the detachment of 9 lorries still stand is in very bad condition now, the road being scarcely recognisable. These lorries still carry for the working party attached to III Corps, dismounted reinforcements attached to XV corps, 141 field ambulance & R.E. field squadron, with one Kelly lorry as spare & also for fetching water for the camp.	

T.134. Wt. W708—776. 500000. 4/15. Sir J. C. & S.

Instructions regarding War Diaries and Intelligence Summaries are contained in F. S. Regs., Part II. and the Staff Manual respectively. Title pages will be prepared in manuscript.

WAR DIARY
or
~~INTELLIGENCE SUMMARY.~~
(Erase heading not required.)

5 Cav. Supply Col. Army Form C. 2118.

(160)

Place	Date	Hour	Summary of Events and Information	Remarks and references to Appendices
			Ambala section lorries delivered at 11.0 a m this morning & afterwards proceeded to BUSSY to fetch wood, coal, & supplies from BUSSY dump for use of Divn Lorries returned to camp at 7.0 P.m.	
CAMP EN AMIENOIS	5 10/16		Rained again in morning. ~~Staff~~ Sgt FORD is under orders to proceed to England immediately to take up munition work under War office authority. Fetched Sgt Childs from BUSSY camp to Supply column to take place of Cpl BRAY who is relieving Sgt FORD. Lieut D. CAMPBELL reported today as medical officer in place of Lt FAIRCLOUGH.	
"	" 6 10/16		Lieut GREGORY A.S.C joined Column today as a supply officer. Weather fine.	
"	" 7 10/16		8 lorries delivered rations at 7.0 a m this morning & afterwards took reliefs from Ambala & Sec'bad Bgdes to digging party near FRICOURT. Remainder of AMBALA Bgd lorries delivered rations at 10.0 a m & afterwards proceeded to rail head to draw wood & coal. 3 lorries from Divl Troops section delivered at 10.30 a m & afterwards proceeded to CANAPLES to draw grocery rations for SS.O.	
"	" 8 10/16		Rain again fell in the morning & evening. Lieut GREGORY was sent to BUSSY to take over supply duties from Capt BIRD ordered to England by W.O telegram. Divine service was	

T.134. Wt. W708-776. 500000. 4/15. Sir J. C. & S.

Instructions regarding War Diaries and Intelligence Summaries are contained in F. S. Regs., Part II. and the Staff Manual respectively. Title pages will be prepared in manuscript.

WAR DIARY
or
~~INTELLIGENCE SUMMARY.~~
(Erase heading not required.)

Army Form C. 2118.

161

Place	Date	Hour	Summary of Events and Information	Remarks and references to Appendices
			held at 2.0 P.M. today.	
CAMP EN AMIENOIS	9/10/16		Loading at railhead was at 9.0 a.m. this morning instead of 6.0 a.m. Interpreter Glecquier went on leave to England this morning for 7 days. Weather fine. Foot parade of 'A' section at 2.0 P.M.	
" "	10/10/16		Lieut SMITH promoted captain in London Gazette. Weather fine. Recd telegram that train would be 6 hours late at railhead this morning. Found that train was in to time as usual. Delivered early with sec'bad section, & afterwards drew 10 tons of coal & 7 tons of wood from railhead for distribution to units today.	
" "	11/10/16		Lt Col Jackson, new O.C. A.S.C. visited the column yesterday. Weather fine. Inspected 'B' section lorries, cookhouse, billets etc. Found all perfectly correct.	
" "	12/10/16		Weather still fine. Train did not arrive until 11.45 a.m. Pte Owens sent in to ABBEVILLE by lorry today & handed over to the North Staffordshire Regt for trial by court martial.	
" "	13/10/16		Train again late today, arriving at 9.30 a.m. Sent one car to O.C. A.S.C. Second car undergoing repairs & overhaul, 3rd car at railhead. Required car to visit A.A. & Q.M.G. also to reconnoitre roads in accordance with instructions from O.C. A.S.C.	

T.134. Wt. W708–776. 500000. 4/15. Sir J. C. & S.

Army Form C. 2118.

(162)

Instructions regarding War Diaries and Intelligence Summaries are contained in F. S. Regs., Part II. and the Staff Manual respectively. Title pages will be prepared in manuscript.

WAR DIARY
or
~~INTELLIGENCE SUMMARY.~~
(Erase heading not required.)

Place	Date	Hour	Summary of Events and Information	Remarks and references to Appendices
			no car available, very inconvenient. Orders were received at 6.0 P.m. that all	
CAMP EN AMIENOIS			supplies drawn from rail head today were to be checked before issue tomorrow, & all supplies drawn from rail head tomorrow are to be checked before issue on the following day. One lorry of "A" section which drew at rail head this morning has dumped its rations at Divn H.d Qrs in preparation for reporting to H.d Qrs of X Corps at PONT REMY tomorrow morning at 7.0 a.m.	
" "	14/10/16		Twelve lorries were ordered to deliver at 8.0 a.m to Brigades this morning & afterwards to take up reliefs for the digging parties from the various regiments. Lorries returned to camp at 10.0 P.m. Weather fine.	
" "	15/10/16		Weather was fine again ~~today~~. Col Mark Synge O.C. A.S.C, & Major Noake left the Division today. Some rain during the night.	
"	16/10/16		Recd orders to deliver rations by 9.0 a.m. in future. This suits every one much better. We can now have parades in the afternoon. Four of Sec 'B's lorries are to call at S.O.D.T.'s office daily after delivery in case there is any coal to be collected from the station. Capt WORLEY R.A.M.C joined unit this evening at 7.0 P.m for duty. Weather fine & dry.	

Instructions regarding War Diaries and Intelligence Summaries are contained in F. S. Regs., Part II. and the Staff Manual respectively. Title pages will be prepared in manuscript.

WAR DIARY
or
~~INTELLIGENCE SUMMARY.~~
(Erase heading not required.)

Army Form C. 2118.

(163)

Place	Date	Hour	Summary of Events and Information	Remarks and references to Appendices
CAMP EN AMIENOIS	17 10/16		wet today, roads bad. Rations were delivered this morning at 9.0 a.m. everything was satisfactory	
" "	18 10/16		weather dull. Nothing of importance to report today. Time of loading and delivery were the same as yesterday.	
" "	19 10/16		Major V. Hunt has taken over the position of S.S.O today from Capt G. O. Hunt. One lorry was supplied today at 7.0 a.m. at AIRAINES for use of 41st Divn to assist them in moving. Rained off & on all day	
" "	20 10/16		Fine & dry with strong wind. Roads getting in good condition. Train arrived at 11.30 a.m. Strength of column today 443 all ranks.	
" "	21 10/16		Train was very late again today & trucks were mixed up with those of another unit necessitating much shunting at the siding. Last lorries left rail head loaded at 5.0 P.m. The usual weekly relief of dismounted men for digging party was carried out. 83 Coy car was lent to Ambala Regtl officer. Frost last night & cold today.	
" "	22 10/16		One lorry was sent to OISEMENT at 5.0 P.m. to assist 6th Divn to move according to instructions recd from O.C. A.S.C. Church parade at 2.0 P.m. weather fine & dry.	

T.134. Wt. W708–776. 500000. 4/15. Sir J. C. & S.

Instructions regarding War Diaries and Intelligence Summaries are contained in F. S. Regs., Part II. and the Staff Manual respectively. Title pages will be prepared in manuscript.

WAR DIARY
or
~~INTELLIGENCE SUMMARY.~~
(Erase heading not required.)

Army Form C. 2118.

(164)

Place	Date	Hour	Summary of Events and Information	Remarks and references to Appendices
CAMP EN AMIENOIS	23/10/16		Weather still fine. Six lorries of "B" section were lent to D.A.D.O.S this morning to help convey blankets etc from CAVILLON to DARGNIES the new Divn H^d Qrs when we move. A motor car was also lent to B.R.O Ambala Bgd from 1.30 P.M to 5.0 P.M.	
" "	24/10/16		A 3 ton lorry was lent to 6th Divn again today to assist them in their move. The lorry was supplied by "B" section. Rain last night & this morning. Discs are being fitted to the rear part of the canopy of every lorry, the discs being adjustable so that every sixth lorry can show a disc to the vehicle behind to ensure proper spacing of lorries on the road. Recd notification that new railhead is WOINCOURT when we move.	
" "	25/10/16		Went to QUERRIEU & obtained permission from Q branch of Fourth army to billet detachment on BUSSY–ALLONVILLE road in the village of BUSSY. Made arrangements for Lt BECK & 45 other officers & men to move into their billets tomorrow. Very wet all day.	
" "	26/10/16		Lieut GREGORY reported last night from BUSSY detachment. He will take over column supply officer duties in a few days from Lt RAISON. Wet in morning, fine in afternoon. Detachment moved in billets at BUSSY.	
" "	27/10/16		Very wet again all day. One days ration of rum for Divn was drawn from ABBEVILLE at 8.30	

T.134. Wt. W708–776. 500000. 4/15. Sir J. C. & S.

Instructions regarding War Diaries and Intelligence Summaries are contained in F. S. Regs., Part II. and the Staff Manual respectively. Title pages will be prepared in manuscript.

WAR DIARY
or
~~INTELLIGENCE~~ SUMMARY.
(Erase heading not required.)

Army Form C. 2118.

(165)

Place	Date	Hour	Summary of Events and Information	Remarks and references to Appendices
			P.m. this evening & issued to units immediately on return of lorries. Visited new rail head & position of column billets at WOINCOURT with O.C. A.S.C. this afternoon.	
CAMP EN AMIENOIS	28/10/16		Recd orders for T. Capt D. G. SMITH to proceed to take command of No 2 Auxiliary (omnibus) company No 91 MT Coy A.S.C. Weather finer & no rain. Strength of company 442 all ranks.	
"	29/10/16		T. Capt Smith left at 2.30 P.m. by car for CHOQUES. Nine lorries of sec'bad red A's were sent at 8.30 a.m. this morning to assist in bring back 21 tons of horse regs from WOINCOURT to present divisional area, the remainder of the lorries being provided by the Ammn Park. Duty was completed at 4.45 P.m. B section drew 25 tons of coal from rail head & conveyed it to the dump in HANGEST.	
"	30/10/16		Pte Young returned with the car at 9.30 a.m. this morning after taking Capt Smith to CHOQUES, delay in his return being caused by No 91 Coy A.S.C having moved from their original position at MORBECQUE.	
"	31/10/16		Visited WOINCOURT with interpreter in afternoon to arrange billets for column which is moving in tomorrow. Found all billets already taken by Canadian Cav Bgd.	

T.134. Wt. W708–776. 500000. 4/15. Sir J. C. & S.

Instructions regarding War Diaries and Intelligence Summaries are contained in F. S. Regs., Part II. and the Staff Manual respectively. Title pages will be prepared in manuscript.

WAR DIARY
or
INTELLIGENCE SUMMARY.
(Erase heading not required.)

Army Form C. 2118.

166

Place	Date	Hour	Summary of Events and Information	Remarks and references to Appendices
			Reported to A A & Q.M.G. & obtained order from him to billet in the village. "A" section loaded at the station at 4.0 P.m returned to camp at 7.0 P.m. left camp at 8.0 P.m with rations which were dumped in new divisional area. Lieut J. W. H. McNab reported to day in the place of Capt Smith. 5 M.T. drivers reported from Base.	
	1/11/16	8.30am	All lorries returned to camp after delivering rations last night by 5.30 a.m.	

C A Crawley-Boevey Major
O C No 2 I C S C

1/11/16

T.134. Wt. W708–776. 500000. 4/15. Sir J. C. & S.

2nd Indian Cav. DIV

2nd Ind Cav Ammo Park
(72 CAV ASC)

1914 SEP → 1916 OCT

TO 5 CAV DIV
BOX 1163

1

2 IND CAV DIVISION

AMMUNITION PARK

72 COY ASC

1914 SEPT – 1916 OCT

Secunderbad ~~[illegible]~~ Cavalry Brigade Ammunition Park

WAR DIARY
or
INTELLIGENCE SUMMARY.
(Erase heading not required.)

76 Coy ASC.

Army Form C. 2118.

Instructions regarding War Diaries and Intelligence Summaries are contained in F. S. Regs., Part II. and the Staff Manual respectively. Title pages will be prepared in manuscript.

Hour, Date, Place	Summary of Events and Information	Remarks and references to Appendices
Portsmouth 19th Sept 1914	Company completed to Establishment in Personnel Vehicles, Stores & Equipment.	
20th Sept.	Company marched to AVONMOUTH.	
21st – " –	Embarked on 'SS ULTONIA'	
23rd – " –	Ship sailed at 5 am	
25th – " –	Landed at HAVRE 7 am. Men & vehicles disembarked.	
27th – " –	Company marched to ROUEN	
28th – " –	" " " NONANCOURT	
29th – " –	" " " VERSAILLES	
1st October	" " " MONNERVILLE	
2nd – " –	" " " ORLEANS.	

(Marginal note bracketed against 27th Sept – 2nd Oct: Weather generally fine – Roads excellent –)

(73989) W4141—463. 400,000. 9/14. H.&J.Ltd. Forms/C. 2118/10.

Instructions regarding War Diaries and Intelligence Summaries are contained in F. S. Regs., Part II. and the Staff Manual respectively. Title pages will be prepared in manuscript.

WAR DIARY
or
INTELLIGENCE SUMMARY.
(*Erase heading not required.*)

Army Form C. 2118.

Hour, Date, Place	Summary of Events and Information	Remarks and references to Appendices
1914 3rd to 24th October	At ORLEANS, doing local transport work, general repairs to vehicles, collecting Ordnance Stores, fitting lorries with super-structures etc.	
25th October	Company marched to ALLONES	
26th — " —	" " " LOUVIERS	
27th — " —	" " " NEUFCHATEL	
	(ALLONES to NEUFCHATEL:) Weather generally fine – roads good.	
28th — " —	" " " ABBEVILLE	
30th — " —	" " " AIRE	
	(ABBEVILLE to AIRE:) Weather wet & cold. Roads indifferent	
31st — " —	" " " ST VENANT	
1st Nov.	Ordered to move to CHOCQUES & to halt there as a convenient centre between railhead at AIRE & the Secunderabad Amm'n Column at LES LOBES.	

Instructions regarding War Diaries and Intelligence Summaries are contained in F. S. Regs., Part II. and the Staff Manual respectively. Title pages will be prepared in manuscript.

WAR DIARY
or
INTELLIGENCE SUMMARY.
(Erase heading not required.)

Army Form C. 2118.

Hour, Date, Place	Summary of Events and Information	Remarks and references to Appendices
November 1914 2nd to 16th	At CHOCQUES. Ammunition supplied regularly to the column as required. A motor cyclist was detached to the column permanently for communication, & telephone communication by means of the post office was established as well. The roads, especially the roads some of how very bad & cut up, & some difficulty was experienced in getting lorries along them. The weather generally was very wet.	Appendix "A" Showing details of Ammunition supplied.
17th Nov to 31st December 1914	Ordered to move to LILLERS. – railhead at AIRE & ammunition supplied to the Ammunition Column as above. – Weather, except for a few days of bright & frosty conditions, continued very wet & bad. No serious trouble with vehicles was experienced in any of the period covered	

(73989) W4141—463. 400,000. 9/14. H.&J.Ltd. Forms/C. 2118/10.

Instructions regarding War Diaries and Intelligence Summaries are contained in F. S. Regs., Part II. and the Staff Manual respectively. Title pages will be prepared in manuscript.

WAR DIARY
or
INTELLIGENCE SUMMARY.
(*Erase heading not required.*)

Army Form C. 2118.

Hour, Date, Place	Summary of Events and Information	Remarks and references to Appendices
	by the above report, & there is no special circumstance to record. All demands for Ammunition from the Column were complied with without any delay or difficulty. H. W. S. Crawford, Major R.A. O.C. 2nd Indian Cavalry Amn Park.	

(73989) W4141—463. 400,000. 9/14. H.&J.Ltd. Forms/C. 2118/10.

APPENDIX 'A' to Vol. 1.
of War Diary of
Secunderabad Cavalry Brigade Amn. Park.

Particulars of Ammunition Supplied to 31st Decr. /14.

Dates	13 Pr.	S.A.A.
3 Nov. 14	—	62,000
4th " "	—	50,000
6th " "	152	—
8th " "	—	70,000
9th " "	112	50,000
10th " "	188	—
11th " "	456	—
14th " "	16	—
16th " "	48	53,000
18th " "	—	72,000
19th " "	228	—
22nd " "	64	—
24th " "	224	—
25th " "	116	—
26th " "	—	38,000
27th " "	40	45,000
29th " "	88	4,000
	1732	444,000

Dates	13 Pr.	S.A.A.
1st Decr /14	96	[illegible]4,000
4th	—	14,000
12th	—	90,000
15th	—	28,000
18th	232	—
19th	228	—
20th	56	—
21st	56	—
22nd	452	—
23rd	224	—
24th	480	—
29th	—	[illegible]8,000
30th	124	—
	1948	174,000
	1732	444,000
TOTAL	3680	618,000

H. A. S. Crawford
Major A.C.
Comdg. 2nd Ind. Cavy. Amn. Park.

Serial No. 55

JB
21/3.

121/4719

72 Coy ASC

WAR DIARY

with Appendix.

OF

2nd Indian Cavalry Ammunition Park.

From 1st February 1915 To 29th February 1915

To Nov. 1917

Instructions regarding War Diaries and Intelligence Summaries are contained in F. S. Regs., Part II. and the Staff Manual respectively. Title pages will be prepared in manuscript.

WAR DIARY
or
INTELLIGENCE SUMMARY.
(Erase heading not required.)

Army Form C. 2118.

Hour, Date, Place	Summary of Events and Information	Remarks and references to Appendices
AIRE February 1915.		
7th	2/Lieut Chatterton A.S.C. joined for duty	
8th	2 Lieut Bray A.S.C. left for duty at ROUEN	
11th	2 Lt Malony R.F.A. joined for duty.	
	There is nothing further to record during the month of February. The weather during practically the whole of January & February was exceedingly bad nearly every day being wet & windy. There was hardly any cold or frosty weather	
	H.A.G. Crawford. Major O.C. 2nd Indian Cav. Am Park	
	28th Feb. 1915	

(73989) W4141—463. 400,000. 9/14. H.&J.Ltd. Forms/C. 2118/10.

2nd Indian Cavalry Ammunition Park (late Secunderabad Cavalry Bde Ammn Park)

Army Form C. 2118.

WAR DIARY
or
INTELLIGENCE SUMMARY.
(Erase heading not required.)

Instructions regarding War Diaries and Intelligence Summaries are contained in F. S. Regs., Part II. and the Staff Manual respectively. Title pages will be prepared in manuscript.

Hour, Date, Place	Summary of Events and Information	Remarks and references to Appendices
January 1915. to Feb 28th 1915 AIRE	8th – Moved from LILLERS to AIRE to join extra lorries and personnel brought out from England under Lieut Sorel A.S.C. & formed the column into the 2nd Indian Cavalry Ammn Park.	Statement showing Ammunition delivered during the period 1st January to 28th February 1915, attached Appendix A
	10th – Got into touch with the 3 Ammunition Columns of the Division – i.e. the Secunderabad, Mhow, & Meerut Amn. Columns.	
	13th – ~~Surplus~~ Lorries surplus to establishment left the column & were distributed as follows: 1st Ind Cav Bde Ammn Park --- 3 OC Army Troops Supply Col G.H.Q. --- 4	
	27th Lieut W.L. Sorel ordered to proceed to England for duty	
	29th Received orders to be ready to move at 2 hours notice, but was not ordered to move.	

APPENDIX A

2nd Indian Cavalry Amn Park.

Statement showing ammunition delivered by above unit during the Period 1st Jany to 28th Feb 1915.

Date 1915.	Nature of Amn	No of rounds	To whom delivered	Remarks.
Jany 16	S.A. ball ·303.	53.000	Meerut Bde Amn Column	
21	Cartgs Signall ball light (Very Pistol)	100	Poona Horse	
24	do	48	Skinners Horse.	
Feb 4	do	120	18th Lancers.	
6	Ball pistol Webley	2760	Secunderabad Amn Col.	
10	S.A. ball ·303	3000	2nd Lancers.	
	Ball pistol Webley	276	Hd Qrs 2 I.C. Divn	
15	do	276.	Hd Qrs I Cav Corps.	
21	13 pr Q.F.	16	Mhow Amn Col.	
22	Ball pistol Webley	552	Poona Horse	
24	Bombs Trench mortar.	50	N Batty RHA	
24	Q.F. 13 pr	796.	X Bty RHA	X changed for defective amm which was sent to Railhead.

H.R.S. Crawford.

Major RFA

Comdg 2 ICAP

Serial No. 55

121/5114

WAR DIARY

OF

2nd Indian Cavalry Ammunition Park.

From 1st March 1915 To 31st March 1915

72 Company ASC. 2nd Indian Cavalry Ammn Park.

WAR DIARY

or

INTELLIGENCE SUMMARY.

(Erase heading not required.)

Army Form C. 2118.

Instructions regarding War Diaries and Intelligence Summaries are contained in F. S. Regs., Part II. and the Staff Manual respectively. Title pages will be prepared in manuscript.

Hour, Date, Place	Summary of Events and Information	Remarks and references to Appendices
March 1915. AIRE 1st	2nd Lieut T.H.E. Oakes RFA proceeded to 7th Division for duty.	
14th	Draft of 10 men arrived from the Base	Ammunition Issued Appx A.
Remainder of Month.	There is nothing else of importance to record during the month of March. The weather generally speaking was fine during the month. About 80 per cent of the men were inoculated against enteric fever, during the month. The Company was exercised in musketry, firing 10 rounds per man.	

H. H. S. Crawford
Major
OC. 2nd Ind Cav. A.P.

2nd Indian Cavalry Amn Park

Appx "A" to War Diary dated 31 3/15

Ammunition Issues.

Date	To whom	Nature of Amn	No of rds	Remarks.
1.3.15	C.R.A. 2nd I.C.D.	Pistol ball	288.	
2.3.15	O.C. V Bty R.H.A.	Trench Mortar	50.	
3.3.15	O.C. 71 M.T. Coy A.S.C.	S.A.A. .303 ball	3000	
3.3.15	O.C. Secunderabad A. Col	-do-	1000.	
6.3.15	Mhow Cav Bde. Amn Col	-do-	13000.	
8.3.15	H.Qrs. 2nd I.C. Div	Pistol ball	300	
8.3.15	H.Qrs Indian Corps.	do.	276	
9.3.15	Signal Squadron H.Q.	do	300.	
9.3.15	2nd Lancers	S.A. ball .303	7000	
10.3.15	Jodhpur Lancers	Pistol ball	1104	
17.3.15	O.C. 83 Coy A.S.C.	S.A. ball .303	1000	
17.3.15	Secunderabad Am Col	Pistol ball	276	
20.3.15	I.C. H.d.Qrs.	do.	276	
26.3.15	2nd Signal Squadron	do.	30.	
27.3.15	I.C.C. H.Qrs.	do	828	
28.3.15	2nd I.C. Dn Supply Col	do.	276.	
29.3.15	Supply Offr Mhow Cav Bde	do.	228	
~~29~~ 30.3.15	2nd Ind Cavy Dvn Supply Col	do.	288.	
31 3/15	Bde Supply Depot Mhow Bde	do.	156.	
31 3/15	I.C.C. H.qrs	do	276	
31 3/15	A.D.M.S. 2nd I.C.D.	do	48	

H.A.S. Crawford
Major R.A.
Comdg 2nd I.C. A.P.

121/5504

Serial No. 55

WAR DIARY

With appendices.

OF

2nd Indian Cavalry Ammunition Park.

From 1st April 1915 To 30th April 1915

2nd Indian Cavalry Ammunition Park.

Instructions regarding War Diaries and Intelligence Summaries are contained in F. S. Regs., Part II. and the Staff Manual respectively. Title pages will be prepared in manuscript.

WAR DIARY
or
INTELLIGENCE SUMMARY.
(*Erase heading not required.*)

Army Form C. 2118.

Hour, Date, Place	Summary of Events and Information	Remarks and references to Appendices
APRIL 1915 AIRE.	During April nothing of importance to record, occurred. All lorries were overhauled & given a workshop test during the month. The weather generally was fine. The health of the men during the month was excellent the amount of sickness being practically negligible. H. H. S. Crawford Major OC 2nd I. C. Am Park.	

2nd Ind. Cavy. Ammn. Park.

Appendix "A" to War Diary for April 1915.

Ammunition Issues.

Date	To Whom	Nature of Ammn.	No. of Rounds	Remarks.
6-4-15	Indian Cavy. Corps. H. Qr.	Pistol Ball	276	
7-4-15	2nd Lancers	S.A.A. ·303	2,000	
10-4-15.	Divisional Ammn. Column	13 Pdr. Q.F.	144	
10-4-15	—— do —— do ——	S.A.A. ·303.	15,000	
12-4-15	Signal Squad.	Pistol Ball	400	
13-4-15	Indian Cavy. Corps H. Qrs.	—do—	276	
18-4-15.	2nd Lancers.	—do—	552	
21-4-15	Ind. Cavy. Corps H. Qrs.	—do—	276	
22-4-15	2nd Lancers	—do—	1656	
23-4-15.	Divisional Ammn. Column	S.A.A. ·303	5,000	
24-4-15	Divisional Ammn. Column	S.A.A. ·303	14,000	
24-4-15	Ind. Cavy. Corps. Signal Squad.	Pistol Ball	276	
29-4-15	2nd Ind. Cavy. Supply Column	Pistol Ball	276	

H. H. L. Crawford.
Major
A.S.C.
O.C. 2nd Ind. Cavy. Ammn. Park

Appendix XVII

"C" Form (Original).

Army Form C. 2123.

MESSAGES AND SIGNALS.

No. of Message

Prefix SM Code 86 Words 42	Received	Sent, or sent out	Office Stamp.
Charges to Collect	From aak	At ... m.	YCO 30 IV 15 ARMY
	By WCC OL	To	
Service Instructions. 1st Div		By	

Handed in at the ... Office, at 2.35 p.m. Received here at 2.48 p.m.

TO C R A 2nd Ind Cav Div

*Sender's Number.	Day of Month.	In reply to Number.	AAA
BM 104	30th		

Although cannot yet say when Batteries will be required it is desirable if local conditions admit to send one officer and a detachment from each Battery as soon as possible to construct emplacements and observing stations aaa Personnel would be attached to 26th and 39th FA Bdes aaa Report if this can be done and time of arrival of personnel

FROM 1st Divn 2·15pm

PLACE

TIME

*This line should be erased if not required.

W. 5375—423. 75,000 Pads—12/12—B. & F.—Forms/C.2123/1.

Serial No. 55.

121/6128

WAR DIARY

with appendices.

OF

Ammunition Park, 2nd Indian Cavalry Division

From 1st May 1915 To 30th June 1915.

Army Form C. 2118.

Instructions regarding War Diaries and Intelligence Summaries are contained in F. S. Regs., Part II and the Staff Manual respectively. Title pages will be prepared in manuscript.

WAR DIARY
or
INTELLIGENCE SUMMARY.
(Erase heading not required.)

Hour, Date, Place	Summary of Events and Information	Remarks and references to Appendices
May 1915 AIRE		
2nd	Orders to move 75 rounds per Gun to LILLERS to join 1st Corps, temporarily	
3rd	½ Gun section of Park with above, proceeded to LILLERS & reported to 1st Amm. Park.	
4th	Park inspected by D.D. of Transport G.H.Q. – reported on satisfactorily	
16th	2 Dennis Lorrys transferred to GHQ Troops Supply Colm 2 Berna Lorries received in exchange.	
21st	T/Lieut Lees promoted Captain T/2 Lt Lee Evans promoted Lieut	
25th	13 Pr Section returned to AIRE Issue of 13 Pr Am stopped until further orders nothing other than above to record. All lorries of park in good order. Weather generally during May, good.	
12th July 1915.	H.H. Crawford Major OC 2 [illegible]	

(73989) W4141—463. 400,000. 9/14. H.&J.Ltd. Forms/C. 2118/10.

2nd Indian Cavalry Ammn. Park.

Appendix "A" to WAR DIARY for MAY 1915.

AMMUNITION ISSUES.

Date.	To whom	Nature of Ammn.	No. of Rounds.	Remarks.
May 6.	2nd Ind. Cavy. Divn. Ammn. Col.	13 Pr. Shrap.	270	
" 6	do	13 Pr. "	1080	
" 7	Indian Cavy. Corps H. Qrs.	Webley Pistol	276	
" 9	2nd Ind. Cavy. Divn. Ammn. Col.	13 Pr. Shrap.	1800	
" 10	do	do	1500	
" 14	do	do	3140	
" 15	do	do	300	
" 15.	Inniskilling Dragoons	Webley Pistol	276	
" 16	2nd Ind. Cavy. Divn. Ammn. Col.	13 Pr. Shrap.	1500	
" 17	do	do	1800	
" 17	Jodhpur Lancers	Webley Pistol	1656	
" 18	2nd Ind. Cavy. Divn. Ammn. Col.	13 Pr. Shrap.	900	
" 19	do	do	608	
" 20	do	do	600	
" 22	do	do	640	
" 23	Ind. Cavy. Corps H. Qrs.	Webley Pistol	276	
" 24	2nd Ind. Cavy. Divn. Ammn. Col.	13 Pr. Shrapn.	48	
" 26	2nd Lancers	Webley Pistol	552	
" 29	1st Ind. Cavy. Ammn. Park.	13 Pr. Shrapn.	1280	

[illegible] Major

O.C. 2nd I.C.A.P.

Instructions regarding War Diaries and Intelligence Summaries are contained in F. S. Regs., Part II. and the Staff Manual respectively. Title pages will be prepared in manuscript.

WAR DIARY
or
INTELLIGENCE SUMMARY.
(*Erase heading not required.*)

Army Form C. 2118.

Hour, Date, Place	Summary of Events and Information	Remarks and references to Appendices
June 1915		
AIRE 3rd	1 Dennis Lorry sent G.H.Q. in exchange for a Berna Lorry	
17th	2 Extra Halley lorries received to carry extra S.A.A.	
	Nothing beyond above to record on particular dates.	
	During the month the establishment of 13 Pr Am was altered as follows 35 %. High Explosive 65 % Shrapnell Amm'n was exchanged accordingly All lorries were repainted & overhauled during the month. Men were exercised in Regimental Drill Parades.	
	H.H. Crawford Major OC 2nd ICAP	

72 M.T. Co. A.S.C.
12 JUL. 1915
INDIAN CAV. AMMTN. PARK

2nd Indian Cavalry Ammn Park.

Appendix "A" to War Diary for month of June 1915

Ammunition Issues.

Date	To Whom issued.	Nature of Ammn	No. of rounds.	Remarks.
June 3	2nd Lancers	·303" S.A.A.	3,000	
" 3	— Do —	Webley Pistol	276	
" 7	2nd Ind. Cavy. Divn. Ammn Column	·303" S.A.A.	2,000	
" 7	— Do —	Webley Pistol	1380.	
" 8	Jodhpur Lancers	— Do —	828	
" 8	13th Hussars	Very Pistol	54	
" 10	2nd Lancers	·303" S.A.A.	1,000	
" 14	2nd Ind. Cavy. Divn. Ammn Column	·303" S.A.A.	2,000	
" 14	— Do. —	Webley Pistol	276	
" 16	Returned to O.O. Railhead	13 Pr. Shrapnel	220	
" 19	2nd I.C.D. Batteries & Column.	13 Pr. H.E.	360	
" 20	2nd Ind. Cavy. Divn. Ammn Column	S.A.A. ·303"	2000	
" 20	— Do —	Webley Pistol	1104	
" 22	Strazeele Railhead	13 Pr. Shrapnel	280	
" 23	2nd Lancers	S.A.A. ·303"	2000	
" 25	2nd I.C.D. Batteries & Amn. Column.	13 Pr. H.E.	720	

[signature]
Major A.S.C.
O.C. 2nd Ind. Cavy. Amn. Col.

Serial No. 55.

121/1650.2

WAR DIARY
with appendices
OF

2nd Indian Cavalry Ammunition Park

FROM 1st July 1915. TO 31st July 1915

2nd Indian Cavalry Ammunition Park.

Instructions regarding War Diaries and Intelligence Summaries are contained in F. S. Regs., Part II. and the Staff Manual respectively. Title pages will be prepared in manuscript.

WAR DIARY
or
INTELLIGENCE SUMMARY.
(Erase heading not required.)

Army Form C. 2118.

Hour, Date, Place	Summary of Events and Information	Remarks and references to Appendices
AIRE : July 1915.		
1st	All new pattern rifles withdrawn, being replaced by the old pattern long rifle, except in the case of car drivers & the "2nd men" on lorries, whose arms have not been replaced.	
4th	H.E. Ammun: brought up to a strength of 25%.	
6th	Coy. inspected by Lt Col Burlton OC ASC 2nd ICD.	
16th	Coy inspected by General James DA & QMG. Ind Cav Corps.	
17th	H.E. Ammn brought up to a proportionate strength of 50%	
30th	Orders received for the Company to move on the 1st August.	
	Nothing further to record during the month. Regimental drill parades were held; the painting & overhauling of all vehicles was proceeded with. The weather generally, during the month was unsettled.	
	H. H. W. Crawford, Major A.S.C. OC 2nd IC Am Pk	

2nd Indian Cavalry Ammn. Park.

Appendix "A". to WAR DIARY for month of JULY 1915

Ammunition ISSUES

Date.	To whom issued	Nature of Ammn.	No. of rounds.	Remarks.
July 6	Indian Cavy. Corps H. Qrs.	Webley Pistol	276	
" 9	2nd Ind. Cavy. Divn. Ammn. Col.	— " —	1104	
" 13	2nd Lancers	Very Pistol	552	
" 28	— " —	·303" SAA.	1000.	

H. A. L. Crawford

Major A.S.C.

O.C. 2nd Ind. Cavy. Ammn. Park

Serial No 55

Confidential

121/6948

War Diary

with appendices

of

2nd Indian Cavalry Ammunition Park.

FROM 1st August 1915. TO 31st August 1915.

Confidential

2nd Indian Cavalry Ammunition Park.

Army Form C. 2118.

Instructions regarding War Diaries and Intelligence Summaries are contained in F. S. Regs., Part II. and the Staff Manual respectively. Title pages will be prepared in manuscript.

WAR DIARY
or
~~INTELLIGENCE SUMMARY.~~

(*Erase heading not required.*)

Hour, Date, Place	Summary of Events and Information	Remarks and references to Appendices
August 1915		
2.30 pm 1st Aire:	Company marched via THEROUANNE, VERCHOCQ to HUMBERT & billetted there. Weather fine, roads good. Captain A.H. Lees posted to 27th Amn: Sub Park.	
2.30 pm 2nd HUMBERT.	Marched via ABBEVILLE to DOMQUER & billetted there — some trouble experienced owing to weak radius rods on Halley lorries. Weather fine, roads good.	
2 pm 3rd DOMQUER.	Marched via L'ETOILE to LONGPRÉ (les Corps Saints) & billetted there. — weather fine, roads good, no breakdown or casualties of any description	
2 pm 7th LONGPRÉ	Marched to FOURDRINOY & billetted there.	
6 pm 13th FOURDRINOY.	Marched via AMIENS to PONT NOYELLE & billetted there. Park now attached to the 10th Corps Amn. Park.	
15th — " —	Captain Wheatley Indian S & T.C. joined.	

2

Army Form C. 2118.

WAR DIARY
or
~~INTELLIGENCE SUMMARY.~~

(Erase heading not required.)

Instructions regarding War Diaries and Intelligence Summaries are contained in F. S. Regs., Part II. and the Staff Manual respectively. Title pages will be prepared in manuscript.

Hour, Date, Place	Summary of Events and Information	Remarks and references to Appendices
PONT NOYELLE 15th - 31st	Nothing further to record during the month, except Ammunition transactions which will be found in the Appendix. Weather generally during the month was fine, & state of the roads good. All lorries & other vehicles in good order & no casualties or breakdowns to record. H. H. Crawford, Major A.S.C. OC 2nd ?C Amn Park. B.E.F.	

(73989) W4141—463. 400,000. 9/14. H.&J.Ltd. Forms/C. 2118/10.

2nd Indian Cavalry Ammn. Park

Appendix "A" to WAR DIARY for month of August 1915

Ammunition Issues

Date	To whom issued.	Nature of Ammn.	No. of rounds.	Remarks
1915 Aug. 10	2nd Indian Cavy. Supply Col.	·303" S.A.A.	3,200	Refilled from Railhead FLESSERS
" 12	——— " ———	·303" S.A.A.	400	— " —
" 16	2nd Ind. Cavy. Divl. Ammn. Col.	Bombs for 95m/m trench mortar	48	— " —
" 18	——— " ———	·303" S.A.A.	349,000	— " —
" "	——— " ———	13 Pr. Shrapnel	46	— " —
" "	——— " ———	Webley Pistol.	2,760	— " —
" 20	——— " ———	13 Pr. H.E.	1,200	— " —
" 21	——— " ———	13 Pr. H.E.	780	— " —
" 24	——— " ———	·303" S.A.A.	99,000	— " —
" "	——— " ———	13 Pr. Shrapnel	236	— " —
" 28	——— " ———	S.A.A. ·303"	30,000	— " —
" 30	——— " ———	S.A.A. ·303"	96,000	— " —
" "	——— " ———	13 Pr. Shrap.	200	— " —
" "	4th Inniskilling Dragoons	S.A.A.	6,000	— " —
" "	10th Corps. Ammn. Park	French Bombs.	30.	— " —

H.A.S. Crawford Major A.S.C.
O.C. 2nd Ind. Cavy. Ammn. Park

Serial No. 55.

Confidential

121/7286

32
A.G.6

War Diary

of

2nd Ind: Cavalry Divnl: Ammunition Park

FROM 1st September 1915 TO 30th September 1915.

Confidential 2nd Indian Cavalry Ammunition Park (72 Company ASC)

Army Form C. 2118.

Instructions regarding War Diaries and Intelligence Summaries are contained in F. S. Regs., Part II. and the Staff Manual respectively. Title pages will be prepared in manuscript.

WAR DIARY
or
INTELLIGENCE SUMMARY.
(Erase heading not required.)

Hour, Date, Place	Summary of Events and Information	Remarks and references to Appendices
September 1915		
PONT NOYELLE 1st - 13th	Nothing to record	
14th	Orders received to proceed to FOURDRINOY on 15th inst.	
FOURDRINOY 15th	Marched to FOURDRINOY - no incident to record.	
17th	Marched to CAMPS-EN-AMIENOIS - " -	
CAMPS-EN-AMIENOIS 17th - 21st	Nothing to record	
22nd	Marched to DOMART ~~[illegible]~~ less 7 lorries detailed under Lieut Lee Evans for duty with Ambala Bde	
DOMART 23rd - 30th	Nothing further to record, up to end of month: During the month all S.A.A. of American manufacture was returned to railhead & exchanged. All 13 Pr H.E. of manufacture prior to 7/8/15 was sent to railhead for examination. Weather during the month changeable. Main roads good, but 2nd class roads becoming somewhat cut up.	
	30/9/15 H. G. S. Crawford Major ASC OC 2nd Ind Cav AP.	

2nd Indian Cavalry Ammn Park

Appendix "A" to War Diary for month of September 1915.

Ammunition Issues.

Date	To whom issued.	Nature of Ammn	No of rounds.	Remarks.
1915.				
Sept 1st	2nd I.C.D. Ammn Column	S.A.A "303"	124.000	—
" 3rd	" " " "	S.A.A "303"	60.000	—
" 4th	2nd Lancers.	S.A.A "303"	9.000	—
" 7th	2nd I. C. D. Ammn Column	Shrapnel	240 rds.	—
" 13th	2nd I. C. D. Ammn Column	Shrapnel H.E.	284 36	— —
" 20th	2nd I. C. D. Ammn Column	Shrapnel H E S.A.A	4 12 7.000	— — —
" 25th	2nd I. C. D. Ammn Column	S.A.A.	101.000	—
" 25th	Meerut Cal. Bdge. Secunderabade Cal. Bdge.	S. A. A S. A. A	60.000 60.000	— —
" 26th	2nd I. C. D. Ammn Column	Shrapnel S. A. A S. A. A.	24 11.000 30.000	— — —

W Wheeler Capt
~~Major. A.S.C~~
O.C. 2nd I.C.A.P.

Serial No. 55

Confidential

121/7601

War Diary

with appendices.

of

2nd Indian Cavalry Ammunition Park.

FROM 1st October 1915 TO 31st October 1915.

Instructions regarding War Diaries and Intelligence Summaries are contained in F. S. Regs., Part II. and the Staff Manual respectively. Title pages will be prepared in manuscript.

WAR DIARY
or
INTELLIGENCE SUMMARY.
(Erase heading not required.)

Army Form C. 2118.

Hour, Date, Place	Summary of Events and Information	Remarks and references to Appendices
October 1915		
Domart. 1st to 8th inst inclusive	Nothing to record.	
Domart. 9th inst.	Captain (Temporary Major) H. A. B. Crawford. A.S.C. left to take up the command of the 2nd G.H.Q. Ammn. Park. Captain W. P. R. Wheatley. S.T.C. took over command at 10 AM.	
Domart 10th and 11th inst	Nothing to record.	
Domart. 12th inst	Orders received at 8 pm to proceed to L'Etoile & to be clear of Domart by 10 AM. 13th inst.	
L'Etoile. 13th inst.	Left Domart at 9.40 AM. & marched to L'Etoile.	
L'Etoile 14th – 20th	Nothing to record.	

Instructions regarding War Diaries and Intelligence Summaries are contained in F. S. Regs., Part II. and the Staff Manual respectively. Title pages will be prepared in manuscript.

WAR DIARY
or
INTELLIGENCE SUMMARY.
(Erase heading not required.)

Army Form C. 2118.

Hour, Date, Place	Summary of Events and Information	Remarks and references to Appendices
October 1915.		
21st inst. ~~B~~ L'Etoile	Ambala Cavalry Brigade Detacht under Captain Lee-Evans rejoined — orders received to move to Bienecourt on 23rd inst.	
Bienecourt 22nd inst.	Nothing to record.	
Bienecourt 23rd inst.	Left L'Etoile at 8.45 A.M. & marched to Bienecourt arriving there at 11-45 A.M. Distance about 20 miles.	
24th-31st inst inclusive Bienecourt.	During the first half of the month the weather was fair to good & the roads good – towards the end of the month a good deal of rain fell, & the going, except on main roads became very heavy.	
	[signature] Captain. O.C. 2nd Ind: Cav: Amm. Park.	
31.10.15.		

(73989) W4141—463. 400,000. 9/14. H.&J.Ltd. Forms/C. 2118/10.

2nd Indian Cavalry Ammn. Park.

Appendix "A" to War Diary for month of October 1915.

Ammunition Issues.

Date.	To whom issued.	Nature of Ammn.	No of rounds.	Remarks
1915. Oct 4th	2nd I. C. D. Ammn. Column.	S.A.A. "303".	11.000.	
" 7th	" " " " "	" "	2.000.	
" 10th	" " " " "	" "	10.000.	

W Wheatley
Captain S&T. C
O.C. 2nd I.C.A.P.

Serial No. 55

121/7780

Confidential

War Diary

with appendices.

of

2nd Indian Cavalry Ammunition Park

FROM 1st November 1915 TO 30th November 1915

Instructions regarding War Diaries and Intelligence Summaries are contained in F. S. Regs., Part II. and the Staff Manual respectively. Title pages will be prepared in manuscript.

WAR DIARY
or
INTELLIGENCE SUMMARY.
(*Erase heading not required.*)

Army Form C. 2118.

Hour, Date, Place	Summary of Events and Information	Remarks and references to Appendices
B Nov. 1st 2nd + 3rd (BIENCOURT)	Nothing to report	
" 4th	Capt. Wheatley returned from leave	
" 5th 6th & 7th + 9th	Ordnance stores drawn & distributed to units	
" 10th	Indian Cavalry Corps Commander inspected the unit	
" 13th	Capt. H.G. Norman White arrived from GHQ to take over command from Capt. W.P.R. Wheatley	
" 14th 15th + 16th	Nothing to record.	
17th	Park left BIENCOURT for DRUEIL. Arrived complete at 4 pm. Distance 16 miles.	
(DRUEIL) " 19th	Drew ordnance stores from Railhead	
" 20th	Capt. W.P.R. Wheatley left for MARSEILLES. 10 Service Benz lorries arrived to replace ten of the present lorries	

(73989) W4141—463. 400,000. 9/14. H.&J.Ltd. Forms/C. 2118/10.

Instructions regarding War Diaries and Intelligence Summaries are contained in F. S. Regs., Part II. and the Staff Manual respectively. Title pages will be prepared in manuscript.

WAR DIARY
or
INTELLIGENCE SUMMARY.
(Erase heading not required.)

Army Form C. 2118.

Hour, Date, Place	Summary of Events and Information	Remarks and references to Appendices
DRUEIL		
Nov. 21st 1915	Drew ordnance stores from railhead	
" 22. 23. 24.	Weather very fine	
" 25th	17 Swiss Berna lorries arrived from ABBEVILLE bringing the total up to 27 of this make.	
" 26th	2/Lt Mulroney RHA proceeded on 8 days leave.	
" 27th	14 lorries were sent to ABBEVILLE replaced.	
" 29th	1 lorry sent to ABBEVILLE replaced	
" 30	Two lorries sent to the 1st Divl Supply Column	
	From the 12th pro. there have been several sharp frosts & falls of snow. No damage has been caused by them to equipment	
	1st December 1915 [illegible] Captain O.C. 2nd Ind Cav Div. Am Park	72 M.T. Co. A.S.C. 11 DEC 1915 INDIAN CAV. AMMTN. PARK

2nd Ind. Cavy. Ammn Park.

Appendix "A" to War Diary for month of November 1915.

Ammunition Issues.

Date	To whom issued	Nature of ammn	No of rounds	Remarks.
20th Nov.	Mobile Vety. Section, Meerut Cavy. Brigade.	S.A.A.	1000	
21 "	Divl. Ammn Column.	H.E.	24.	
"	" " "	S.A.A.	30,000.	

H. Mnemmert [illegible]

Captain. I.A.R.

Comdg. 2nd I.C.A.P.

CONFIDENTIAL.

WAR DIARY

of

DETACHMENT 2nd CAV. DIV. AMM. Pk ATTACHED TO 46th DIV. AMM. SUB Pk

Z Z

from 30/11/15 to 31/12/15

(VOLUME 1.)

Army Form C. 2118.

Instructions regarding War Diaries and Intelligence Summaries are contained in F.S. Regs., Part II. and the Staff Manual respectively. Title pages will be prepared in manuscript.

WAR DIARY

~~or~~

~~INTELLIGENCE SUMMARY.~~

(Erase heading not required.)

Hour, Date, Place	Summary of Events and Information	Remarks and references to Appendices
12 noon 30/11/15 AVROULT (Map HAZEBROUCK 5A, ⑤ 8,6.)	Left 2nd Cavalry Division Ammunition Park with eleven lorries, one motor car and two motor Cycles and proceeded to Aire (map. Sheet 36a, H28 Central) where I detached Sgt Symonds with three lorries and one motor cycle to proceed to 7th Div. Amm. Sub Park, at BAS RIEUX (Map Sheet 36a, U 24, A, 9,5) as seperate Detachment, whilst I continued with remainder to ST. VENANT (map Sheet 36a, P4, c, 1, 0) to be attached to 46th Div. Amm. Sub Park, arriving at 3 P.M. No road trouble. Reported to O.C. 46th Div. A.S.P. Motor Cyclist orderly reported 4-30 P.M. that Sgt Symonds had arrived safely at 7th Div. Amm. Sub Park.	
6 P.M.	Rendered "Marching in State" here.	
	30/11/15 John Pilbury Lieut. A.S.C. O/c Detachment 2nd Cav Div. Amm PK attached to 46th Div. A.S.P.	

(9 26 6) W 257—976 100,000 4/12 H W V 79/3298

Army Form C. 2118.

WAR DIARY

~~or~~

~~INTELLIGENCE SUMMARY.~~

(Erase heading not required.)

Instructions regarding War Diaries and Intelligence Summaries are contained in F. S. Regs., Part II. and the Staff Manual respectively. Title pages will be prepared in manuscript.

Hour, Date, Place	Summary of Events and Information	Remarks and references to Appendices
10 AM. 1 12/15 ST. VENANT	Reported to O.C. Town and sent in "Marching in State" and Billeting Particulars to him.	
10.30 A.M.	Went and found Ammunition Column at Q36 a,9,5 (Map Sheet 36 a) and saw O.C. there.	
12 NOON	Sent in Daily Ammunition return.	
5 P.M.	Received communication from O.C. R.H.A. asking me to report to him.	
9 A.M. 2 12/15	Went to Railhead to arrange about Supply of Ammunition.	
3 P.M.	Reported to O.C. R.H.A. at Lacouture (Map Sheet 36 a X 5, a, 5, 8), who wants four lorries daily for carrying bricks and slag for horse standings.	
11 A.M. 3 12/15	Reported to O.C. XIth Corps Parks at MERVILLE (Map Sheet 36 a K 29, d 1,5) Told to report all fatigue work done by lorries.	
2.30 PM.	Saw Sgt Symonds, who reported everything satisfactory	
4.0 PM.	Received instructions from O.C. R.H.A. to detail three lorries daily for carrying bricks and slag for horse standings.	
8 A.M. 4 12/15	Despatched three lorries on R.H.A Fatigues to Amm. Column.	
9.30 AM.	Rendered weekly returns to C.C. Amm. Park.	
11.30 AM.	Park lorries on Detachment here examined by M.T. Inspectors.	
7.30 A.M. 5 12/15	Despatched two lorries on R.H.A Fatigues to Amm. Column.	
11 A.M.	Rendered weekly billeting Details to O.C. 46th Div. a.S.P.	
11.30 A.M.	Sent weekly Ammunition Return to Amm. PK.	
7.30 AM. 6 12/15	Despatched three lorries on R.H.A. Fatigues to Amm. Column.	
11. AM	Sent Return of Personell and Vehicles to O.C. R.H.A. as requested.	

JmR.

Army Form C. 2118.

WAR DIARY

~~or~~

~~INTELLIGENCE SUMMARY.~~

(Erase heading not required.)

Instructions regarding War Diaries and Intelligence Summaries are contained in F. S. Regs., Part II. and the Staff Manual respectively. Title pages will be prepared in manuscript.

Hour, Date, Place	Summary of Events and Information	Remarks and references to Appendices
8 A.M. 7/12/15 ST. VENANT	Despatched three lorries on R.H.A. Fatigues to Amm. Column.	
11.30 A.M.	Replied to enquiry from O.C. R.H.A. that all Time Detonators had been removed from H.E. Shell.	
8.30 A.M. 8/12/15	Despatched three lorries on R.H.A. Fatigues to Amm. Column.	
2.30 P.M.	Received visit from Park Gunner officer, who brought new officer who is taking over, to inspect Ordnance Stores.	
6.30 P.M.	Received Demand from Amm. Colum for 360 Rounds Shrapnel to be sent up next morning.	
8 A.M. 9/12/15	Despatched 360 Rounds Shrapnel to Amm. Column and three lorries for R.H.A. Fatigues.	
11 A.M.	Refilled at Railhead.	
5.30 P.M.	Pte Pepper reported for Duty here with Sunbeam Car No 1752.	
8 A.M. 10/12/15	Despatched three lorries on R.H.A. Fatigues to Amm. Column.	
2 P.M.	Sent Sunbeam Car to tow Unic back to Park and return with Spares.	
8.30 A.M. 11/12/15	Despatched two lorries on R.H.A. Fatigues to Amm. Column.	
10 A.M.	Rendered weekly Returns to O.C. Amm. Park.	
3 P.M.	Cyclist Orderly returned from Park with Instructions from O.C. to send Sunbeam car to bring Gunner officer here to-morrow morning.	
6 P.M.	Received Demand from Amm. Column for 300 Rounds Shrapnel to be sent up in the morning	

JmR

(9 26 6) W 257—976 100,000 4/12 H W V 79/3298

Instructions regarding War Diaries and Intelligence Summaries are contained in F. S. Regs., Part II. and the S[...]f Manual respectively. Title Pages will be p[...]red in manuscript.

WAR DIARY
or
~~INTELLIGENCE SUMMARY~~
(Erase heading not required.)

Army Form C. 2118

Place	Date	Hour	Summary of Events and Information	Remarks and references to Appendices
ST VENANT	12 12/15	8.30 AM	Despatched 300 Rounds Shrapnel to Amm. Column and two lorries for R.H.A. Fatigues. Refilled at Railhead.	
		9.0 AM	Despatched Sunbeam Car to Park for Gunner Officer.	
		10.30 AM	Sent weekly Ammunition Return to Park.	
		11.0 AM.	Rendered Billeting Details to O.C. 46th Div. Amm. Sub Park here.	
		2.30 P.M.	Gunner Officer reported for Duty here.	
	13 12/15	8.30 AM.	Despatched three lorries on R.H.A. Fatigues to Ammunition Column.	
		2-0 P.M.	Despatched Sunbeam Car with Gunner Officer to O.C. R.H.A. 2nd Cavalry Division. O.C. R.H.A asked that next Issue of Shrapnel should contain No 85 Fuses.	
	14 12/15	8 AM.	Despatched three lorries on R.H.A. Fatigues to Ammunition Column.	
		11 A.M.	Received Demand from Ammunition Column for 600 Rounds Shrapnel and supplied same and refilled at Railhead. Reported to O.C. R.H.A. that no No 85 Fuses were available in Shrapnel Shell (as per note G.H.Q. a1011 d/14 12/15).	
	15 12/15	8.30 AM	Despatched three lorries on R.H.A. Fatigues to Ammunition Column.	
		5 P.M.	Issued Pay to Company Detachment.	
	16 12/15	8.30 AM.	Despatched three lorries on R.H.A. Fatigues to Ammunition Column.	
		9. A.M.	Returned Lorry No 3341 to Park with request that smaller lorry be sent for Duty here as the great width of Body on this lorry made it very difficult to pass other vehicles on these narrow roads.	
		11.30 AM	L/Cpl Hodgson reported accident to his motor cycle through Skid:- front wheel buckled, luggage carrier bent, bottom lug loose on Steering Head	
		2 P.M.	Lorry No 6095 arrived here in place of No 3341	

J.M.R.

Instructions regarding War Diaries and Intelligence Summaries are contained in F. S. Regs., Part II. and the St[illegible]f Manual respectively. Title Pages will be p[illegible]red in manuscript.

WAR DIARY
~~or~~
~~INTELLIGENCE~~ SUMMARY

(Erase heading not required.)

Army Form C. 2118

Place	Date	Hour	Summary of Events and Information	Remarks and references to Appendices
ST. VENANT	17/12/15	8 AM.	Received Demand from Ammunition Column for 428 Rounds Shrapnel. Delivered same and refilled at Railhead.	
		8.30 AM.	Sent three lorries on R.H.A. Fatigues to Ammunition Column.	
		10. AM.	Despatched Sunbeam Car to Park with L/Cpl Hodgson and damaged motor cycle together with Report of accident.	
		3 P.M.	L/Cpl Hodgson reported here with another motor cycle.	
		6 P.M.	Dr. Pepper reported having got back with Sunbeam Car, he having been delayed on journey owing to compensating Pin in Rear Brake Shoe breaking. This was repaired in AIRE (Map Sheet 36a H 28) by No 6 G.H.Q. Amm. PK. Workshops. O/c No 6 G.H.Q. Amm. PK. Workshops sent Report of Repairs done by him.	
	18/12/15	8 AM.	Despatched three lorries on R.H.A. Fatigues to Ammunition Column.	
		8.30 AM.	Received Demand from Amm. Column for 160 Rounds Shrapnel. Delivered same and refilled at Railhead.	
		11 AM.	Rendered Weekly Returns to O.C. Park per Sunbeam Car and returned with Spares	
	19/12/15	10 AM.	Despatched three lorries on R.H.A. Fatigues.	
		10.30 AM.	Received Demand from Amm. Column for 160 Rounds Shrapnel. Delivered same and refilled at Railhead.	
		11 AM.	Rendered Billeting Details to O.C. 46th Div. A.S.P. here.	
		11.30 AM.	Rendered Lorry Fatigue Details to O.C. XI Corps Parks.	

[signature]

1875 Wt. W593/826 1,000,000 4/15 J.B.C. & A. A.D.S.S./Forms/C. 2118.

Army Form C. 2118

Instructions regarding War Diaries and Intelligence Summaries are contained in F. S. Regs., Part II. and the Staff Manual respectively. Title Pages will be prepared in manuscript.

WAR DIARY

~~or~~

~~INTELLIGENCE SUMMARY~~

(Erase heading not required.)

Place	Date	Hour	Summary of Events and Information	Remarks and references to Appendices
ST. VENANT	20 12/15	8.15 AM.	Despatched three lorries on R.H.A. Fatigues to Ammunition Column.	
		3 PM.	Received Demand for 200 Rounds Shrapnel from Ammunition Column. Delivered same and refilled at Railhead	
	21 12/15	8.15 AM.	Despatched three lorries on R.H.A. Fatigues.	
		1 P.M.	Received Demand from Amm. Column for 200 Rounds Shrapnel and 14 Rounds H.E. Shell. Delivered same and refilled at Railhead with Shrapnel but not H.E.	
		2 P.M.	Sent Gunner Coyne back to Park as per Instructions received from O.C. and returned with Spares.	
		4 P.M.	Received Leave Warrant for Pte Newstead from Adj. XI Corps Parks.	
	22 12/15	8.15 AM.	Despatched three lorries on R.H.A Fatigues.	
		9.30 AM.	Received notification from O.C. 46th Div. A.S.P. for me to attend F.G. Court Martial to-morrow at 11 A.M. here.	
		10.30 AM.	Refilled at Railhead with H.E. Shell	
		2.30 P.M.	Received Demand from Amm. Column for 200 Rounds Shrapnel. Delivered same and refilled at Railhead.	
		3 P.M.	Received enquiry from Adj. XI Corps Parks re 44/80 Fuses in H.E. Shell.	
	23 12/15	8.15 AM.	Despatched three lorries on R.H.A. Fatigues.	
		10 A.M.	Received Demand from Amm. Column for 216 Rounds Shrapnel. Delivered same and refilled at Railhead.	
		11 A.M.	Attended F.G. Court Martial here.	
		2.30 P.M.	Despatched Sunbeam Car to Park for Spares.	

JmR

Instructions regarding War Diaries and Intelligence Summaries are contained in F. S. Regs., Part II. and the Staff Manual respectively. Title Pages will be prepared in manuscript.

WAR DIARY

~~or~~

~~INTELLIGENCE SUMMARY~~

(Erase heading not required.)

Army Form C. 2118

Place	Date	Hour	Summary of Events and Information	Remarks and references to Appendices
ST.VENANT	24 12/15	8.30AM.	Despatched three lorries on R.H.A. Fatigues to Ammunition Column.	
		10A.M.	Received Demand from Amm. Column for 300 Rounds Shrapnel. Delivered same and refilled at Railhead.	
		10.30AM.	Went to Merville (MERVILLE, Map Sheet 36 a K 29 a 7,6) on Sunbeam Car with Requisition signed by O.C. 46th Div. A.S.P. here for Twelve Hundred Francs. Received this amount from Field Cashier, returned and issued Pay to Detachment.	
		5 P.M.	Received Demand from Ammunition Column for 760 Rounds Shrapnel. Delivered same and refilled at Railhead at LAPUGNOY (Map Bethune Combined Sheet D 21 d 1,7.) none being available at our Railhead here.	
		6.30P.M.	Reported to O.C. 38th Div. A.S.P. here that we should be attached to them to-morrow as per Instructions from O.C. XI Corps Parks.	
	25 12/15	9AM.	Sent in "Marching in State" to O.C. 38th Div. Amm. Sub-Park.	
		11.A.M.	Sent weekly Returns to O.C. Park per Sunbeam Car and took Pte Chisholme back to Park as per Instructions from O.C. and brought back Pte Ellison.	
	26 12/15	8.30AM.	Despatched three lorries on R.H.A. Fatigues to Amm. Column.	
		9.30AM.	Rendered weekly Ammunition Returns to O.C. Park and Billeting Details to O.C. here. Went to Ammunition Column and examined state of roads taken by our lorries on their daily run.	
		11AM.	Received Demand from Amm. Column for 16 Primers 13 Pdr Q.F. These were obtained at and supplied from Railhead here.	

1875 Wt. W593/826 1,000,000 4/15 J.B.C. & A. A.D.S.S./Forms/C. 2118.

JmR

Instructions regarding War Diaries and Intelligence Summaries are contained in F. S. Regs., Part II. and the Staff Manual respectively. Title Pages will be prepared in manuscript.

WAR DIARY

~~or~~

~~INTELLIGENCE SUMMARY~~

(Erase heading not required.)

Army Form C. 2118

Place	Date	Hour	Summary of Events and Information	Remarks and references to Appendices
ST. VENANT	27 12/15	8.15 AM.	Despatched three lorries on R.H.A. Fatigues to Amm. Column.	
		9.30 AM.	Secured Lock-up Shed and have transferred Stores into same.	
		11 AM.	Obtained Shelter suitable for Lorries whilst being painted.	
		12 Noon	Lorry 2160 put under Shelter to be painted.	
	28 12/15	8.30 AM.	Despatched three lorries on R.H.A. Fatigues to Amm. Column.	
		2 P.M.	Despatched Sunbeam Car to Park for Spares.	
		5 P.M.	Received Demand for 148 Rounds Shrapnel from Amm. Column, to be sent up in the morning.	
	29 12/15	8.15 AM.	Despatched three lorries to Amm. Col. on R.H.A. Fatigues and sent up 148 Rounds Shrapnel and refilled at Railhead	
		3.45 PM.	Received Demand from Amm. Column for 198 Rounds Shrapnel. Delivered same and refilled at Railhead.	
		6 P.M.	Received Leave Warrant for Sergt Delamere from O.C. XI Corps Parks.	
	30 12/15	9 AM.	Despatched three lorries on R.H.A. Fatigues to Amm. Column.	
		10 A.M.	Found 13 Boxes of S.A.A. and one Box Cordite, in Billets previously occupied by troops, and salvaged same.	
		2 P.M.	Sent Sunbeam Car to Park for Spares.	
	31 12/15	8.30 AM.	Despatched three lorries on R.H.A. Fatigues to Amm. Column.	
		3 P.M.	O.C. Park called here and inspected Detachment.	
		5.30 PM.	Pte Coles returned his Motor Cycle from Amm. Column and reported broken front forks on same.	

31 12/15

J. Rubury Lt A.S.C.
O/c 2nd Cav. Div. Amm. PR Detachment
attached 38th Div. A.S.P.

1875 Wt. W502/826 1,000,000 4/15 J.B.C. & A. A.D.S.S./Forms/C. 2118.

Amm. Parks.

CONFIDENTIAL

WAR DIARY

DETACHMENT 2nd CAV. DIV AMMn Pk ATTACHED TO 46th DIV. A.S.P.

FROM 30/11/15 — TO 6/1/16

Vol

Instructions regarding War Diaries and Intelligence Summaries are contained in F. S. Regs., Part II. and the Staff Manual respectively. Title Pages will be prepared in manuscript.

WAR DIARY

~~or~~

~~INTELLIGENCE SUMMARY~~

(Erase heading not required.)

Army Form C. 2118

Place	Date	Hour	Summary of Events and Information	Remarks and references to Appendices
ST VENANT	1/1/16	8.30AM	Despatched three lorries on R.H.A. Fatigues to Ammunition Column.	
		10.0AM	Rendered weekly Returns to O.C. Park at BAS RIEUX, where Park has moved to to-day (Map Sheet 36A V 19 b 4.3.)	
		10.30AM	Received Demand from Amm. Column for 24 Primers Q.F. 13 Pdr. Obtained these from Railhead and despatched same to Amm. Col. per Sunbeam Car.	
		2 P.M.	Went out on Sunbeam Car and procured Front Forks for Pte Coles' Motor Cycle.	
		6.30PM	Returned one Lorry Load of Empty Shell cases to Railhead.	
	2/1/16	9 AM.	Despatched three lorries on R.H.A. Fatigues.	
		9-30AM	Rendered weekly Ammunition Return to O.C. Park	
		10 AM	Rendered weekly Billeting Details to O.C 38th Div. Amm. Sub. Park here.	
	3/1/16	2 P.M.	Went to Park on Sunbeam Car for Spares.	
		6 P.M.	Received Demand from Ammunition Column for Spare Gun Parts	
	4/1/16	9.AM	Despatched Spare Gun Parts to Ammunition Column and indented on Ordnance for same.	
		11 AM.	Lorry No 2160 finished being painted.	
		3 P.M.	Lorry No 5546 moved under Shelter to be painted	
	5/1/16	7AM.	Despatched Lorry No 6098 to ISBERGUES (Map Sheet 36A O,4,c,1,1.) to be re-tyred.	
		8A.M.	Despatched Lorry to Amm. Column for empty Shell cases and returned same to Railhead.	
		8P.M	Lorry No 6098 returned from being re-tyred.	
	6/1/16	8.30AM	Despatched Sunbeam Car to take Gunner Officer to report to O.C. R.HA. 2nd Cav. Div. He returned at 10AM. with Orders for Detachment to rejoin main portion of Ammunition Park at BAS RIEUX same day	
		2P.M.	Reported to O.C. 38th Div. Amm. Sub Park that we were ordered to rejoin our own Park and rendered Billeting Details for portion of current week. also sent in Report of move to O.C. Town.	
		4.30PM	Moved Detachment to BAS RIEUX arriving 6 P.M. no trouble with lorries on the way.*	

[illegible] Lt. A.S.C.

* joined up with the rest of the Park at TAILLY [illegible] O/c Detachment 2nd Cav. Div. Amm. PK

1875. Wt. W593/826 1,000,000 4/15 J.B.C. & A. A.D.S.S./Forms/C. 2118.

SERIAL NO 55

Confidential

War Diary

of

2nd Indian Cavalry Ammunition Park

FROM 1st December 1915 TO 31st December 1915

N.2011

Army Form C. 2118.

Instructions regarding War Diaries and Intelligence Summaries are contained in F. S. Regs., Part II. and the Staff Manual respectively. Title pages will be prepared in manuscript.

WAR DIARY
or
INTELLIGENCE SUMMARY.
(Erase heading not required.)

Hour, Date, Place	Summary of Events and Information	Remarks and references to Appendices
DRUEIL		
Dec. 1st + 2nd	Weather fine. Parades + driving exercises carried out.	
" 3rd 4th + 5th	Ammunition + fuzes drawn from Railhead + distributed.	
" 6th 7th 8th 9th + 10th	Parades + driving exercises carried out when weather permitted	
" 11th 12th + 13th	Drew ammunition from Railhead + distributed same.	
" 14th 15th + 16th	Parades carried out when weather permitted.	
" 17th	Park left DRUEIL at 3 pm on transfer to SENARPONT, arriving	
" "	there complete at 6 pm. An accident occurred when	
" "	leaving DRUEIL whereby an old lady was knocked over by a	
" "	cyclist. Her leg was broken + the cyclist's hand badly cut.	
" 18th 19th 20th 21st 22nd 23rd + 24th	Parades + driving exercises carried out when possible.	
" 25th	Xmas day observed as a holiday.	
26th 27th 28th	Ammunition drawn from railhead + delivered.	
29th 30th + 31st	Parades carried out when possible.	
NOTE	The whole month has been particularly wet, with very few intervals of sun shine. Opportunity was taken of all suitable times for parades + cleaning lorries.	

[illegible]
Capt. I.A.R.
OC 2nd Ind Cav. Div. Amm. Park

2nd Indian Cavalry Ammnᵗⁿ Park

Appendix "A" to War Diary for month of

December 1915.

Date.	To whom issued.	Nature of Ammnᵗⁿ	No of Rounds	Remarks
1-12-15.	Ammnᵗⁿ Column	S.A.A.	30,000.	
		Pistol Webley	1380.	
26-12-15.	Machine Gun School	S.A.A.	8,000	

H. E. Mormanwhite [signature]

Captain I.A.R.
O.C. 2nd I.C.A.P.

SERIAL NO 55

Confidential

War Diary

of

2nd Indian Cavalry Ammunition Park

(72 Coy ASC)

FROM 1st January 1918 TO 31st January 1918

Instructions regarding War Diaries and Intelligence Summaries are contained in F. S. Regs., Part II. and the Staff Manual respectively. Title pages will be prepared in manuscript.

WAR DIARY
or
INTELLIGENCE SUMMARY.
(*Erase heading not required.*)

Army Form C. 2118.

Hour, Date, Place	Summary of Events and Information	Remarks and References to Appendices
SENARPONT		
January 1st, 2nd.	Grenades drawn from Railhead CORBIE and distributed to units.	
" 3rd, 4th, 5th.	Nothing to report.	
" 6th	Interpreter A Lebrun was transferred from the Park and Interpreter Boussaller arrived	
" 7th, 8th, 9th, 10th, 11th, 12th, 13th, 14th, 15th, 16th	Nothing to report. Usual parades & driving exercises carried out. When weather permitted.	
" 17th	Very pistol ammunition drawn from CORBIE railhead.	
" 18th, 19th	Nothing to report.	
" 20th	Delivery of Very Pistol ammunition to 8th Hussars, 13th Hussars & 9th Horse	
" 21st	Lt (Temporary Capt) P.S. Whitcombe ASC arrived from No 2 GHQ Ammunition Park to take over the Command of the Park.	
" 22nd	Delivery of Very pistol ammunition completed. 1 box to each regiment in the division and also the Signal Squadron	
" 23rd	Capt H. G. N. White, IAR left for England. SAA Ammunition drawn from Railhead CORBIE	

Instructions regarding War Diaries and Intelligence Summaries are contained in F. S. Regs., Part II. and the Staff Manual respectively. Title pages will be prepared in manuscript.

Army Form C. 2118.

WAR DIARY
or
INTELLIGENCE SUMMARY.
(Erase heading not required.)

Hour, Date, Place	Summary of Events and Information	Remarks and References to Appendices
SENARPONT		
January 24th to 30th	Nothing to report.	
" 31st	Exchanged 295 rds Shrapnel uncapped for same number capped from Ammunition Column & issued SAA & Pistol Webley.	
	Weather during the month has been very mild, but the roads have usually wet and the going heavy.	
	1st February 1916. P. S. Whitcombe. Capt ASC O.C. 2nd Ind. Cav. Div. Amm Park	

2nd Indian Cavalry Ammn Park.

Appendix "A"

To "War Diary" for January.

DATE.	TO WHOM. ISSUED.	NATURE OF AMMN	No OF ROUNDS.	REMARKS.
11.1.16.	Machine Gun School.	S. A. A.	30,000.	
31.1.16.	2nd Ind Cav Ammn Column.	S. A. A Webley Pistol	35,000 3864.	

1/2/16

P. S. Whitcombe Captain ASC
O.C. 2nd I.C.A.P.

SERIAL NO 55.

Confidential

War Diary

of

2nd Indian Cavalry Ammunition Park

FROM 1st February 1916 TO 29th February 1916

Instructions regarding War Diaries and Intelligence Summaries are contained in F. S. Regs., Part II. and the Staff Manual respectively. Title pages will be prepared in manuscript.

WAR DIARY
or
INTELLIGENCE SUMMARY.
(*Erase heading not required.*)

Army Form C. 2118.

Sheet II

Hour, Date, Place	Summary of Events and Information	Remarks and references to Appendices
SENARPONT		
February 1st & 2nd	Grenades drawn from Railhead CORBIE and distributed to units. SAA delivered to Amn Column.	
" 3rd 4th 5th & 6th	Nothing to report	
" 7th	S.A.A and explosives delivered to Column.	
" 8th	Nothing to report.	
" 9th	Delivery of S.A.A. ammunition to Supply Column	
" 10th	Delivery of MG. S.A.A. to Machine Gun School.	
" 11th 12th & 13th	Nothing to report.	
" 14th	Explosives drawn from Railhead CORBIE.	
" 15th	Nothing to report	
" 16th	Orders received from Division for 13 pr Section to be ready to proceed with RHA Bde to 1st Army Area on 18th inst.	
" 17th	No 2 Section (Capt Lee Evans) getting ready to proceed if necessary to 1st Army Area. Orders received 7.30 pm for 13 pr Section to proceed at 6.30 am tomorrow (18th) to St VENANT, to be attached to 38th Amn Sub Park	
" 18th	No 2 Section left for St VENANT at 6.30 am, moving via OISEMONT – ABBEVILLE, HESDIN, FRUGES, THEROUANNE, AIRE, making midday halt at FRUGES. Information received from A.G.'s Office Base that percentage of [illegible] have been reduced to 25.	

Instructions regarding War Diaries and Intelligence Summaries are contained in F. S. Regs., Part II. and the Staff Manual respectively. Title pages will be prepared in manuscript.

WAR DIARY
or
INTELLIGENCE SUMMARY.
(Erase heading not required.)

Army Form C. 2118.

Sheet II

Hour, Date, Place	Summary of Events and Information	Remarks and references to Appendices
SENARPONT		
February 19th	Nothing to report.	
" 20th	Information received through Supply Column that D of T would inspect the Park tomorrow 21st inst. at 11.45 am. Wire from No 2 Section that they had reached St VENANT at 6.45 pm on 18th.	
" 21st	D of T arrived about 12.15 pm and inspected the workshops and some of the lorries & left again about 12.45 pm. All leave by DIEPPE cancelled.	
" 22nd	Webley Pistol ammunition delivered to Camp Commandant 2nd Indian Cav Div.	
" 23rd	S.A.A. Pistol Webley Amn and Explosives drawn from Railhead CORBIE.	
" 24th	S.A.A. drawn from Railhead. Explosives delivered to 30th Lancers.	
" 25th	Snowing all day & roads very bad	
" 26th	Explosives delivered to Amn Column. 6 inches of snow on ground & roads slippery	
" 27th	Nothing to report. Some snow & a slight thaw.	
" 28th & 29th.	No lorries out owing to thaw scheme coming into operation. Opportunity taken of a general clean up of the lorries & lines.	
	Apart from the snow at the end of the month, the weather on the whole has been fine & the going fairly good.	

1st March 1916. P. S. Whitcombe Capt ASC
O.C. 2nd Ind Cav Amn Park.

Appendix "A"

To War Diary for month of February.

Ammunition Issues.

Date.	To whom issued.	Nature of Ammn.	No. of Rounds.	Remarks
1. 2. 16.	2nd I.C.D. Ammn. Col.	S.A.A.	10,000	
7. 2. 16.	— do — do —	S.A.A.	20,000	
9. 2. 16.	— do Supply Column	S.A.A.	2,000.	
10. 2. 16.	Machine Gun School.	S.A.A.	4,000.	
22. 2. 16.	Camp Commandant 2nd I.C. Div.	Webley Pistol	864.	

R. S. Whitcombe Captain A.S.C.
O.C. 2nd I.C.A.P.

SERIAL NO 53

Confidential

War Diary

of

2nd Indian Cavalry Ammunition Park (Detached Section)

FROM 18th February 1916 TO 29th February 1916

ORIGINAL.

WAR DIARY

OF

DETACHMENT

2ND INDIAN CAVALRY AMM: PARK

ATTACHED TO

38TH DIVISION

FEB 18TH TO FEB 29TH 1916

VOLUME I.

Sheet 1

Instructions regarding War Diaries and Intelligence Summaries are contained in F. S. Regs., Part II. and the Staff Manual respectively. Title pages will be prepared in manuscript.

WAR DIARY
or
~~INTELLIGENCE SUMMARY.~~
(Erase heading not required.)

Army Form C. 2118.

1916 Hour, Date, Place	Summary of Events and Information	Remarks and references to Appendices
Friday Feb 18th	The detachment left SENARPONT at 6.30 am and marched via ABBEVILLE, FRUGES, AIRE to St VENANT arriving at the latter place at 4.45 pm. In accordance with orders reported to O.C. 38th ~~Amm~~ Sub Park and parked lorries in the town. Weather very wet.	
Saturday Feb 19th	Reported to SAA + DMG ~~+~~ to CRA 38th Division and enquired as to position of Amm Column	
Sunday Feb 20th	Arranged with O.C. Amm column as to Refilling Point.	
Monday Feb 21st	Weather + roads much improved. Very heavy firing heard from the South all night. Aeroplane engines heard overhead during the night.	
Tuesday Feb 22nd	Nothing to record. Weather very bad. Frost at night.	
Wednesday Feb 23rd	Nothing to record. Weather cold + frosty with snow.	
Thursday Feb 24th	Nine lorries were lent to the 38th Park to carry ammunition as a dump was being hastily made in anticipation of a thaw. All lorries returned safely	

Sheet 2

Instructions regarding War Diaries and Intelligence Summaries are contained in F. S. Regs., Part II. and the Staff Manual respectively. Title pages will be prepared in manuscript.

WAR DIARY
or
~~INTELLIGENCE SUMMARY~~.
(Erase heading not required.)

Army Form C. 2118.

Hour, Date, Place	Summary of Events and Information	Remarks and references to Appendices
Friday Feb 25th	Seven lorries made a second journey for the 38th Park and returned at noon. 200 rounds of Shrapnel were delivered to the wagon line of N Battery as the Amm Col had moved right back. This Ammunition was formed a dump and was not replaced from railhead. 80 rounds Shrapnel were delivered to the Amm Column. Heavy fall of snow during the night.	
Saturday Feb 26th	80 rounds Shrapnel drawn from Railhead. Rain & thaw began.	
Sunday Feb 27th	Nothing to record. Thaw continued & roads very wet.	
Monday Feb 28th	do.	
Tuesday Feb 29th	Two enemy aeroplanes over town at about 11.0 am. One was shot down by our machines and fell about 1 mile E of CALONNE-sur-Lys. The other made off towards the NE pursued by our machines.	

1.3.16

G Lee [illegible] Capt
O/c Detachment 2nd Ind Cav Amm Park

SERIAL NO 55

Confidential

War Diary

of

2nd Indian Cavalry Ammunition Park

FROM 1st March 1916 TO 31st March 1916

Confidential

WAR DIARY

of

2nd IND. CAV. DIVn AMn PARK

1st March to 31st March 1916

VOL XV

Instructions regarding War Diaries and Intelligence Summaries are contained in F. S. Regs., Part II. and the Staff Manual respectively. Title pages will be prepared in manuscript.

WAR DIARY
or
INTELLIGENCE SUMMARY.
(Erase heading not required.)

Army Form C. 2118.

Sheet I

Hour, Date, Place	Summary of Events and Information	Remarks and references to Appendices
SENARPONT		
March. 1st	Thaw scheme still in operation: no lorries working. 2000 rds N type SAA returned by 30th Horse, and 2000 rds issued to replace.	
2nd	Thaw scheme continued for a fourth day. Exchange of N type SAA with Amm. Column & turn over of explosives.	
3rd	Grenades drawn from railhead CORBIE and explosives returned to RE Park MONDICOURT.	
4th	Grenades drawn from railhead yesterday issued to units. Information received that G.O.C. 2nd Ind. Cav. Div. would inspect the Park on Wednesday.	
5th	SAA and Pistol drawn from Railhead CORBIE and N type returned. 2nd Ind Cav Div attached to 4th Army from today. Amm. Railhead changed to AUTHIEULE	
6th	Nothing to report	
7th	S.A.A. & Webley Pistol Amm. delivered to Amm. Column. G.O.C Division's inspection postponed till Thursday, March 9th	
8th	Nothing to report.	
9th	Inspection at 3 pm by G.O.C. 2nd Ind Cav Div, who expressed his satisfaction at the state of the lorries & men.	
10th	Nothing to report.	
11th.	Capt Lee Evans came in from Detached Section and reported they were at HERISSART attached to 10th Corps Park.	

Instructions regarding War Diaries and Intelligence Summaries are contained in F. S. Regs., Part II. and the Staff Manual respectively. Title pages will be prepared in manuscript.

WAR DIARY
or
INTELLIGENCE SUMMARY.
(Erase heading not required.)

Army Form C. 2118.

Sheet II

Hour, Date, Place	Summary of Events and Information	Remarks and references to Appendices
SENARPONT		
March 12th	S.A.A delivered to Amn Column. 16 men arrived from Base MT Depot bringing the Park up to Establishment.	
13th	SAA and Explosives drawn from CORBIE railhead. One of the 16 men who arrived from Base sick with Scarlet Fever and remainder had to be placed in quarantine for 16 days	
14th	SAA and Explosives delivered to Amn Column.	
15th, 16th, 17th	Nothing to report.	
18th	O.C ordered to report to DD of S&T 4th Army, with weekly returns, at 12 noon.	
19th	Nothing to report.	
20th	Lorry sent to railhead for SAA reported it had been moved to PUCHEVILLIERS. SAA delivered to Amn Column. Leave reopened.	
21st	New lorry indented for under authority from GHQ for carriage of grenades. Total Establishment of Park now to be 30 lorries and SAA Establishment to be 679,680 rds and 2600 grenades.	
22nd, 23rd, 24th	Nothing to report.	
25th	DD of T, Capt Davidson RE down from GHQ to look at Swiss Berna Springs.	
26th	Nothing to report. 13 men who were in quarantine now free.	
27th, 28th, 29th, 30th, 31st	Issuing SAA & Pistol Amn to regiments to complete them to new Establishment. R.S.M Spalding RHA attached to the Army Gunnery School of Instruction on 28th. With the exception of heavy snow at the beginning of the month and some snow showers at the end the weather has been fine & the roads good.	

1/4/16. P. S. Whitcombe Capt ASC
OC 2nd Indian Cav Amn Park

(73989) W4141—463. 400,000. 9/14. H.&J.Ltd. Forms/C. 2118/10.

Appendix "A" to "War Diary"

for the month of March 1916. for:–

2nd Indian Cavalry Ammunition Park.

Date.	To whom issued.	Nature of Ammn.	No. of rounds.	Remarks.
2-3-16	2nd I.C.D. Ammn. Column	S.A.A. + Webley Pistol	102,000. 5244.	
7.3.16	– do – do – do.–	S.A.A. + Webley Pistol	42000 1104.	
12.3.16	– do – do – do –	S.A.A. + Webley Pistol	9,000 1104.	
14-3-16	– do – do – do	S.A.A. Webley Pistol	21000 552	
16.3.16	Machine Gun Squadron.	S.A.A.	6000.	
20.3.16	2nd I.C.D. Ammn. Column	S.A.A.	2000.	
22-3-16	Camp Comd 2nd I.C.D.	Webley Pistol	390	
26-3-16	Signals 2nd I.C.D.	do do	276.	
27-3-16	2nd I.C.D. Ammn. Column	S.A.A. Webley Pistol	36000 3036	
" " "	8th Hussars	S.A.A.	21000	
" " "	9th Hodsons Horse	S.A.A.	20000	
" " "	20th Deccan Horse	S.A.A. Webley Pistol	25,600. 276.	
28.3.16	13th Hussars.	S.A.A.	23,000	
" " "	3rd Skinners Horse	Webley Pistol	276	
" "	Meerut M. G. Squadron	S.A.A.	21,000	
" "	30th Lancers	S.A.A.	29000.	
29.3.16	Meerut: M. G. Squad	S.A.A.	12,000	
" " "	18th Lancers.	S.A.A.	26000	
" " "	Skinners Horse.	S.A.A.	20000	
" " "	9th Hodsons Horse	S.A.A.	5,000	
30.3.16.	30th Lancers.	S.A.A.	4,000	

G. S. Whitcombe Captain ASC
O.C. 2nd I.C.A.P.

WAR DIARY

DETACHMENT

2nd INDIAN CAVALRY AMM PARK.

"

MARCH 1916

VOLUME II.

Instructions regarding War Diaries and Intelligence Summaries are contained in F. S. Regs., Part II. and the Staff Manual respectively. Title pages will be prepared in manuscript.

WAR DIARY

or

~~INTELLIGENCE~~ SUMMARY.

(Erase heading not required.)

Army Form C. 2118.

Hour, Date, Place	Summary of Events and Information	Remarks and references to Appendices
March 1916.		
1st to 6th	Detachment parked at St VENANT. Lorries sent daily to 38th A.S.P.	
6th.	300 rounds of N picked up from N Battery dump.	
8th.	Orders received at 7.0 pm to proceed to TALMAS on following day.	
9th	Marched at 9.0am with ten supply lorries 2nd Ind Cav Supply Col. Arrived TALMAS 4.15pm. Received orders to proceed to 10th Corps Amm Park. Arrived HERISSART 7.15pm & reported 10th Corps Amm Park. Billeted in HERISSART.	
10th to 31st.	Arranged refilling points with Amm Col. Supplied lorries for fatigue work, as required, to the 2nd Ind Cav Digging Park & also to RE Labour Battalion. No ammunition supplied to Column.	

[illegible] Capt A.S.C.

O/c Detachment 2nd Ind Cav Amm Park

(9 29 6) W2794 100,000 8/14 H W V Forms/C. 2118/11

SERIAL NO. 55

Confidential

War Diary

of

2nd Indian Cavalry Divisional Ammunition Park

FROM 1st April 1916 TO 30th April 1916

Instructions regarding War Diaries and Intelligence Summaries are contained in F. S. Regs., Part II. and the Staff Manual respectively. Title pages will be prepared in manuscript.

WAR DIARY
or
INTELLIGENCE SUMMARY.
(*Erase heading not required.*)

Army Form C. 2118.

Sheet I.

Hour, Date, Place	Summary of Events and Information	Remarks and References to Appendices
SENARPONT		
April 1st	Grenades for practice purposes issued to units.	
2nd	Nothing to report	
3rd	6000 rds SAA issued to Secunderabad Machine Gun Squadron. 13pr Section of Park rejoined from 10th Corps Amn Park, arriving SENARPONT at noon. Lorries running well and in good order.	
" 4th	SAA issued to XXth Deccan Horse.	
" 5th	All 13 pr HE Amn checked, counted, & oiled. Cleaning and overhauling lorries all day.	
" 6th, 7th	Nothing to report.	
" 8th, 9th & 10th	All 13 pr Shrapnel returned to railheads at CORBIE and PUCHEVILLERS, half to each. Also boxed shrapnel from Amn Column and Batteries collected and returned.	
" 11th.	Remainder of Shrapnel returned to railhead CORBIE. Grenades No 5 drawn from railhead PUCHEVILLERS to complete new establishment of Division. Information received from O.C. ASC. that establishment of cars of the Park was to be reduced to 3. Sending away Vehicle No 17542.	
" 12th.	Grenades No 5 issued to each Cavalry regt except 13 Hussars and 3rd Skinners Horse.	
" 13th & 14th	Nothing to report. Leave stopped.	
" 15th	SAA issued to all Cavalry regts except 13th Hussars and 3rd Skinners Horse. SAA, Pistol Very Amn, and the remaining grenades (except Nos 1 & 2) drawn from railhead PUCHEVILLERS.	

Instructions regarding War Diaries and Intelligence Summaries are contained in F. S. Regs., Part II. and the Staff Manual respectively. Title pages will be prepared in manuscript.

WAR DIARY
or
INTELLIGENCE SUMMARY.
(Erase heading not required.)

Army Form C. 2118.

Sheet II

Hour, Date, Place	Summary of Events and Information	Remarks and References to Appendices
SENARPONT		
April 16th.	SAA and Cavalry explosives drawn from railhead PUCHEVILLERS.	
" 17th.	SAA issued to Meerut Brigade, and grenades No 5 to 18th Lancers & 3rd Skinners Horse.	
" 18th	Nothing to report.	
" 19th	Lorry for carriage of Grenades fetched from 4th Army Troops S.C. Park now complete in new Establishment of 30 lorries. Information received that all HE 13 pr Amn except that with 85 or 100 fuses to be changed for that with No 100 fuzes & No 2 gaines.	
" 20th	Nothing to report.	
" 21st GOOD FRIDAY.	13 pr HE Amn collected from Amn Column for return to railhead.	
22nd	Nothing to report.	
" 23rd EASTER DAY.	All 13 pr HE returned to railhead CORBIE. Cavalry explosives drawn from railhead PUCHVILLERS. Church parade 2 pm.	
" 24th	Nothing to report.	
" 25th, 26th.	New 13 pr HE amn drawn from railhead CORBIE to complete division to new Establishment, and issued to Amn Column & Batteries. Establishment of Park in HE 13 pr Amn now is 666 rds. Leave reopened.	
" 27th	Nothing to report.	
" 28th, 29th, 30th.	Remainder of old pattern 13 pr HE amn collected from Amn Column and Batteries and returned to railhead CORBIE. Bi-monthly grenades (except Nos 1, 2) drawn from railhead PUCHVILLERS.	P. S. Whitcombe Capt ASC

NOTE: The middle of the month was very wet but the roads on the whole have been fairly good. Parades: have been carried out as often as possible.

11/5/16 O.C. ... Cavalry Amn Park

Appendix "A" to War Diary for month of

April. 1916.

2nd Indian Cavalry Ammunition Park.

Date.	To whom issued.	Number of Rounds.	Nature of Ammn.	Remarks.
April. 3.	Secunderabad M.G. Squadron	6,000	S.A.A.	
" 4.	20th Deccan Horse.	4,700.	"	
" 8.	Returned to Railhead.	1324.	13pdr. Shrap.	
" 9.	" " "	1320.	"	
" 11.	" " "	436.	"	
" 12.	9th Hodsons Horse.	552.	Pistol	
" 15.	20th Deccan Horse.	16,000	S.A.A.	
" 15.	9th Hodsons Horse.	16,000.	"	
" 15.	18th Lancers.	16,000	"	
" 15.	7th Dragoon Guards.	16,000	"	
" 15.	Poona Horse.	16,000	"	
" 15.	8th Hussars.	16,000	"	
" 15.	30th Lancers.	16,000	"	
" 17.	Meerut Brigade.	32,000.	"	
" 26.	Ammn. Column 2nd I.C.D.	990.	H.E. 13pdr.	
" 26.	"V" Battery R.H.A.	264	"	
" 26.	"X" " "	264	"	
" 23.	Returned to Railhead.	2649.	"	
" 29.	" " "	864	"	

SERIAL NO ....

Confidential

War Diary

of

2nd Indian Cavalry Ammunition Park (Detachment)

FROM 1st April 1916 TO ~~30th~~ 3rd April 1916.

Instructions regarding War Diaries and Intelligence Summaries are contained in F. S. Regs., Part II. and the Staff Manual respectively. Title pages will be prepared in manuscript.

WAR DIARY
or
~~INTELLIGENCE SUMMARY.~~
(Erase heading not required.)

Army Form C. 2118.

Hour, Date, Place	Summary of Events and Information	Remarks and references to Appendices
April 1st	Received orders to march on the 2nd to ST OUEN.	
2nd	Marched at 10.0 am and arrived ST OUEN at noon. Met the Amm Col & X Battery at ST OUEN. An orderly was sent to Hdqrs 2nd Ind Cav Division asking for march orders for the following day. Received orders to return to SENARPONT.	
3rd	Marched at 8.45 am and reached SENARPONT at noon & reported to Hdqrs 2nd Ind Cav Amn Park. – Handed in stores & rations.	

G Ker Shaw
2nd Lt R.S.C.
O/c Detachment 2nd Ind Cav Amn Park

(73989) W4141—463. 400,000. 9/14. H.&J.Ltd. Forms/C. 2118/10.

SERIAL NO 55.

Confidential

War Diary

of

2nd Indian Cavalry Divisional Ammunition Park.

FROM 1st May 1916 TO 31st May 1916.

Instructions regarding War Diaries and Intelligence Summaries are contained in F. S. Regs., Part II. and the Staff Manual respectively. Title pages will be prepared in manuscript.

WAR DIARY
or
INTELLIGENCE SUMMARY.
(Erase heading not required.)

Army Form C. 2118.

Sheet I.

Hour, Date, Place	Summary of Events and Information	Remarks and references to Appendices
SENARPONT		
May 1st	SAA & Pistol Amn issued to Amn Column. Bi-monthly grenades distributed to units.	
" 2nd	Nothing to report	
" 3rd	Explosives to complete to new establishments drawn from Railhead CORBIE.	
" 4th	Explosives distributed to regiments.	
" 5th	Nothing to report.	
" 6th	2nd Ind Cav Supply Column left SENARPONT for GAMACHES. Park was the only unit in this village	
" 7th	SAA issued to Amn Column.	
" 8th	Moved the lorries and parked them in the square vacated by the Supply Column	
" 9th, 10th, 11th, 12th	Nothing to report.	
" 13th	Cavalry explosives returned to RE Park MONDICOURT. Bi-monthly grenades SAA & Pistol Amn drawn from Railhead POCHVILLERS.	
" 14th	Nothing to report	
" 15th	Bi-monthly grenades issued to regiments.	
" 16th, 17th	Nothing to report.	
" 18th	SAA issued to Amn Column.	
" 19th	SAA issued to Amn Column and Ambala Brigade	
" 20th	Nothing to report.	
" 21st	SAA issued to 30th Lancers.	
" 22nd, 23rd, 24th	Nothing to report.	

Instructions regarding War Diaries and Intelligence Summaries are contained in F. S. Regs., Part II. and the Staff Manual respectively. Title pages will be prepared in manuscript.

WAR DIARY
or
INTELLIGENCE SUMMARY.
(Erase heading not required.)

Army Form C. 2118.

Sheet 2.

Hour, Date, Place	Summary of Events and Information	Remarks and references to Appendices
SENARPONT		
May 25th	SAA issued to Amⁿ Column and 30th Lancers.	
" 26th, 27th, 28th, 29th	Nothing to report	
" 30th	SAA issued to 9th Hodson's Horse	
" 31st	Orders received for Capt Lee Evans to report to Base M T Depot ROUEN for duty, and for Capt E. G. Pelly from 8th Divⁿ Supply Column to report here to replace him	
	NOTE The weather throughout the month has been fine, and the roads good on the whole though the surface is rough.	
	F. S. Whitcombe Capt ASC	
	1/6/16. OC 2nd Indian Cav. Amⁿ Park	

(73989) W4141—463. 400,000. 9/14. H.&J.Ltd. Forms/C. 2118/10.

2nd. INDIAN CAVALRY AMMUNITION PARK.

Appendix "A" to War Diary for month of MAY. 1916.

DATE.	TO WHOM ISSUED.	Nature of Ammn.	No. of Rounds	Remarks.
May 1st.	2nd Ind. Cavy. Divl. Ammn. Column.	S. A. A.	18,000.	
" "	" " " " "	Webley Pistol.	3,036.	
" 7th	" " " " "	S. A. A.	12,000.	
" 18th	" " " " "	"	25,000.	
" 19th	Ambala Cavalry Brigade.	"	21,000.	
" "	2nd Ind. Cavy. Divl. Ammn. Column.	"	25,000.	
" 21st	30th Lancers.	"	17,000.	
" 25.	2nd I.C.D. Ammunition Column.	"	61,000.	
" "	30th Lancers.	"	1,000.	
" 30th	9th Hodsons Horse.	"	1,000.	

72 M.T. Co. A.S.C.
31 MAY. 1916
INDIAN CAV. AMMTN. PARK

P. S. [illegible] Captain. A.S.C.
Comdg. 2nd Ind. Cavalry
Ammn. Park.

SERIAL NO. 55.

Confidential War Diary

of

2nd. Indian Cavalry Divisional Ammunition Park.

FROM 1st June 1916 TO 30th June 1916.

Army Form C. 2118.

Instructions regarding War Diaries and Intelligence Summaries are contained in F. S. Regs., Part II. and the Staff Manual respectively. Title pages will be prepared in manuscript.

WAR DIARY
or
INTELLIGENCE SUMMARY.
(*Erase heading not required.*)

Sheet 1.

Hour, Date, Place	Summary of Events and Information	Remarks and References to Appendices
SENARPONT		
June 1st	Capt E.G. PELLY arrived from 8th Div^n Supply Column and took over Command of the 13 pr Section from Capt G. LEE. EVANS, who left for Base MT Depot.	
" 2nd	2 lorries drawing SAA from railhead PUCHVILLIERS.	
" 3rd	SAA issued to Machine Gun Squadron. Orders received 2 pm that Park would move to GAMACHES on 6th inst.	
" 4th	Park left SENARPONT complete at 2 pm and moved via BLANGY to GAMACHES and parked in the street.	
GAMACHES		
" 5th	Cleaning lorries and arranging various billets and temporary stores.	
" 6th	SAA issued to Ambala Machine Gun Squadron. Information received that D.D of S&T Fourth Army would inspect the Park on 8th inst. Orders received to fill up with 13 pr Shrapnel for the division as soon as it became available at railhead, a total of 24 lorry loads.	
" 7th	Nothing to report.	
" 8th	D.D of S&T arrived 11.45 am and inspected the Park and left at 12.15 pm.	
" 9th	SAA for Machine Gun practice issued to Brigades, and 13 pr Am^n to Am^n Column.	
" 10th	Ammunition drawn from railhead CORBIE	
" 11th	SAA issued to Am^n Column.	
" 12th	8 lorry loads of shrapnel drawn from CORBIE railhead.	
" 13th	More shrapnel 13 pr drawn from railhead CORBIE, and issued to Am^n Column and X and N Batteries to complete them. Also SAA issued to Am^n Column. 21 lorries out on duty in all.	

Instructions regarding War Diaries and Intelligence Summaries are contained in F. S. Regs., Part II. and the Staff Manual respectively. Title pages will be prepared in manuscript.

WAR DIARY
or
INTELLIGENCE SUMMARY.
(Erase heading not required.)

Army Form C. 2118.

Sheet 2.

Hour, Date, Place	Summary of Events and Information	Remarks and References to Appendices
GAMACHES June 14th.	Balance of 13pr Shrapnel to complete the Division drawn from Railhead CORBIE. SAA issued to Amn Column. Summer time taken in and clocks advanced 1 hour at 11pm.	
" 15th	O.C. ASC, 2nd Ind Cav Divn interviewed Pte Deacon re his application for a Commission.	
" 16th	V. Battery completed with 13pr Shrapnel. Surplus grenades collected from regiments.	
" 17th	Nothing to report.	
" 18th	SAA issued to 13th Hussars. Surplus ammunition and grenades collected from Meerut Brigade, which is leaving the Division and being replaced by the Canadian Bde.	
" 19th	SAA issued to 18th Lancers and more SAA collected from Meerut Bde.	
" 20th	Nothing to report.	
" 21st	Collected SAA from Supply Railhead GAMACHES left there by 13th Hussars. SAA and explosives drawn from railhead CORBIE and grenades collected from Meerut Bde returned. Orders received 2pm for Park to move to OISEMONT at 2pm on 22nd inst; also that in the event of a forward move the Canadian Amn Park would be attached to this Park.	
" 22nd	Owing to lorries being retained for fatigues by the division, 5 lorries were sent on to OISEMONT in the morning, the loads dumped, and the lorries returned to GAMACHES at 12.30 pm. Park left GAMACHES complete at 2 pm and arrived at OISEMONT at 3.15 pm and parked in the Square.	
OISEMONT June 23rd	SAA and new explosives issued to Amn Column. Conference at O.C. ASC's office PONT REMY between OC's of the MT units of the Division and Canadian Bde about evacuating the lorries of the Meerut Bde. 14 lorries, 1 workshop, 1 Store, 1 Car, 3 motor Bicycles, 1 officer, 12 artificers, 2 Sgts, 38 drivers, and 12 RA ordered to be withdrawn from Park by GHQ, but as a result of conference, 8 lorries only were ordered to be held in readiness to go with proportion of personnel by O.C. ASC.	

Instructions regarding War Diaries and Intelligence Summaries are contained in F. S. Regs., Part II. and the Staff Manual respectively. Title pages will be prepared in manuscript.

WAR DIARY
or
INTELLIGENCE SUMMARY.
(Erase heading not required.)

Army Form C. 2118.

Sheet 3.

Hour, Date, Place	Summary of Events and Information	Remarks and References to Appendices
OISEMONT June 24th	Amn for 1½" Pistol Illuminating issued to 4 of the Regts and Secunderabad Machine Gun Squadron.	
" 25th	Information received that Park would move on 27th inst to QUERRIEUX area, time place, and route to be communicated later.	
" 26th	Proportion of all types of ammunition for Meerut Bde returned to railhead CORBIE. Orders received 7.30 pm for Park to move to BUSSY LES DAOURS at 6.30 am on 27th inst. At 8.30 pm orders received for the 8 lorries, held in readiness to go to be sent to GHQ Troops Supply Column HESDIN before the Park moves tomorrow.	
" 27th	8 lorries and 20 drivers left for GHQ Troops SC under Captain PELLY at 4 am, the latter to return to meet Park at BUSSY LES DAOURS after handing them over. Park left OISEMONT at 6.30 am and moved via AIRAINES - PICQUIGNY - AMIENS to BUSSY LES DAOURS arriving complete at 10.15 am. Weather very wet, and road allotted to Park unfit for lorries. Another road allotted at 11.20 am and parked there. CAPTAIN PELLY arrived back ~~about~~ at 3.15 pm	
BUSSY LES DAOURS " 28th	Ammunition for 1" Pistols Illuminating drawn from railhead CORBIE and all units completed to scale. OC Ordered to report at Q Office, Reserve Army at 11 am, when following instructions were received - While the Amn Columns of the Cavalry Division were located near the River D'ANCRE, Ammunition Parks would not be moved. Ammunition railhead to be CONTAY. In case of an advance necessitating lorries crossing the River D'ANCRE, the lorries to move by the PONT NOYELLES - ALBERT road and supply up the ALBERT - BAPAUME road. On the following day ammunition railhead to be ALBERT and the Parks to be moved there under orders from Reserve Army.	

Instructions regarding War Diaries and Intelligence Summaries are contained in F. S. Regs., Part II. and the Staff Manual respectively. Title pages will be prepared in manuscript.

WAR DIARY
or
INTELLIGENCE SUMMARY.
(Erase heading not required.)

Army Form C. 2118.

Sheet 4.

Hour, Date, Place	Summary of Events and Information	Remarks and references to Appendices
BUSSY LES DAOURS. June 29th	Standing by all day. Orders received 8.30 pm for Workshop and Store Lorries with Officer and artificer personnel, 1 car, 3 motor bicycles, 2 Sergeants, 5 drivers and 8 RA to be sent to GHQ Troops Supply Column HESDIN on 30th inst. The Canadian Bde Amn Park to take over the repair of the lorries and vehicles of this Park and necessary spare parts and stores to be handed over to them. Started packing up workshops and handing over stores at once. Permission given for car to be retained tomorrow and sent on July 1st.	by OC ASC
" 30th "	Revolver amn issued to 8th Hussars and Ambala Bde.	
11 am	2Lt DIAMOND, Workshop Officer, Workshop lorry, Store lorry, 3 bicycles, 12 artificers, 2 Sgts, 5 drivers, and 8 RA left the Park on transfer to GHQ Troops Supply Column. 2nd Lt CHATTERTON went to GHQ to interview the DAT with reference to his application for a regular Commission in the ASC.	
	NOTE The weather during the month on the whole was bad, with a few fine days. The roads were usually wet, but with the exception of the last 4 days transport was never difficult.	
	P. S. Whitcombe. Capt. ASC. OC. 2nd Indian Cav Amn Park	
	1st July 1916.	

(73989) W4141—463. 400,000. 9/14. H.&J.Ltd. Forms/C. 2118/10.

Appendix "A" to War Diary for the month of June 1916 for:– 2nd Indian Cavalry Ammnt. Park.

Date.	To whom issued.	Nature of Ammt.	No. of rounds.
3-6-16	Machine Gun Squadron.	S.A.A.	6,000.
" " "	" "	Webley Pistol	276.
6. 6. 16	Ambala Machine Gun Squadron	S.A.A.	6,000.
9. 6. 16	Meerut Brigade.	S.A.A	14000
" " "	S'bd Brigade	S.A.A	14,000
" " "	Ambala Brigade	S.A.A.	15,000.
" " "	2nd Ind. Cav Div Ammnt. Col.	H.E.	68.
11. 6. 16	2nd Ind Cav Div Ammnt. Col.	S.A.A	19,000.
13 6. 16	2nd Ind Cav Div Ammnt. Col.	Shrapnel	2,472
" " "	" " " " "	S.A.A.	19,000.
" "	"X" Battery, R.H.A.	Shrapnel	792.
" "	"N" "	"	792.
14. 6. 16	2nd Ind Cav Div Ammnt. Col	S.A.A.	24,000
"	" " " " "	Webley Pistol	1380.
16. 6. 16	"V" Battery.	Shrapnel	792.
18. 6. 16	13th Hussars.	S.A.A	15,000
19. 6. 16	18 Lancers.	S.A.A	10,000.
23. 6. 16	2nd Ind Cav Ammnt. Col.	S.A.A	45,000
28. 6. 16	17th Ammnt. Sub Park.	S.A.A.	7,000.
29. 6. 16	2nd Ind Cav Ammnt. Park	Webley Pistol	552.
30. 6. 16	Ambala Brigade	Webley Pistol	276.
30. 6. 16	8th Hussars.	Webley Pistol	276.

G. S. Whitcombe Captain ASC.
O.C. 2nd Ind. C.A.P.

SERIAL NO 55.

Confidential

War Diary

of

2nd Indian Cavalry Ammunition Park.

FROM 1st July 1916 TO 31st July 1916.

Army Form C. 2118.

Instructions regarding War Diaries and Intelligence Summaries are contained in F. S. Regs., Part II. and the Staff Manual respectively. Title pages will be prepared in manuscript.

WAR DIARY
or
INTELLIGENCE SUMMARY.
(Erase heading not required.)

Sheet I

Hour, Date, Place	Summary of Events and Information	Remarks and References to Appendices
BUSSY-LES-DAOURS		
JULY 1st	The two Parks Canadian and Indian Cavalry, were amalgamated for purposes of ammunition supply and transport, under the command of Major MORRISON, Canadian ASC, but were ordered to remain as separate units for interior economy and discipline. Three more lorries of the Indian Cavalry Park ordered to be held in readiness to be transferred to GHQ Troops Supply Column. The division moved up to BUIRE in the morning about daybreak, the Park remaining in its present position but the Division returned to BUSSY in the evening.	
2nd	Major MORRISON CASC ordered to report for duty to 1st Canadian Sub Park. Command of the combined Indian Cavalry and Canadian Parks taken over by Captain COCHRANE Canadian Field Artillery. The 2 lorries ordered to be in readiness to be transferred to GHQ Troops SC still standing by.	
3rd	Pistol Webley ammunition issued to Amn Column. The 3 lorries to be transferred ordered to proceed to GHQ Troops SC, HESDIN, tomorrow morning, after first dumping today at MERICOURT surplus stores of the Canadian Park.	
4th	SAA issued to 9th Hodson's Horse. The 3 lorries to be transferred left the Park for HESDIN at 4 am.	
5th	The remaining 2 lorries of those originally ordered to be transferred to be sent off to HESDIN tomorrow morning. Information received from 2Lt DIMOND that all the lorries from this Park at GHQ were under him and formed a Detachment from the 2nd Indian Cavalry Amn Park, the workshop being used for repairing L of C vehicles	

Instructions regarding War Diaries and Intelligence Summaries are contained in F. S. Regs., Part II and the Staff Manual respectively. Title pages will be prepared in manuscript.

WAR DIARY
or
INTELLIGENCE SUMMARY.
(*Erase heading not required.*)

Army Form C. 2118.

SHEET II

Hour, Date, Place	Summary of Events and Information	Remarks and references to Appendices
BUSSY LES DAOURS		
July 6th	SAA issued to 7th D.Gs. The two lorries for G.H.Q. with the drivers and 2 R.A. left the Park at 6.30 am.	
" 7th	Nothing to report	
" 8th	Webley Pistol Amn issued to Amn Column and Grenades No 5 to Poona Horse.	
" 9th	Webley Pistol Amn and Grenades No 5 issued to Amn Column	
" 10th	Nothing to report.	
" 11th	Various small quantities of Amn drawn from railhead CONTAY to complete	Appendix A.
" 12th	Nothing to report.	
" 13th	Division moved up to DERNANCOURT during the day, the Park remaining in present position.	
" 14th	Nothing to report	
" 15th	Secunderabad Brigade reported to have been in action, and a small quantity of Shrapnel and Grenades No 5, were sent up to the Amn Column near DERNANCOURT at 6 pm, also 2 gun wheels. O.C. ordered to report	
" ~~15th~~	to O.C. XV Corps Park, and informed that the Park would probably be under his orders for purposes of movement and would probably move tomorrow to VILLE SUR ANCRE. Aircraft raid over the lines about 11 pm apparently on AMIENS; 2 aeroplanes were heard but seemed to be driven off by the anti aircraft batteries. Amn Railhead changed to CORBIE.	
" 16th	Informed about 2 pm the Park would not move today. O.C. went to MERICOURT to reconnoitre for a place for the Park and reported on road in J.10.a.3.9. Map 62D. Ordered to move there tomorrow morning by O.C. XV Corps Park. Orders issued accordingly to move at 9.30 am.	

Instructions regarding War Diaries and Intelligence Summaries are contained in F. S. Regs., Part II. and the Staff Manual respectively. Title pages will be prepared in manuscript.

WAR DIARY
or
INTELLIGENCE SUMMARY.
(Erase heading not required.)

Army Form C. 2118.

Sheet III

Hour, Date, Place	Summary of Events and Information	Remarks and References to Appendices
BUSSY-LES-DAOURS JULY 17th	Park left BUSSY at 9.30 am and moved via QUERRIEUX - HEILLY - and RIBEMONT to MERICOURT arriving at 11.15 am and parked in a [illegible] outside. The road was very narrow and greasy and the lorries had to be backed up.	
MERICOURT JULY 18th	Grenades No 5 issued to Amm Column and [illegible] drawn from railhead CORBIE working all day on the road to enable lorries to pass.	
" 19th	Captain WHITCOMBE ASC [illegible] to take over Command of combined Parks with effect from 3.7.16.	
" 20th	Captain COCHRANE Canadian RFA left the Park to report for duty to the Canadian Corps.	
" 21st 22nd	Nothing to report.	
" 23rd	Division moved back to BUSSY LES DAOURS park remaining at MERICOURT.	
" 24th	Nothing to report.	
" 25th	SAA issued to Amm Column	
" 26th, 27th, 28th	Nothing to report.	
" 29th	SAA and Pistol Amm drawn from railhead CORBIE.	
" 30th	SAA and Pistol Amm issued to Amm Column. Information received that GOC division would inspect the Park at 10.30 am on Tuesday August 1st.	
" 31st	Inspected by O.C. ASC, 2nd Indian Cav Divn at 10.30 am.	
	NOTE The weather during the month [illegible] fine on the whole, though [illegible] changeable during the first fortnight. The roads are all very narrow and the going bad.	

1/8/16.

P. S. Whitcombe. Capt ASC.
OC 2nd Indian Cavalry Amm Park

(9 29 6) W 3332—1107 100,000 10/13 H W V Forms/C. 2118/10.

2nd Indian Cavalry Ammunition Park.

Appendix "A"

to

War Diary

July. 1916.

Date.	To whom issued.	Nature of Ammⁿ	Nº of Rounds.	Remarks.
3rd July	Ammⁿ Column 2nd Ind. Cavy. Divn.	Webley Pistol	3,312.	
"	" " " " "	S.A.A.	6,000	
"	" " " " "	Colt	900.	
"	" " " " "	Webley Pistol	1,656.	
4th	9th Hodson's Horse.	·303" S.A.A.	8,000.	
"	Canadian M.G. Squadron.	" "	13,000.	
6th	7 Dragoon Guards.	" "	2,000.	
8th	Poona Horse.	No 5 Grenades.	96.	
"	Ammⁿ Column. 2nd Ind. Cavy. Divn.	Webley Pistol	2,208.	
9th	" " " " "	" "	2760.	
"	" " " " "	No 5 Grenades.	96	
12th	Reserve Park.	Webley pistol	276.	
"	Canadian Brigade.	·303" S.A.A.	3,000	
15th	Ammⁿ Column. 2nd Ind. Cavy. Divn.	13 pdr. Shrap.	20.	
"	" " " " "	No 5. Grenades.	96.	
18th	" " " " "	No 5 Grenades.	108	
25th	" " " " "	·303" S.A.A.	31,000	
27th	" " " " "	13 pdr. Shrap.	2	
30th	" " " " "	·303" S.A.A.	18,000.	
"	" " " " "	Webley pistol	552.	

P.S. Wilcox Captain A.S.C.
Comdg. 2nd Ind. Cavy.
Ammⁿ Park

SERIAL NO. 55.

Confidential

War Diary

of

2nd Indian Cavalry Division Ammunition Park

FROM 1st August 1916 TO 31st August 1916

Instructions regarding War Diaries and Intelligence Summaries are contained in F. S. Regs., Part II. and the Staff Manual respectively. Title pages will be prepared in manuscript.

WAR DIARY
or
INTELLIGENCE SUMMARY.
(Erase heading not required.)

Army Form C. 2118.

2nd D.C. Amn Park

Sheet I

Hour, Date, Place	Summary of Events and Information	Remarks and References to Appendices
MERICOURT		
AUGUST 1st.	G.O.C. Division arrived at 10.45 am and inspected the Park and left again at 11.30 am.	
" 2nd	Pistol Amn and Cartridges Illuminating 1 inch supplied to Amn Column. Orders received from A.D. of S.&T. Fourth Army to fit 2 pairs of each of the various types of Lorry Springs now in charge and to have them ready for an inspection by a representative from the D of T.	
" 3rd 4th	Nothing to report.	
" 5th	Pistol Amn issued to Amn Column and 12 damaged rds 18 pr HE exchanged.	
" 6th	Nothing to report.	
" 7th	SAA issued to Canadian Amn Column. Orders received 6 pm to move tomorrow at 5 am to BOUILLANCOURT. Orders issued for move at once.	
" 8th	Park left MERICOURT 5 am and moved via CORBIE - VEQUEMONT - AMIENS - TERRAMESNIL - MOLLIENS - SENARPONT to BOUILLANCOURT arriving at 11 am. Canadian Park followed at 5 minutes interval but was delayed on the road and arrived at 2 pm. 2nd Lt CHATTERTON ASC (SR) gazetted 2nd Lt ASC dated July 23rd.	
BOUILLANCOURT AUGUST 9th	Nothing to report.	

Instructions regarding War Diaries and Intelligence Summaries are contained in F. S. Regs., Part II. and the Staff Manual respectively. Title pages will be prepared in manuscript.

Army Form C. 2118.

WAR DIARY
or
INTELLIGENCE SUMMARY.
(Erase heading not required.)

Sheet II

Hour, Date, Place	Summary of Events and Information	Remarks and References to Appendices
BOUILLANCOURT AUGUST 10th	OC ASC came in at 11.30 am with orders to move to RAMBURES at 2 pm. Moved accordingly via HATTEBLERY arriving at 2.30 pm and parked in the village.	
RAMBURES AUGUST 11th	Nothing to report.	
12th	SAA issued to Armoured Cars. Park inspected at 2 pm by Inspectors from DQT; lorries all in good order and clean. Orders received for section of 13 pr lorries for one battery to proceed tomorrow to SOUES for attachment to XV Corps. 4 lorries got ready to go under Captain PELLY.	
" 13th	Grenades No 5 and SAA issued to Strathcona Horse. Capt PELLY with 4 lorries and one motor cycle and proportion of amn for X Battery left RAMBURES at 12.30 pm and proceeded to SOUES via BISEMONT and AIRAINES for attachment to XV Corps. TLt J. DRURY ASC. arrived from MT School at St OMER for duty.	
" 14th	Capt PELLY arrived back in the evening having handed over the 4 lorries for X Battery to be attached to No 14 ASP.	
" 15th	TCapt PELLY ASC ordered to report to DQ S&T, base Office being replaced by TLt J. DRURY ASC.	
" 16th	Capt PELLY left for England.	
" 17th to 24th (incl)	Nothing to report.	

(9 29 6) W 3332—1107 100,000 10/13 H W V Forms/C. 2118/10.

Instructions regarding War Diaries and Intelligence Summaries are contained in F. S. Regs., Part II. and the Staff Manual respectively. Title pages will be prepared in manuscript.

WAR DIARY
or
INTELLIGENCE SUMMARY.
(Erase heading not required.)

Army Form C. 2118.

Sheet III

Hour, Date, Place	Summary of Events and Information	Remarks and References to Appendices
RAMBURES. AUGUST 25th	Inspector from GHQ arrived to inspect Lorry Springs. Information received from that Park (less SAA Section) would probably move East tomorrow.	
" 26th	Orders received 7.30 am for Park to proceed to AILLY. Less SAA Section & 2nd Ind Cav Section of Park would move thence on 27th under orders of O.C. RHA Bde and Canadian Section of Park to move on 28th under orders of O.C. Canadian RHA Bde. After interview with AA & QMG, 2nd ICD, orders were issued for 13pr Sections of Park only to proceed. HQ and Workshops remaining with SAA Section. Lt DRURY with 1 car, 4 lorries and 1 motor cycle (proportion of Park for N battery) and Lt YOUNG Can ASC with 1 car, 7 lorries and 1 motor cycle (for Canadian batteries) left RAMBURES at 2 pm and moved via OISEMONT, AIRAINES, PIQUIGNY to AILLY. 2Lt CHATTERTON ASC took over SAA Section & workshops of Canadians from Lt YOUNG during his absence.	
" 27th	Authority received for 13pr Amn to be drawn from railhead CORBIE to replace that expended by Canadian Batteries. Authority forwarded to Canadian Detachment for compliance. Church Parade 11.30 am.	
" 28th	Nothing to report.	
" 29th	Establishment of 12th reduced by 48 N and 12 NX owing to [illegible] [illegible] Bde [illegible] [illegible].	
" 30th 31st	Nothing to report.	

(9 29 6) W 3332—1107 100,000 10/13 H W V Forms/C. 2118/10.

NOTE. The bottom part of the track [illegible] very stony, but the lorries [illegible] quickly and were clean [illegible].

P. S. Whitcombe Capt ASC
OC 2nd Indian Cav Amn Park.
1/9/16

2nd Indian Cavy Ammn Park.

Appendix "A" to War Diary for month of:-

August. 1916.

Date.	To whom issued.	Nature of Ammn	Number of Rounds.	Remarks.
Aug. 2nd	Ammn Column 2nd Ind. Cavy Divn	Webley pistol	552.	
" "	" " " " " "	1" illuminating	600.	
" 3rd	" " " " " "	Webley pistol	1656.	
" 5th	" " " " " "	" "	2208.	
" "	" " " " " "	H. E.	12.	
" 7th	Ammn Column 2nd I.C.D. (Canadian portion)	Webley pistol	3864	
" "	" " " " "	·303" S.A.A.	18,000.	
" "	" " " " "	Colt.	200.	
" 12	No 1 Light Armoured Car Battery	·303" S.A.A.	10,000	
" 13	Strathcona Horse.	Grenade No 5	60.	
" "	" "	·303" S.A.A.	9,000	

P. S. Whitcombe Capt. A.S.C.
Comdg. 2nd Ind. Cavy. A. Park

1/9/16.

SERIAL NO 55.

Confidential

War Diary

of

2nd Indian Cavalry Ammunition Park

FROM 1st September 1916 TO 30th September 1916.

Army Form C. 2118.

Instructions regarding War Diaries and Intelligence Summaries are contained in F. S. Regs., Part II. and the Staff Manual respectively. Title pages will be prepared in manuscript.

WAR DIARY
or
INTELLIGENCE SUMMARY.
(Erase heading not required.)

Sheet 1.

Hour, Date, Place	Summary of Events and Information	Remarks and References to Appendices
RAMBURES September 1st	Nothing to report.	
" 2nd	SAA issued to Amn Column and Strathcona's Horse.	
" 3rd 4th	Nothing to report.	
" 5th	SAA issued to Amn Column. Information rec'd 10 pm that Division should be prepared to move at 4 am tomorrow. Orders were issued to pack up at once and be prepared to move at half an hours notice.	
" 6th	Information received at 2 am that Division would be at CAVILLON for night of 6/7th Sept. Orders for move of Park would be issued later. Orders received 4 pm for Park to move to BUSSY-LES-DAOURS. Park left RAMBURES 5.35 pm and moved via SENARPONT – HORNOY – MOLLIENS-VIDAME – AMIENS to BUSSY, arriving 11 pm and parked on the ALLONVILLE road.	
BUSSY-LES-DAOURS " 7th	SAA drawn from Railhead CORBIE and 3 pr Amn issued to No 9 Armoured Car Battery.	
" 8th	Nothing to report.	
" 9th	SAA issued to Canadian M.G. Squadron and R[?] Grenadiers No's to No 9 Armoured Car Battery. Information received that Detachments of Park for "N" & "X" Batteries would return to Park.	

Instructions regarding War Diaries and Intelligence Summaries are contained in F. S. Regs., Part II. and the Staff Manual respectively. Title pages will be prepared in manuscript.

WAR DIARY
or
INTELLIGENCE SUMMARY.
(*Erase heading not required.*)

Army Form C. 2118.

Sheet II.

Hour, Date, Place	Summary of Events and Information	Remarks and References to Appendices
BUSSY-LES-DAOURS September 10th	Detachments for "N" & "X" Batteries returned in afternoon, the former fed up with ammunition, the latter empty. Information received that Park was at the disposal of the GOC RA Cavalry Corps for the purpose of forming a dump	
11th	Orders received 7.30 pm for all available lorries to proceed at 5am tomorrow morning to LA BOISSELLE and dump 13 pr and SAA amn. Then return to railhead at EDGEHILL and draw up to complete Dump at LA BOISSELLE to establishment of 10,000 rds N, 10,000 rds NX, 3600 A, 3600 AX, 300 E, and 500,000 SAA. Fatigue parties for dump at LA BOISSELLE and also for another at LA BRIQUETERIE, near MONTAUBAN, to be picked up at 5.15 am and taken up with the lorries. Orders were issued for 2Lt CHATTERTON to take charge of 18 lorries for the Dump and 2Lt MALONY to take charge at Railhead.	
12th	2Lt CHATTERTON left Park at 5 am with 18 lorries and proceeded to work on forming the Dump at LA BOISSELLE. 2 of the lorries were sent on to LA BRIQUETERIE with the fatigue party for the other dump. Ammunition train did not arrive	

Instructions regarding War Diaries and Intelligence Summaries are contained in F. S. Regs., Part II. and the Staff Manual respectively. Title pages will be prepared in manuscript.

WAR DIARY
or
INTELLIGENCE SUMMARY.
(Erase heading not required.)

Army Form C. 2118.

Sheet III

Hour, Date, Place	Summary of Events and Information	Remarks and References to Appendices
BUSSY LES DAOURS September 12th	at EDGEHILL till 5 pm and the lorries had to wait there for it. SAA and nearly half the 13 pr Amn was got up to the Dump during the day. Informed at EDGEHILL that A and AX ammunition must be drawn at CONTAY. Canadian 13 pr Detachment returned to Park at 6 pm empty.	
13th	Work on the Dump was delayed during the night by heavy shelling of the road and round the Dump from 9.30 pm last night to 6 am. Lorries continued to work on the Dump all day and completed all amn except A and AX from CONTAY by 3 pm. Half the amn from CONTAY was then taken up and the men given 3 hours rest. Orders were received at 10 am for the Canadian 13 pr lorries to collect the amn left with XV Corps Park and complete the Amn Column to establishment at once. This was completed by 10 pm. ~~Owing~~ Orders were received at 5 pm for the Park to move up to ALBERT. Owing to every available lorry being employed on the Dump, sanction was obtained from Cavalry Corps to move tomorrow morning (14th inst). Orders were therefore issued to move at 9 am. Orders were received that the Dump was to be kept up to establishment by the Park. It was therefore arranged that a motor cyclist should remain at the Dump to communication.	

(9 29 6) W 3332—1107 100,000 10/13 H W V Forms/C. 2118/10.

Instructions regarding War Diaries and Intelligence Summaries are contained in F. S. Regs., Part II. and the Staff Manual respectively. Title pages will be prepared in manuscript.

WAR DIARY
or
INTELLIGENCE SUMMARY.
(*Erase heading not required.*)

Army Form C. 2118.

Sheet IV.

Hour, Date, Place	Summary of Events and Information	Remarks and References to Appendices
BUSSY LES DAOURS September 14th. ALBERT.	The Park left BUSSY at 9 am and moved via QUERRIEUX - RIBEMONT - DERNANCOURT to MOULIN D HUILE, ALBERT arriving at 11 am and parked in an open space in front of the mill. The last load of ammunition was got up to the Dump at 12 noon and the Dump reported complete accordingly. 7 lorries then returned to CONTAY to fill up the Park to Establishment in SAA getting back to the Park at ALBERT at 6 pm. Information received from Cavalry Corps at 5 pm that Amn Railhead in future would be CONTAY. Orders were issued to draw up balance of 18 pr amn to complete Park to Establishment tomorrow morning.	
September 15th	Lorries left 9 am to draw up balance of 18 pr amn from CONTAY. A few shells fell in ALBERT during the day but none near the Park.	
16th	All 13 pr amn with 44/80 fuze was examined and cleaned. ALBERT was shelled from 6 pm to 9 pm. At 7.15 pm shells began to [illegible] in the vicinity of the Park; the lorries were therefore at once started up and spread out as far as possible in a neighbouring field and down a lane. One shell fell on the edge of the square just as the last lorry was got out. The men behaved well and the lorries were clear of the square within 5 minutes of the order to start up. There were no casualties. Lorries left spread out during the night.	

Instructions regarding War Diaries and Intelligence Summaries are contained in F. S. Regs., Part II. and the Staff Manual respectively. Title pages will be prepared in manuscript.

WAR DIARY

or

INTELLIGENCE SUMMARY.

(Erase heading not required.)

Army Form C. 2118.

Sheet V.

Hour, Date, Place	Summary of Events and Information	Remarks and References to Appendices
ALBERT September 17th	Division moved back to BUSSY. The lorries that were ditched overnight in spreading out were got out and the lorries parked in as open an order as the locality would admit. The HE and Shrapnel lorries were placed as far away from the others as possible and the Grenade lorry away to the side in a field. It was impossible to get more than 10 yards between each lorry, owing to there being only one road into the Park; nothing more could be done in the event of further shelling. Orders were therefore issued for the men to get under cover and await orders in this eventuality.	
" 18th	Weather very wet and the men were engaged all day in improving the lorry standings.	
" 19th	The town was shelled in the middle of the day and again about 9 pm when the shells came rather close. Owing to the state of the ground it was impossible to move the lorries by night, and the men were therefore got under cover.	
" 20th	Proportion of the Spare Gun Parts handed over to the Ord^n Officer. ALBERT was shelled at intervals at ~~night~~ last night and during the morning, but none fell very near the Park.	
" 21st	Shells fell very near the Park from 2.30 pm to 4 pm. The Dump at LA BOISSELLE was hit by a shell at 9.15 pm and blew up, the bicycle belonging to the orderly from the Park being destroyed.	

Instructions regarding War Diaries and Intelligence Summaries are contained in F. S. Regs., Part II. and the Staff Manual respectively. Title pages will be prepared in manuscript.

WAR DIARY
or
INTELLIGENCE SUMMARY.
(*Erase heading not required.*)

Army Form C. 2118.

Sheet VI

Hour, Date, Place	Summary of Events and Information	Remarks and References to Appendices
ALBERT September 22nd	Report was sent in [illegible] area round the Park had been frequently shelled during the past few days and it was considered only a matter of time before the ammunition lorries were hit. Verbal orders were received from AQMG Cav Corps to move somewhere in the neighbourhood of the 1st Ind Cav Park. After a position had been found the Park left ALBERT at 5 pm and moved down the ALBERT–BRAY road to a field half a mile South of MEAULTE and parked there, arriving 6 pm.	
MEAULTE September 23rd	Orders received from Division 7.30 pm to move to BUSSY at 10 am. Left accordingly and proceeded via MERICOURT – CORBIE – DAOURS arriving BUSSY 12 noon and parked on ALLONVILLE–BUSSY road.	
BUSSY LES DAOURS September 24th	SAA Grenades No 5 + 13 pr am[illegible] issued to Amn Column.	
25th	Orders received at midnight (25th–26th) for SAA Section to move to RAMBURES at 7.30 am 26th. Orders issued accordingly.	
26th	SAA Section, consisting of 10 lorries, 1 car and 1 motorcycle, left with 2/Lt CHATTERTON at 7.30 am for RAMBURES via AMIENS and MOLLIENS VIDAME. Orders rec'd for 2nd Ind 13 pr Section to proceed to AILLY for attachment to XV Corps Park and Canadian 13 pr Section to proceed to MARICOURT to XIV Corps Park. These orders were cancelled at 10 pm.	
27th	Grenades drawn from CONTAY. Information received from 2/Lt CHATTERTON SAA Section were at MONTAGNE, having been ordered there shortly after arriving at RAMBURES on 26th inst.	

(9 29 6) W 3332—1107 100,000 10/13 H W V Forms/C. 2118/10.

Army Form C. 2118.

Instructions regarding War Diaries and Intelligence Summaries are contained in F. S. Regs., Part II. and the Staff Manual respectively. Title pages will be prepared in manuscript.

WAR DIARY
or
INTELLIGENCE SUMMARY.
(*Erase heading not required.*)

Sheet VII

Hour, Date, Place	Summary of Events and Information	Remarks and References to Appendices
AUSSY LES DAOURS.		
September 28th	Grenades drawn yesterday sent on to SAA Section at MONTAGNE.	
" 29th 30th	Nothing to report.	
	Note. The weather on the whole during the month was fine, and the roads dry, though very rough & worn.	
	P. S. Whitcombe Capt. ASC.	
	OC. 2nd Indian Cavalry Amn Park.	
	1/10/16	

(9 29 6) W 3332–1107 100,000 10/13 H W V Forms/C. 2118/10.

2nd Indian Cavalry Ammunition Park

Appendix "A" to War Diary

for month of September. 1916.

Date.	To whom issued.	Number of Rounds.	Nature of Amm.n	Remarks.
2-9-16.	Lord Strathcona's Horse.	552	Webley Pistol.	
" " "	" "	200	Colt.	
" " "	2nd Indian Cavalry Divl. Amm.n Column.	6,000.	S.A.A.	
5-9-16.	" " " " " "	37,000.	"	
" " "	" " " " " "	2,208.	Webley Pistol.	
7-9-16.	No 9 Light Armoured Car Battery.	2,000.	S.A.A.	
" " "	" " " " "	16	3pdr.	
" " "	Fort Garry Horse	3,000.	S.A.A.	
9-9-16	Canadian M.G. Squadron.	15,000.	S.A.A.	
" " "	No 9. Light Armoured Car Battery.	216.	Grenades No 5	
12-9-16.	Ammunition Dump.	10,000.	N.	
13-9-16	" "	10,000.	N.X.	
14-9-16.	" "	3,600	A.	
	" "	3,600	A.X.	
	" "	300.	E.	
	" "	500,000.	S.A.A.	
16-9-16.	2nd Ind. Cavy. Divl. Amm.n Column.	2 boxes.	1" Pistol illuminating	
24-9-16.	" " " " " "	552.	Webley Pistol	
" " "	" " " " " "	432.	Grenades No 5.	
" " "	" " " " " "	4.	N.	
" " "	" " " " " "	4.	N.X.	
25-9-16	" " " " " "	144	Grenades No 5.	

P. Whitehead Captain, ASC.
Comdg. 2nd Ind. Cavy. A. Park.

Duplicate

Lieut. Wrench

R/946

CONFIDENTIAL

WAR DIARY

of

2nd INDIAN CAVALRY AMN PARK

October 1st to 31st 1916

Vol XXII

Instructions regarding War Diaries and Intelligence Summaries are contained in F. S. Regs., Part II. and the Staff Manual respectively. Title pages will be prepared in manuscript.

WAR DIARY

or

INTELLIGENCE SUMMARY.

(*Erase heading not required.*)

Army Form C. 2118.

Hour, Date, Place	Summary of Events and Information	Remarks and References to Appendices
BUSSY LES DAOURS OCTOBER 1st 2nd	Nothing to report.	
3rd	Afternoon No 5 [illegible] from BUSSY by [illegible] Section and [illegible]	
4th	Nothing to report.	
5th	Orders rec'd for Canadian 17pr Section to proceed to MARICOURT for attachment to XIV Corps Park. Section left about 11 am under Lt YOUNG. Orders rec'd for Indian 17pr Section to move tomorrow to BUIRE for attachment to XV Corps Park.	
6th	3rd Indian 17pr Section under Lt DRURY left at 10 am and proceeded via QUERRIEUX, RIBEMONT to BUIRE for attachment to No 14 A.S.P. H.Q. Section of Park left BUSSY at 2.15 pm and moved back to [illegible] SAA section at MONTAGNE, via AMIENS and MOLLIENS VIDAME arriving at 6 pm.	
MONTAGNE 7th	SAA issued to Poona Horse.	
8th 9th 10th 11th	Nothing of importance to report.	
12th	SAA issued to Amm Column.	
13, 14, 15, 16	Nothing to report.	
17th	SAA issued to Deccan Horse.	
18th	A.D.O.S. 7 Cav Corps [illegible] arrived with OC ASC about 3.30 pm and inspected [illegible]	
19th	Shooting competition arranged for men at a French Machine gun range in the village.	

Army Form C. 2118.

Instructions regarding War Diaries and Intelligence Summaries are contained in F. S. Regs., Part II. and the Staff Manual respectively. Title pages will be prepared in manuscript.

WAR DIARY
or
INTELLIGENCE SUMMARY.
(Erase heading not required.)

Hour, Date, Place	Summary of Events and Information	Remarks and References to Appendices
MONTAGNE. October 20th	[illegible] at CONTAY. [illegible] BUIRE. [illegible]	
21.22.23rd [illegible]	Nothing of importance to report. Weather very bad.	
27th	[illegible] to 18th Section at BUIRE.	
28th	[illegible] and proceed to DARONIES [illegible]	
29th	[illegible] left for DARONIES at [illegible] about 4.30 pm.	
30th	Nothing to report.	
31st	[illegible] BUIRE. [illegible] at CUST MAREST [illegible] MONTAGNE [illegible] MOLLIENS VIDAMES [illegible] MONTAGNE [illegible] AIRAINES [illegible] MAREST at 5 pm.	
	NOTE. [illegible]	P. S. [illegible] 1/11/16

(9 29 6) W 3332—1107 100,000 10/13 H W V Forms/C. 2118/10.

B.W.F. FRANCE & FLANDERS.

2 IND CAV DIV TROOPS.

O.C. ARMY SERVICE CORPS.

1914 DEC TO 1916 DEC.

DIVISIONAL SUPPLY COLUMN

(71 COY A.S.C.)

1914 SEPT TO 1915 MAR.

1916 JULY TO 1916 SEPT.

2 INDIAN CAV AMMUNITION

PARK(72 COY A.S.C.)

1914 SEPT TO 1916 OCT.

1184

B.W.F.FRANCE & FLANDERS

2 IND CAV DIV TROOPS.

D.C. ARMY SERVICE CORPS

1914 DEC TO 1916 DEC.

DIVISIONAL SUPPLY COL

(71 COY A.S.C.)

1914 SEPT TO 1915 MAR.

1916 JULY TO 1916 SEPT

2 INDIAN CAV AMMUNITION

PARK(72 COY A.S.C.)

1914 SEPT TO 1916 OCT.

1184

www.ingramcontent.com/pod-product-compliance
Lightning Source LLC
Chambersburg PA
CBHW080828010526
44112CB00015B/2473
9781474501675